Crossing Borders, Latin American Migrations:
Collections and Services for/from New Library Users

SALALM Secretariat
Latin American Library
Tulane University

Crossing Borders, Latin American Migrations: Collections and Services for/from New Library Users

Papers of the Fifty-First Annual Meeting of the
SEMINAR ON THE ACQUISITION OF
LATIN AMERICAN LIBRARY MATERIALS

Santo Domingo, Dominican Republic
March 19–22, 2006

Adán Griego
Editor

SALALM Secretariat
Latin American Library
Tulane University

ISBN: 0-917617-81-9

Contents

Keynote Address

Caribbean Migrations

Cuban Diaspora

The Exports of Migration

Migration: The Mexican Experience

Libraries, Librarians, and Library Resources

Library Resources: The Canadian Experience

Women Writers across Latin American Borders

Preface

Preparations for the Santo Domingo SALALM conference started in mid-December 2004 with the first of three visits to meet with the local arrangements committee: Aida Montero from the Fundación Global Democracia y Desarrollo (FUNGLODE) and Dulce María Núñez Tavera from the Pontificia Universidad Católica Madre y Maestra (Catholic University). Planning continued even during the crucial post-Katrina days in September 2005 when the executive secretariat moved from the University of Texas at Austin to Tulane University's Latin American Library in New Orleans. After extensive discussions, SALALM's Executive Board decided that the 51st conference would continue as planned and the next months proved to be one of the most challenging experiences for SALALM as an organization.

In choosing the conference theme, "Crossing Borders, Latin American Migrations: Collections and Services for/from New Library Users," I wanted to revisit the concept of "migrations" as the year 2006 marked the 500th anniversary of the death of Christopher Columbus. It was his first voyage in 1492 that had sparked a movement of peoples across the Atlantic, a movement that continued for the next 400 years. In the late-nineteenth century, this east-west pattern of migration added a new direction: south-north and places as far away as New York and New Orleans hosted a thriving Spanish language press, which served emerging immigrant communities.

This new pattern continued with people fleeing the 1910 Mexican Revolution and in the 1940s with the Mexican "bracero" or guest worker program. Earlier, in the 1930s, Puerto Ricans had also left the island and settled in the New York area. The Cuban Revolution and the 1980s political upheaval in Central America produced similar displacements with immigrants settling in various parts of the United States.

The conference's eighteen panels provided an array of presentations focusing on the notion of "crossing borders" with the keynote speech by New York–based writer Jaime Manrique highlighting the important role of libraries as national identities move across national borders. Several other papers presented here address a diasporic movement in its many manifestations: from migration patterns throughout the Caribbean region and Mexico; to the presence of women throughout the literary frontier; as well as the development of Latin American studies services and collections at Canadian academic libraries.

In an effort to ensure SALALM's presence long after the conference had ended, two other activities were organized: a MARC 21 Pre-Conference attended by more than thirty enthusiastic participants from several Santo Domingo institutions; and a donation of more than three hundred books collected by SALALM attendees to be shared with our host institutions.

Collectively, the papers and activities of SALALM's 51st annual conference in Santo Domingo reflect the enduring commitment of a membership that came together at a time of great uncertainty for the organization.

Adán Griego

Acknowledgments

A very special word of *agradecimiento* to Laura Gutierrez-Witt who continued her volunteer work as SALALM's executive secretariat after her term expired. Likewise, Hortensia Calvo, as the new executive secretary, managed to carry out her duties with much success at a time of personal uncertainty.

I am indebted to my supervisors at the Stanford University Libraries for providing support and release time so that I could focus on SALALM. Both Everardo Rodriguez at Standford and Jockasta Santos at FUNGLODE deserve a special mention for their ability to "massage" electronic files and solve many a crisis with much patience. But, it is really to SALALM's members to whom I owe much for their support throughout the many challenging times onsite. *Muy agradecido* also to our hosts in the Dominican Republic at FUNGLODE and the Catholic University for giving SALALM the opportunity to learn and share, which in the end is part of our overarching mission as area studies librarians.

Last, but not least, thanks to Mark L. Grover and Shannon Thurlow who patiently awaited the arrival of much delayed documents. I claim any dangling modifiers and any other errors due to *cálculo semántico y lingüístico.*

Keynote Address

1. Soy escritor bilingüe y transnacional

Jaime Manrique

Mi infancia y mi adolescencia transcurrieron en Colombia, los años en que empecé a formarme como ser humano y como escritor. El bilingüismo y la transnacionalidad cultural jugaron un papel importante en mi vida desde la más temprana edad, cuando el esquema de lo que sería mi vida de adulto apenas empezaba a insinuarse. Como mis padres no estaban casados entre sí, a los cinco años fui matriculado en el Colegio Hebreo Unión de Barranquilla, mi ciudad natal. A los judíos, aparentemente, no les importaba mi ilegitimidad. Así fue como aprendí hebreo antes de aprender a leer en español (aunque lamentablemente, con el paso de los años, perdí todo conocimiento de esa lengua) y me convertí en practicante consumado de danzas israelitas. Mis primeros recuerdos felices están ligados a ese colegio. Casi todos los estudiantes eran hijos de judíos europeos que habían llegado a Barranquilla durante la Segunda Guerra Mundial o poco después. Mi mejor amigo era un niño sueco llamado Stick Luster. Era rubio cenizo, larguirucho. Su familia había llegado a Barranquilla porque su padre era ingeniero de la compañía de teléfonos. Entonces podría afirmar que, mi primer amor, también fue un amor transnacional.

Crecí en un hogar sin libros. Mi madre no había terminado la escuela primaria y no había en mi casa nadie que leyera libros o apreciara la vida de la mente. Sin embargo, el momento más importante de mi infancia fue el instante exacto cuando aprendí a leer en español. Yo iba en el bus del colegio al medio día, absorto en la tira cómica de "Tarzán" del periódico dominical. Durante un par de años había seguido las aventuras de Tarzán en las tiras cómicas interpretando los dibujos de colores de los cuadros. De repente, entendí las palabras. Me quedé sentado allí en silencio, temblando, sin hacer ruido, inmóvil, como si estuviera atrapado en un temblor que estremecía al mundo. No pude voltearme hacia el niño que estaba sentado a mi lado para explicarle lo que estaba pasando. Fue como si desde entonces entendiera que los sentimientos más profundos son imposibles de comunicar y que en últimas no significan nada para los demás. Sentí lo que Balboa debió haber sentido cuando vio el Pacífico por primera vez: una vastedad desconocida abriéndose ante mis ojos; comprendí que mi vida sería más rica para siempre, que había grandes tesoros esperándome en el futuro, que nunca sería el mismo, que había encontrado algo que representaba una vida nueva que iba a estar disponible para mí mientras estuviera vivo.

El transplante y la inmigración fueron una constante desde mi infancia. Tenía siete años cuando mi madre decidió buscar mejor fortuna en Bogotá, la capital de Colombia. Fue allí donde, de manera indirecta, se desarrolló mi amor por la literatura. Una joven de nombre Elisa llegó a trabajar a nuestra casa. Elisa se encariñó con mi hermana y conmigo. Era atlética, tenía el pelo largo y usaba trenza, piernas torneadas y musculosas, y ojos vivos y cálidos. Por las noches, Elisa (que había abandonado la escuela secundaria porque sus padres necesitaban que trabajara) venía a nuestra habitación y nos contaba historias de *Las mil y una noches*. También nos relataba varios de los cuentos de hadas de Hans Christian Andersen y de los Hermanos Grimm. Nos dormíamos con estas historias. Elisa era una extraordinaria narradora de cuentos, y durante todo el día yo esperaba el momento en que ella se convertía en nuestra Scherezade. Cuando cerraba los ojos después de que se apagaban las luces nocturnas, mi mente quedaba encendida en la oscuridad. Estaba ansioso por hacerme mayor para poder leer todos esos libros. Comencé a sentirme intensamente vivo. Supe que había una vida más allá del mundo físico, una vida de la mente, donde las cosas más maravillosas podían suceder. Me sentí liberado de la tiranía de la lógica del mundo, que no dejaba mucho espacio para la magia.

Cuando cumplí ocho años un amigo me regaló mi primer libro, *Las Aventuras de Dick Turpin,* un Robin Hood moderno. Ese fue el primer libro que leí de principio a fin. El segundo libro que leí fue *Las fábulas de Esopo,* en la biblioteca del Colegio Colón, en Barranquilla, ciudad a la cual habíamos regresado después de tres años en Bogotá. Este fue otro momento decisivo de mi vida. *Las fábulas de Esopo* me parecieron inexplicables y llenas de sabiduría. Nada había encendido mi imaginación de la misma manera desde las historias de Elisa y *Las mil y una noches.*

Los años de mi adolescencia fueron marcados por mi voracidad por la lectura. Nuestros vecinos en Barranquilla tenían una colección de libros empastados en cuero llamada *Las grandes novelas de la literatura universal.* Las leí con un fervor que no ha evocado nada más desde entonces. La colección incluía a los grandes novelistas del siglo XIX. Leí *Crimen y castigo* que me impresionó tanto que lo guardaba debajo de mi almohada; *Ana Karenina* y *Resurrección* de Tolstói; *Padres e hijos* y *Relatos de un cazador* de Turguéniev. Mi cuerpo vivía en Barranquilla, pero mi mente estaba llena de la Rusia del siglo XIX. Esto cambió cuando leí a *Jane Eyre* y, más importante, *Cumbres Borrascosas,* novela que releí dieciocho veces. Mientras caminaba por las calurosas calles de Barranquilla imaginaba estar explorando los páramos salvajes y melancólicos de Inglaterra. Quería morir de tuberculosis como las Bronte. Me sentaba en el pupitre en el colegio, en la parte de atrás del salón de clases, y tosía todo el día, con la esperanza de desarrollar una tuberculosis. Después leí varias veces *Madame Bovary* de Flaubert, y luego pasé a *Bouvard et Pecuchet* que, para mí, parecía una extraña historia de amor homosexual. Devoré *Rojo y negro* de Stendhal, *Papá Goriot* y *Eugenie Grandet* de Balzac,

Oliver Twist y *David Copperfield* de Dickens, *La feria de las vanidades* de Thackeray (que tenía una heroína malvada y encantadora con cuyos sueños de ascenso social me identificaba), y *El molino del Floss* de George Elliot, una novela cercana a mi corazón porque el vínculo entre Maggie y su hermano se me parecía a mi vínculo con mi hermana.

Es muy posible que no me hubiera convertido en escritor si mis vecinos no hubieran tenido esta colección y no hubieran sido lo suficientemente amables como para prestarme los libros. Cuando miro atrás, sin embargo, nada de lo que me ha sucedido desde entonces me ha marcado de manera tan profunda como la lectura de esas obras.

Mi vida se desarrollaba paralela a las historia de mi madre. A los cuarenta y siete años, sola, sin ninguna preparación, ella decidió inmigrar a los Estados Unidos. Esta terminaría siendo la inmigración que marcaría con más fuerza mi futuro y que determinaría la clase de escritor que soy. Mi madre, quien nunca había tenido un trabajo, se mudo a un país donde sólo tenía una amiga, un país cuya lengua ella desconocía. Ella consiguió trabajo de costurera en una fábrica, y yo en una estación de gasolina. Durante el último año de mi bachillerato, una maestra que observó mi amor por la lectura me animó para que continuara mis estudios.

Fue en Tampa donde descubrí a los grandes narradores de la literatura latinoamericana en le siglo XX. Yo acababa de graduarme de bachillerato y todavía trabajaba en la gasolinera. Soñaba con ser escritor y con estudiar, aunque no tenía una idea clara de cual sería el camino que me enrumbaría hacia mis sueños.

Un día que no estaba trabajando, caminé hasta la biblioteca pública de Tampa. En esa época la biblioteca pública de Tampa quedaba en una edificación vieja y oscura de finales de 1800. Pasé toda mañana explorando el edificio. En una esquina del sótano había un anaquel con libros en español. Allí encontré los libros de los autores que en los próximos años cambiarían irrevocablemente el curso de mi vida. Allá estaban los libros de Borges, Puig, Rulfo, Donoso, Vargas Llosa, Cortázar y García Márquez.

Cuando llegué a los Estados Unidos por primera vez, ya me consideraba escritor y había escrito poemas, narrativa y una espantosa obra teatral de corte seudo existencial. En plena adolescencia, estaba en ese punto en el cual mi dominio del castellano empezaba a expandirse vertiginosamente, sin que conociera el idioma ni su gramática a fondo. Este proceso fue truncado con mi ingreso a la universidad. Recibí una beca para estudiar en la universidad de South Florida, en Tampa y decidí estudiar literatura inglesa (porque la desconocía y porque Borges la amaba). Forzosamente—y con gran ahínco—tuve que sumergirme en el inglés. Un día escribí un cuento en inglés, y luego un poema, y antes de que me diera cuenta estaba escribiendo en ambos idiomas. Empecé a publicar mis primeros esfuerzos en español en los suplementos literarios de periódicos colombianos, y mi ficción en inglés en revistas universitarias.

Ya para esa época estaba consciente de que mi uso del idioma cervantino estaba contaminado por el inglés.

Después de recibirme en la universidad regresé a Colombia, donde viví por casi una década. Eran los años del Boom Latinoamericano y yo quería ser parte de una tradición viva que me inspiraba y enorgullecía. En Colombia publiqué mi primer poemario (por el cual recibí en 1975 el Premio Nacional de Poesía Eduardo Cote Lemus). También publiqué un volumen que incluía una novela corta—*El cadáver de papá*—y varios cuentos; y una compilación de mis reseñas y ensayos sobre el cine, *Notas de Cine: Confesiones de un crítico amateur.* Todo parecía indicar que el castellano iba a ser la lengua en la cual realizaría mi obra. Sin embargo, recién cumplidos los treinta años me transplanté a Nueva York, donde—fuera de una estadía de un año en España, a mediados de los años 70—he residido desde ese entonces.

En 1979 salí de Colombia, que sufría el mal trato de un gobierno represivo y torturador, y me transplanté a Nueva York. Me exilié de Colombia por dos razones: como homosexual no pensaba que podría encontrar en mi patria el espacio necesario para vivir sin secretos; y también porque la experiencia de mis años universitarios me había convertido en un demócrata, a quien se le hacía imposible vivir en una inflexible sociedad de clases y racista.

A raíz de la publicación de mi novela política y de denuncia, *Oro colombiano,* que salió al mercado en inglés en 1983 (y fue publicada en México por Diana en 1985) pasaron casi veinte años antes de que volviera a publicar en mi patria.

A ese auto-exilio se debe el hecho de que en los últimos veinticinco años he producido gran parte de mi obra en inglés, inspirado por el ejemplo del ruso Vladimir Nabokov, la danesa Isaak Dinesen y el polaco Joseph Conrad, quienes escogieron escribir en inglés en su adultez. Los latinoamericanos Manuel Puig y Guillermo Cabrera Infante también incursionaron en ese idioma. Puig escribió su novela *Sangre de amor correspondido* en inglés, y el autor cubano escribió un libro sobre el tabaco en la lengua de Shakespeare. Más recientemente, en el caso dominicano, por ejemplo, tenemos a Junot Diaz y Julia Alvarez que, aunque oriundos de la Republica Dominicana, crecieron en los Estados Unidos y escriben ahora en inglés. Y como ellos hay docenas, tal vez cientos, de escritores de todos los rincones de la tierra, que debido a su migración, a la búsqueda de sus padres o de ellos mismos, han escogido lenguas diferentes a las suyas para escribir una obra que, en muchos casos, es acerca de sus puntos de origen.

Yo, sin embargo, he continuado escribiendo la mayor parte de mi poesía en castellano porque considero mis poemas la parte privada de mi obra y por esa razón acudo al primer idioma que escuché de los labios de mi madre y mis familiares. Al igual que Borges, encuentro que la prosa en inglés me seduce con mayor pasión que la escrita en castellano. Más cuando leo a Quevedo, Góngora, San Juan de la Cruz y Sor Juana, encuentro una música en sus versos que no logro escuchar en inglés. Y es esa música la que me mantiene aferrado a un idioma que, con el paso de los años, se torna cada vez más difícil de aprehender. Es en ese espacio—un limbo lingüístico—donde existe toda mi obra.

Estoy convencido que en el futuro habrá un número mayor de escritores que escribirán—como Nabokov y Puig (quien también escribió una novela en Portugués)—en varios idiomas. En la era moderna, digamos desde la población acelerada de los Estados Unidos en el siglo XIX por diferentes grupos de inmigrantes europeos, los movimientos migratorios son como olas grandes de seres humanos desplazándose de las naciones pobres a las naciones ricas, de las antiguas colonias a la base del imperio. Este proceso se ha vuelto aun más complejo por las guerras civiles, las guerras imperialistas y el genocidio—que impera con tanta impunidad en nuestros días. Es más, el carro, el avión, el teléfono, el cine, la televisión y el Internet—todos invenciones del siglo XX—han acabado derrumbando las barreras geográficas. El resultado es de doble filo—cada vez más existe una homogeneidad cultural de la cual la cultura pop es el hilo que enlaza ese tejido desconcertante. Y por todas estas razones, el inglés se ha convertido en lo que el Esperanto quiso ser.

El tema de mi charla es "el escritor y la transnacionalidad", así que ofreceré un par de reflexiones acerca de mi propia globalización literaria, de como mi bilingualismo me llevó a la transnacionalidad literaria. Mi segunda novela, *Luna latina en Manhattan,* fue escrita en inglés y salió al mercado editorial en 1992. En los nueve años que transcurrieron entre *Oro colombiano* y *Luna Latina* tomé la decisión de tratar de escribir en inglés puesto que en Colombia me había convertido en *persona non grata* y porque cada día se me hacía más difícil reconstruir el habla de mi gente. Durante esos años de transición, escribí, en un inglés atroz, un mamotreto de novela que nadie quiso publicar. Mi crisis literaria era profunda. Sentía que me había quedado sin un idioma. Un día la escritora norteamericana Lorrie Moore me dijo, "Jaime, escribe acerca del metro". Y fue así que empecé a escribir *Luna latina en Manhattan* una novela narrada en primera persona, en mi inglés machacado. Empecé entonces a escribir acerca de los latinoamericanos y colombianos en Nueva York. En Latinoamérica nadie se interesó por el libro, tuvo que esperar hasta que el tema de la diáspora se pusiera de moda para que la novela fuera traducida al español y publicada—doce años después de haber aparecido en inglés.

El haberme quedado sin lenguaje—o haberme quedado con uno híbrido, muy cercano al Spanglish—me llevó a explorar un territorio que ningún escritor Colombiano había minado. Existe en los Estados Unidos una gran colonia colombiana cuyas historias nunca habían sido contadas. En términos literarios, ellos no existían. Así, en vez de llegar a un callejón sin salida, mi obra se convirtió en un puente entre dos culturas.

Hoy día, escribo no sólo acerca de la Colombia que conocí en mi juventud, sino también acerca de la Colombia, la pequeña Colombia, que existe en Queens, Nueva York, y en Manhattan y todos los lugares de los Estados Unidos donde hay colonias de colombianos. Pero también me interesan las historias de la oleada de inmigrantes centroamericanos que han llegado a los Estados Unidos en las dos últimas décadas. Y fue así como, al perder mi lengua materna mi obra adquirió la amplitud de una geografía sin barreras. Hoy día, puedo decir que soy un escritor latino, un colombiano que escribe en inglés en los Estados Unidos, cuyo tema principal es toda Latinoamérica y toda su historia.

El gran novelista argentino Manuel Puig dijo en una ocasión que la principal ventaja que tenía para un escritor latinoamericano vivir en el exterior era que el escritor no tenía que autocensurarse. Yo añadiría que mis experiencias como escritor han ocurrido no en el exterior (más allá de las fronteras de mi patria) sino el interior de mi psique. El lugar geográfico donde he escrito mi obra ha sido importante, por supuesto, mas no tanto como la exploración interna que me ha llevado a destilar mis ideas y emociones y a articular mi visión del mundo, una nueva misión para el escritor del siglo XXI—que para mí consiste en dejar testimonio del ser humano en cualquier parte a través de la historia.

Este mes salió en los Estados Unidos en inglés mi novela *Nuestras vidas son los ríos,* que narra la historia de Manuela Sáenz, la gran heroína de la independencia sur americana y quien fuera el gran amor del Libertador Simón Bolívar. En la actualidad, he empezado a esbozar una novela que sucede principalmente en la España del siglo XVII. Se me ocurre, cuando reflexiono acerca de mi obra más reciente que esa trashumancia de mi madre, que comenzó en mi niñez, cuando yo no tenía ningún control sobre mi destino, me llevó, sin habérmelo propuesto, a convertirme en un escritor sin fronteras.

Caribbean Migrations

2. Our House in the Next World: Building a Dominican Cultural Presence in New York City

Pamela M. Graham

In 1999 the annual book fair held in Santo Domingo, the Dominican Republic, became an international event including contingents of publishers and exhibitors from other nations and designating a country of honor each year. In 2005 the *feria* experienced a different kind of expansion, internal in the sense that it was aimed at recognizing cultural and literary production by Dominicans, but not necessarily published or created on Dominican soil. For the first time, the Commission for Dominican Culture in the United States sponsored a *Programa de la Diáspora,* which included two book-exhibit pavilions and a four-day schedule of readings, panels, and conferences. In addition to these events, during the week of the feria's opening, President Leonel Fernández awarded one of the nation's highest honors, the Order of Merit of Duarte, Sánchez y Mella, to six Dominicans residing in the United States in recognition of their contributions to Dominican culture.[1] The program's pamphlet distributed at the feria included the phrase "un segmento de la dominicanidad se piensa e integra desde la lejanía."

For many observers, these honors represented the culmination of years of effort on the part of Dominicans living abroad to obtain support and recognition for cultural endeavors from the Dominican state. Those with less familiarity with the history of Dominican international migration might question why the cultural work of migrants in the United States and the condition of diaspora were such prominent themes of the feria. How is *dominicanidad* altered by the experience of living abroad and how have Dominicans in the United States, particularly in New York City, become organized as members of a diaspora? What factors affect the extent and nature of such organizing? Does the Dominican state have a vested interest in supporting an expanded concept of dominicanidad and what consequences flow from state policies to recognize and incorporate migrants?

I argue that the formal recognition of diasporic cultural production by home country states is a complex process, fully embedded in a host of economic and political realities that frame and define contemporary international migrations. Efforts to expand the political rights and economic power of migrants with respect to their countries of origin permanently alter concepts of nation and citizenship and thus have an impact on cultural dimensions of migrant life. After providing some brief background on the recent history of Dominican migration and early patterns of cultural organizing, I will provide a preliminary overview of recent efforts by Dominican migrants in New York City to develop a Dominican state-supported cultural center in northern Manhattan. Analyzing this experience provides an opportunity for exploring how states define and support national cultural policy in diasporic contexts and the role of migrants in the construction of such policy when the concept of the nation is no longer tied to territory.

Nature and Characteristics of Dominican Immigration to the United States

Dominicans comprise the third largest Latin American immigrant group in the United States, after Mexicans and Cubans, and the fourth largest Latino or Hispanic group.[2] Since the late 1960s, the Dominican Republic has ranked within the top ten source nations for immigration into the United States. Approximately 845,000 persons have entered the United States as immigrants from the Dominican Republic since the early-twentieth century (fig. 1). There has also been a sizeable flow of undocumented immigration, often occurring through overstays of nonimmigrant visas (fig. 2). Migration has had economically diverse origins including persons declaring working-class and professional occupations.

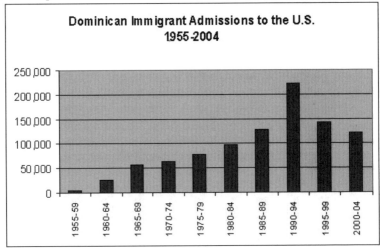

Fig. 1. Dominican Immigrant Admissions to the U.S.: 1955–2004. U.S. Department of Justice, Immigration and Naturalization Service, *Annual Report of the Immigration and Naturalization Service,* 1950–1976; *Statistical Yearbook of the Immigration and Naturalization Service,* 1977–2001; and U.S. Department of Homeland Security, Office of Immigration Statistics, *Yearbook of Immigration Statistics,* 2002–2004.

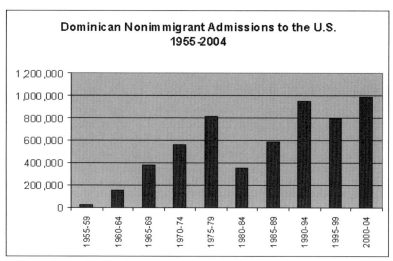

Fig. 2. Dominican Nonimmigrant Admissions to the U.S.: 1955–2004. U.S. Department of Justice, Immigration and Naturalization Service, *Annual Report of the Immigration and Naturalization Service*, 1950–1976; *Statistical Yearbook of the Immigration and Naturalization Service*, 1977–2001; and U.S. Department of Homeland Security, Office of Immigration Statistics, *Yearbook of Immigration Statistics*, 2002–2004.

Census figures, which record numbers of persons living in the United States as opposed to immigrant or nonimmigrant entries, indicate that over 900,000 persons of Dominican origin (born either in the United States or in the Dominican Republic) were resident in the United States as of the year 2000 (Brittingham and de la Cruz 2004, 4). Researchers working with Current Population Survey data have estimated the Dominican population in the United States to be just over 1,000,000 (Castro and Boswell 2002, 5). These estimates translate into the equivalent of 9 to 11 percent of the current population of the Dominican Republic.

The Dominican population in the United States is predominantly female (54 percent) and young (Castro and Boswell 2002, 5–6). By the late 1990s, Dominicans had the highest poverty rate of ethnic and racial groups in New York City, and also had the highest proportion of female-headed households, a marker of poverty and other socioeconomic disadvantages (Duany, 2005, 525; Hernández and Rivera-Batiz 2000, 23–28).

A striking feature of Dominican migration is the high concentration of settlement in the New York metropolitan area, although this has been changing in recent decades. This residential concentration peaked in the 1970s, with 84 percent of Dominican-born persons in the United States living in New York City. While this concentration has declined, New York City still accounts for over one-half of all Dominicans in the United States (New York City Department of City Planning 2004, 19).[3]

Residential concentration within New York City is quite strong, with
the northern Manhattan neighborhood of Washington Heights and neighboring areas of the Bronx being the most populous Dominican sections in
2000 (fig. 3). The close to 100,000 Dominicans living in northern Manhattan
have inscribed this space with their presence: there are public schools and/or
streets named for Juan Pablo Duarte, the Mirabal sisters, Salomé Ureña, and
Juan Bosch; and numerous shops and restaurants refer to the Cibao region
of the country and to Quisqueya, the Taino name for Hispaniola. Northern
Manhattan also possesses local city council and state assembly districts that
have consistently elected Dominican-origin politicians since the early 1990s.

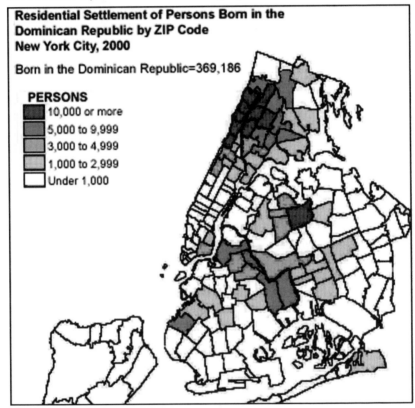

Fig. 3. Residential Settlement of Persons Born in the Dominican Republic by Zip
Code New York City, 2000. New York City Department of City Planning, Population
Division, *The Newest New Yorkers 2000 Briefing Booklet* (2004), p. 18.

Despite having high poverty rates, Dominicans living abroad have become
an important source of economic support for their country of origin. Remittances
sent to the Dominican Republic amounted to almost U.S.$3 billion in 2004.
This figure represents 13 percent of the country's GDP, 47 percent of exports

from free-trade zones, and about 62 percent of income from tourism (Suki 2004, 5).

Developing an Organizational and Cultural Presence in New York

The cultural development of the Dominican community in New York can find a modern starting point in the extensive formation of national and professional associations that took place almost upon arrival of many migrants in New York in the 1960s.[4] This *movimiento clubístico* included groups such as the Centro Cívico Cultural Dominicano, founded in 1962, and the Club Juan Pablo Duarte, formed in 1966 and made up of persons from the Cibao region of the Dominican Republic who had migrated to the United States in the 1950s and early 1960s (Jiménez Belén, 1977, 26–29).[5] Associations of various professions emerged as well: lawyers, doctors, journalists, and artists formed groups, and the Association of Dominican Professionals in New York was established in 1970 (39). By the late 1970s, at least thirty-six clubs and associations existed in Washington Heights neighborhood alone (Sassen-Koob 1979; Sainz 1990).

The other major component of organizational life in New York City were branches or *filiales* of Dominican political parties, such as the Dominican Revolutionary Party (PRD), the Dominican Liberation Party (PLD), and the Social Christian Reformist Party aka *Partido Reformista* (PRSC).[6] Both the PRD and the PRSC were founded abroad; PRD in Havana 1939, and the Reformista Party in New York City in the early 1960s. The political parties have served as a dominant organizing force among migrants living abroad. The partisanship that pervaded most areas of Dominican life existed within the cultural and social organizations abroad and many of these were at least unofficially linked to political parties.

These cultural and social groups focused exclusively on commemorating major Dominican national holidays, and keeping customs and cultural memories alive among those who lived abroad. De la Cruz described the groups as "instruments for combating the nostalgia of living in a society that could not understand them" (2004, 136, author's translation). The return ideology, that is, the intention to return eventually to the Dominican Republic, shaped the focus and activities of these groups, and they thus developed in isolation to the greater New York environment in which they physically existed. In turn, this environment was not receptive to this new and growing immigrant group; often referred to as "invisible immigrants," Dominicans received little attention in the U.S. media and were commonly mistaken for Puerto Ricans. Low naturalization rates to U.S. citizenship reinforced the legal and political isolation of many migrants.[7] The commonly used phrase "dominicanos ausentes" described migrants in terms of where they were not.

Out of this isolation, Dominicans in New York continued to forge an extensive organizational and cultural life. Political and economic realties in both countries drove important changes in the New York–Dominican community. While migrating under regular immigrant visas (or in some cases tourist visas), many of the migrants in the late 1960s and 1970s fled their country for explicit political reasons. Some had been combatants in the civil war of 1965 and/or sympathizers of the overthrown Dominican president, Juan Bosch (Mitchell 1992). In the aftermath of the U.S.-led occupation of the country in 1965 and 1966, and in the context of President Joaquín Balaguer's repression of political opponents during the 1970s, many migrants arrived in New York with a clear and passionate interest in publicizing their cause and promoting political change at home (De la Cruz 2004, 140–141).

These events had several important consequences for migrant organizations and clubs and the organization of culture abroad. Many of the existing cultural groups were drawn into more politically oriented activities, forming committees on human rights, for example. De la Cruz writes that the prospect of Balaguer's reelection in 1974 "provoked the rise of a unified movement of the most diverse political-community sectors in the Dominican Republic, and this movement arrived with force in the community in New York" (2004, 141, author's translation). Opposition political parties abroad were deeply involved in political struggles and this formed a common bridge among migrant organizations. The interest in Dominican politics also reinforced attention paid to the country of origin and on Dominicanness (or dominicanidad) as a focal point of organizing. Throughout Balaguer's years in the presidency, the Dominican state made little to no attempt to engage Dominicans living abroad, many of whom were actively opposed to his leadership.

Alongside this politically motivated movement, migration was also serving as a strategy for economic survival. Levels of economically motivated migration intensified throughout the 1970s and 1980s in response to dramatic changes and crises in the Dominican economy (Hartlyn 1998, 136–146). While remittances of money from migrants to family and kin networks became increasingly important, organizations that had formed around town or region of origin in the Dominican Republic, such as the Macorisanos Ausentes and Núcleo Santiagüero, directed their resources toward helping those home communities through philanthropic work. These activities reinforced ties to the Dominican Republic and the role of those living abroad in the ongoing experience of their country of origin.

As the number of Dominican migrants in New York grew during the 1980s and 1990s, so did the number and kind of organizations within the community. By the mid-1980s, over one hundred Dominican associations existed in New York (Torres-Saillant and Hernández 1998, 102).[8] The permanent settlement of Dominican migrants in the United States prompted a diversification of the organizational landscape and deeper involvement with the New York political scene. For example, Alianza Dominicana, formed in the early 1980s, has focused on social services and advocacy; and the Asociación Comunal de Dominicanos

Progresistas, also started in the 1980s, became involved in politics and social services. These groups, unlike many other community organizations, legally incorporated as nonprofits in New York and sought resources from various levels of U.S. government. The gradual incorporation of Dominicans into the local New York City political scene had its roots in these social service–oriented groups and the desire to improve the quality of life in Dominican neighborhoods (Graham 1998; Sagás 2004).

Yet even as migrant groups began to focus on realities and needs within New York, their interest in the political and economic affairs of the Dominican Republic did not fade. In this context, the first signs of engagement between the Dominican state and the migrant community took place as efforts emerged to develop a cultural center in New York supported by the Dominican government. Control of this government had shifted in the late 1970s from the PRSC and Balaguer to PRD-affiliated leaders, Antonio Guzmán and then Salvador Jorge Blanco. With impetus coming from prominent Dominican community leaders, President Jorge Blanco publicly supported the formation of a Casa Cultural Dominicana in 1982, and in 1985 donated U.S.$100,000 to the Dominican community in New York toward this end. Under the leadership of writer Franklin Gutiérrez, the Casa opened in northern Manhattan in 1985. The Casa was incorporated as a nonprofit organization under New York state law and thus could not legally receive regular funding from a foreign government. From the perspective of the Dominican government, allocation of regular state funding was not possible since the Casa was not institutionalized, that is, incorporated as an official part of the Dominican government. In 1989, the Casa closed for reasons that have never been publicly documented, although lack of regular funding and an inability to raise funding within New York no doubt played a major role in its demise. It should also be noted that the Dominican Republic lacked a cabinet-level ministry for cultural affairs, and this certainly contributed to problems with organizing support for culture in general (Abréu 2005, 367–374; Sánchez and Cabrera 2004).

The project of a state-supported cultural venue in New York languished during the next ten years. Balaguer returned to the presidency from 1986 to 1996, but had little to no interest in the development of a center for Dominican cultural expression abroad. Partido Reformista engagement with the New York community was limited to support for the overseas branches of the Reformista party and ties to a few of the traditional cultural groups. Increasingly contentious elections resulted in regular political crises, where Balaguer's victories at the ballot box were challenged due to corruption and vote rigging. The final straw was the 1994 election where Balaguer claimed to have won a sixth term. This triggered a serious political crisis that prompted electoral and political reform (Hartlyn 1998, 232–268). A constitutional reform that occurred in 1994 allowed those living abroad to retain their Dominican nationality upon acquiring another nation's citizenship. This would be followed in 1997 by an expansion of voting rights in presidential elections to Dominican nationals living abroad (Rodríguez 2005, 518).[9]

Resolution of the 1994 electoral crisis paved the way for a new and younger generation of political leaders, although not without the support of the older generation of leaders who had dominated Dominican politics for over thirty years. In 1996, Leonel Fernández of the PLD won the presidential election. Born in Santo Domingo, Fernández had spent several years of his childhood in New York, attending public schools, and returned to live in the Dominican Republic to attend a university in 1968 (Ozuna 2003, 105). As an active and increasingly important member of the PLD, Fernández traveled frequently to New York in the 1980s and early 1990s and thus had extensive exposure to and contacts within the Dominican community.

From the time Fernández was elected, members of the Dominican community began promoting the reopening of a cultural house in New York. In a visit to New York shortly after Fernández took office, the issue was raised in a meeting with community leaders and in an event in 1998 at the Riverbank Park in northern Manhattan, held to promote the president's state reform project (Ventura 1996, 16). At this event Fernández announced that he had instructed Dominican Consul Bienvenido Pérez to find a date for the opening of a Casa de la Cultura Dominicana (Cruz Tejada 1998, 14). In July 1999, a Casa de la Cultura Dominicana opened at Amsterdam Avenue and 150th Street in northern Manhattan. The Dominican government and the Dominican consulate allocated over half a million dollars to support the Casa and its director, Frank Cortorreal. Months before leaving office, Fernández's government passed a law creating a ministry of culture (Secretaría del Estado de Cultura), the product of a planning process that had begun in 1997 with the formation of a Presidential Council on Culture. The new law referred to the roles of Dominicans living abroad in forming cultural policies and the permanence of national values, but did not assign any representation to the overseas Dominican community within the new ministry's structure.[10]

A year after the Casa's opening, in August 2000, a new government took control of the Dominican presidency when Hipólito Mejía of the PRD was elected. Soon afterwards the Casa ceased being an NGO and became part of the Secretaría del Estado de Cultura. The Casa received a budget of approximately U.S.$43,000 per month. Between its founding in 1999 and 2004, an estimated U.S.$1,000,000 was allocated to the Casa (Gutiérrez 2004, 216).

From its opening to the end of 2002, the Casa sponsored many cultural activities and received coverage in the Spanish language press in New York. Cortorreal was replaced as director of the Casa when the new Dominican administration took office, and during the first part of the Mejía administration, the Casa was directed by Rafael Mendoza and Fr. Ricardo Fajardo, with Hector Amarante as director of the literary section. Activities ranged from book launches, *tertulias* or literary gatherings, poetry readings, to art exhibitions. The Casa also hosted public lectures and discussions about immigration law reform and other community affairs (Pérez and Rodríguez 2001; Medina 2001; Blanchard 2001; Malone 1999). Notably, the *Primer Foro de Cultura y Literatura Dominicana en Nueva York* was held at the Casa in January 2001, with the participation of many noted New York Dominican writers such as Claribel Díaz, Héctor Miolán, Héctor Amarante, Jorge Piña, and Mateo Morrison (Foro de Cultura y Literatura Dominicana en Nueva York 2003).

Despite the Casa's steady programming, its legal incorporation into the new state structures supporting culture, and the allocation of funding to support the Casa, the project was plagued with problems. These disputes were documented in the media, on websites and online discussion boards of Dominican cultural groups, and in books that some more active participants in this process have published (Abréu 2005; De la Cruz 2004; Ventura 2004).[11] Among the problems cited were criticism of relations between the leadership of the Casa and the community of cultural activists in New York, dissatisfaction with secretary Raful's management of the project, complaints over the lack of a clear and transparent organizational and financial management of the Casa, and charges that Dominican political partisanship had infiltrated and thus misdirected the purpose and function of the cultural center.

While many of these charges referred to the entire period of the Casa's existence, under both political parties, specific conflicts surrounded a forum convened in August of 2002 as part of a Dominican national effort to develop a ten-year cultural strategic plan. Dissatisfaction with how this process was structured and managed reinforced the sense of exclusion of Dominicans abroad from the development of national cultural policy. As the Casa experienced increasingly serious financial troubles, and members of the community boycotted events held by the Casa, it was temporarily closed in 2002. At the request of a *comité coordinador de la asamblea,* formed by community activists in early 2003, a consultative council was eventually formed to advise the leadership of the Casa and to improve communication between community cultural groups and the Casa.

Despite efforts to transform and resolve problems plaguing the Casa, poor relations between the Secretaría de Cultura and the community continued. Perhaps most irreconcilable were the charges that political parties had been using the Casa for their own ends. In the literary forum held in 2001 at the Casa, one writer gave a presentation whose title starkly posed the question: "¿Casa de la Cultura Dominicana: órgano de difusión cultural o partido político de turno?" Accounts of the incidents published by Dominican activists and to an online bulletin board for Dominican literature all refer to the large payrolls maintained by the Casa and the employment of members of political parties who had no discernible functions at the Casa.[12]

In the midst of this complicated scenario, a change in presidential administrations took place in the Dominican Republic in 2004. The return of Leonel

Fernández to office brought about changes to the project of developing a state-supported cultural center in New York. Prior to his reelection in 2004, Fernández initiated an effort called the New York-Dominican Strategic Alliance Project, through the Fundación Global Democracia y Desarrollo (FUNGLODE) over which he presided, and in cooperation with academic institutions in the United States, NGOs, and other business and community leaders. In a report published in 2004, an evaluation of the Casa de la Cultura was presented by Franklin Gutiérrez. He listed the reasons for the Casa's failures:

> [the] overwhelming and unnecessary size of the employment machine; the delay of the Dominican government in handing over assigned resources; the internal conflicts between the directors (increasingly acute); the absence of a defined cultural policy with respect to the community served; and the pressures from the cultural sectors of Dominican New Yorkers who feel excluded from the project. (216)

Gutiérrez proposed several measures for the resuscitation of the project, among them, working more closing with other existing Dominican cultural organizations in New York, elevating the director's position to the rank of an undersecretary of the Secretariat of Culture, and achieving greater participation by Dominican writers and intellectuals in the Feria Internacional del Libro held annually in Santo Domingo (Gutiérrez 2004, 221).

During the PLD's campaign for office in 2004, the party put forth a *Program of Government* that included a section on Dominicans living abroad, interestingly as part of their domestic policy program. The document noted the importance of Dominicans abroad and the levels of remittances sent by them to the Dominican Republic. The program also recognized the difficulties of adaptation and reception of Dominicans in their countries of residence and the discrimination often encountered in other countries. The PLD outlined an objective of promoting participation of Dominicans abroad for the benefit of both the Dominican Republic and the migrants themselves. Strategies for achieving this objective included establishing an independent commissioner to serve as a link between the president and overseas communities and the funding of cultural centers in all large communities of Dominicans living abroad. Other political and administrative reforms were outlined, including promoting naturalization to citizenship of the countries in which Dominican emigrants live, along with further development of political rights within the Dominican system (Partido de la Liberación Dominicana 2004, 120–121).

Once in office in August 2004, Fernández created via presidential decree the Comisionado Dominicano de Cultura en USA, who would serve as a director of the Casa de la Cultura (Presidencia de la República Dominicana 2004).[13] The latter name was soon abandoned in favor of the use of "Comisionado," no doubt to distance the project from the controversies of the earlier incarnations of the Casa. The Comisionado's objectives were the following: "primero, pro-teger [*sic*] a los artistas dominicanos residentes en Estados Unidos; segundo, ofrecer a la diáspora dominicana estadounidense un programa de acción que contribuya al man-tenimiento [*sic*] de los valores culturales nacionales y; tercero, dirigir la cultura domini-cana [*sic*] hacia otras comunidades latinas establecidas en Norteamérica" (Comisionado Dominicano de Cultura en USA n.d.). Franklin Gutiérrez once again served as the leader of this organizing effort, this time in the role of commissioner.

Since its establishment, the Comisionado has been sponsoring a full slate of events, including literary gatherings, readings, conferences, and theatrical events. The Comisionado also manages a literary prize for writers in the diaspora, Letras de Ultramar, which awards $5,000 and an invitation to the annual Feria Internacional del Libro in Santo Domingo in addition to publication under the Dominican Editora Nacional's Colección de Ultramar. As noted at the beginning of this article, the Comisionado had a noted presence at the 2005 Feria Internacional del Libro, with about thirty participants from the U.S. cultural community in attendance. In addition to debuting two pavilions featuring La Diáspora Dominicana and one devoted to the Comisionado, three days of the fair were devoted to the diaspora with panels on themes related to Dominican writers living abroad.

Despite these initial accomplishments, debates persist about the cultural center's proper role in the community and its management and whether a change of name can lead to more substantial changes in the center's functioning. As might be predicted, some members of the Dominican community were critical of the Comisionado's involvement in the feria, questioning the criteria for including writers, the level of travel support for invited participants, and the definition of diaspora and the placing of writers in this category instead of recognizing them as simply Dominican writers (Ventura 2005).

Towards an Understanding of the Organization of Culture

This brief review of cultural organizational development and cultural center projects among Dominicans in New York points to several trends. First, support for an official cultural center was related to broader changes in the political development of both the Dominican Republic and the communities of Dominicans living in New York. The increasing visibility of Dominicans in New York as they have undergone a process of incorporation, and their growing role in providing economic support to their country of origin, has provided social and political capital that has undoubtedly helped advance cultural agendas. Developing and advancing such agendas has been complicated by a variety of political factors, however. The prevalence and organizational power of Dominican political parties overseas has had an effect on other kinds of organizing abroad, and it has been difficult to keep partisanship out of the process of promoting culture. On the other hand, the development of voting rights and possible representation of overseas migrants within the Dominican system may provide new access points to the Dominican state that can be used to promote state support for culture abroad.

Changes in the Dominican state have also been important. While earlier waves of migrants maintained strong allegiance to their *patria,* their relationship to the Dominican state was clearly shaped by the exile-like nature of their migration. Dominican governments in the 1960s and 1970s had no incentive to recognize or engage those who had chosen to leave the country. By the 1980s, when the state began to develop more interest in Dominicans living abroad, the lack of a cultural ministry in the Dominican Republic reflected institutional weaknesses in the state that made it difficult if not impossible to carry out the project of organizing and supporting migrants in New York. The first Casa's incorporation under New York state law complicated efforts to strengthen connections with the Dominican state. The creation of a ministry of culture in the Dominican Republic and the institutionalization of the overseas cultural center as part of this ministry have brought the Comisionado solidly within the sphere of the Dominican state. It is not clear, however, whether the institutional position of the Comisionado can allow it to transcend the variations in support migrants may receive in future governments. And since the Comisionado is part of the Dominican state, it will be limited in its ability to raise nongovernmental funding or support from local and federal sources within the United States. Thus the transnational nature of this project remains bounded by nationally oriented norms.

Dominicans abroad have had to navigate a complex course between two national contexts, as is reflected in the objectives defined by the Comisionado in 2004: there is the desire to receive recognition and support from the Dominican state, and there is the desire to improve connections to and a presence within cultural movements in the United States. It is perhaps both necessary and natural to see a constant questioning among writers and artists over the appropriate place for their work in this transnational context. The Dominican state has expanded the boundaries of its concept of the nation through legal and political reform and has had to recognize the vital role of its diaspora in its economic future. Determining the appropriate role for the Dominican state in nonpolitical and noneconomic aspects of life is a central challenge to the state and to the variety of "cultural workers" living abroad.

Clearly the competing visions among Dominicans in New York on the organization of cultural life will not diminish in the near future. Lines of division fall in multiple ways: over whether a writer publishes in English or Spanish, over whether one has become part of the mainstream U.S. academic community and with which academic venues one seeks participation, over how long one has lived abroad, and now over whether one is involved and recognized by the Dominican state. Alongside these divisions are more fundamental debates of the place of writers and artists in society and the role of art within the Dominican community. One's identity as a Dominican, Dominican American, and/or Latino/a will remain a highly personal choice but is constantly being defined by others in and outside of the Dominican cultural community. It is also important to note that extensive activity and organizing among Dominican writers and artists have taken place independently of any overt Dominican state support, such as activities sponsored by Dominican organizations like Alianza Dominicana, and through groups such as Trazarte and PEC (Palabra: Expresión y Cultura), and through literary events at Dominican bookstores in New York City such as Libería Calíope. This begs the question of whether any kind of state support should be sought and the consequences of official support for cultural production.

In the end, there are a few "knowns" around which there appears to be a consensus: cultural production among Dominicans abroad has been rich and varied; organizations and groupings have emerged to channel and support such activities; the Dominican state has begun to recognize such areas of Dominican life abroad; a few Dominicans have received recognition in the mainstream U.S. literary marketplace and academy; and many others have not had recognition and support in the United States or in the Dominican Republic. The extensive migration process that altered the political, economic, and social reality of the Dominican Republic has clearly had an impact on cultural aspects of life. An expanded concept of dominicanidad will be a reality that shapes the ongoing evolution of cultural life abroad.

NOTES

1. Among those honored were academics Silvio Torres-Saillant and Ramona Hernández, founding leaders of the Dominican Studies Institute at the City College of New York; and Daisy Cocco de Filipis, a scholar of Dominican and Dominican-American literature; Orlando Alba; Angel Garrido; and Franklin Gutiérrez, the Commissioner for Dominican Culture in the United States.

2. In the 2000 U.S. Census, Dominicans made up 2.2 percent of the Hispanic population, after Mexicans (58.5 percent), Puerto Ricans (9.6 percent), who are not officially immigrants due to their U.S. citizenship, and Cubans (3.5 percent) (Castro and Boswell 2002, 4).

3. Other major cities of settlement now include Miami; Paterson, New Jersey; Boston and Lawrence, Massachusetts; along with Providence, Rhode Island; and the island of Puerto Rico.

4. Domingo de la Cruz (2004) provides a detailed account of organizations and clubs in this period.

5. This club changed its name to El Instituto Duartiano de los Estados Unidos in the late 1980s. It was closely linked with the Partido Reformista Social Cristiano, of Joaquín Balaguer, and the name change was supposedly at his suggestion (De la Cruz 2004, 136; Torres-Saillant and Hernández 1998, 80).

6. For more on the parties and on political activity by Dominicans living in the United States during the Trujillo era of the 1930s–1961, see Graham 1996, 57–100; and Rodríguez de León 1998, 117–134.

7. Only 7.8 percent of those Dominicans admitted as permanent residents between 1960 and 1970 elected to naturalize by 1980. This rate increased to 17.7 percent one decade later for all Dominicans and to 21.7 percent for those residing in New York City (Grasmuck and Pessar 1991, 207). By the late 1990s, fewer than a third of all Dominican-born immigrants in the United

States were citizens (Duany 2005, 525). By contrast, immigrants from many Asian countries had naturalization rates well above 50 percent during this same time period (525).

8. De la Cruz (2004) lists over seventy organizations that were active between 1984 and 1991 (153–154); see also Rodríguez de León 1998, 185–195.

9. Voting from abroad was not implemented until the presidential elections of 2004, mostly due to logistical issues.

10. Article 50 of the law (Ley No. 41-00) states: "La Secretaría de Estado de Cultura formulará e implementará políticas de integración y desarrollo cultural con las comunidades dominicanas fronterizas y dominicanas residentes en el exterior, estimulando la permanencia de los valores nacionales." Reprinted in Raful 2002, 194.

11. The Yahoo! en Español discussion board *abecedario,* devoted to discussions of Dominican literature, was another site for sharing opinions and debates within the community. Interestingly, this forum includes writers living in the Dominican Republic. See http://espanol.groups.yahoo.com/group/abecedario/ (accessed March 1, 2006).

12. Referred to as "botellas," these individuals apparently showed up only to claim paychecks. In a posting to *abecedario,* one activist who is a well-known writer alleged that 60 percent of the Casa's budget went to paying staff. Toward the end of 2002, only 10 of 24 employees actually worked at the Casa. "Situación Casa de la Cultura/N.Y.," http://espanol.groups.yahoo.com/group/abecedario/message/5097, posted January 3, 2003 (accessed March 1, 2006).

13. See Presidencia de la República Dominicana, Decreto Número 1152-04, http://www.presidencia.gov.do/frontend/amp_decretos.php?id=299 (accessed February 28, 2006).

BIBLIOGRAPHY

Abecedario lista de distribución. http://espanol.groups.yahoo.com/group/abecedario/. Accessed March 1, 2006.

Abréu, Dió-genes. 2005. *A pesar del naufragio: Violencia domestica y el ejercicio del poder: Testimonio dominicano desde New York.* Santo Domingo, Dominican Republic: Mediabyte.

Blanchard, César. 2001. "25 años de cultura con sabrosura." *El Diario/La Prensa,* May 28, p. 10.

Brittingham, Angela, and G. Patricia de la Cruz. 2004. *Ancestry 2000, Census 2000 Brief.* Washington, D.C.: U.S. Census Bureau. http://purl.access.gpo.gov/GPO/LPS54095. Accessed February 2, 2006.

Castro, Max J., and Thomas D. Boswell. 2002. *The Dominican Diaspora Revisited: Dominicans and Dominican-Americans in a New Century.* North-South Agenda Papers no. 53. Coral Gables, Fla.: Dante B. Fascell North-South Center.

Comisionado Dominicano de Cultura en USA. n.d. *Definición.* http://www.geocities.com/comisionadodecultura/definicion.html. Accessed February 28, 2006.

Cruz Tejada, Miguel. 1998. "Leonel Fernández, un estilo diferente, una nueva era." *Impacto,* June 23, p. 14.

De la Cruz, Domingo. 2004. *Comunidad Dominicana en Nueva York: Una historia cultural.* New York: Cruvision.

Duany, Jorge. 2005. "Dominicans." *The Oxford Encyclopedia of Latinos and Latinas in the United States,* edited by Suzanne Oboler and Deena J. González. New York: Oxford University Press. Pp. 520–530.

Foro de Cultura y Literatura Dominicana en Nueva York. 2003. *Primer Foro de Cultura y Literatura Dominicana en Nueva York.* Jackson Hts., N.Y.: Editorial Sitel.

Graham, Pamela M. 1996. "Re-Imagining the Nation and Defining the District: The Simultaneous Political Incorporation of Dominican Transnational Migrants." Ph.D. diss., University of North Carolina at Chapel Hill.

———. 1998. "An Overview of the Political Incorporation of Dominican Migrants in New York City." *Latino Studies Journal* 9, no. 3 (fall): 39–64.

Grasmuck, Sherri, and Patricia R. Pessar. 1991. *Between Two Islands: Dominican International Migration.* Berkeley: University of California Press.

Gutiérrez, Franklin. 2004. "Assessment of the New York Cultural Panorama." *Building Strategic Partnerships for Development: Dominican Republic—New York State.* Santo Domingo, Dominican Republic: Fundación Global Democracia y Desarrollo and CUNY Dominican Studies Institute at City College. Pp. 214–221.

Hartlyn, Jonathan. 1998. *The Struggle for Democratic Politics in the Dominican Republic.* Chapel Hill: University of North Carolina Press.

Hernández, Ramona, and Francisco L. Rivera-Batiz. 2000. *Dominicans in the United States: A Socioeconomic Profile, 2000.* New York: CUNY Dominican Studies Institute.

Jiménez Belén, José. 1977. *Nueva York es Así: Pinceladas dominicanistas en la urbe.* Santo Domingo, Dominican Republic: Editoria Taller.

Malone, J. C. 1999. "El arte dominicano se afianza en Nueva York." *El Diario/La Prensa,* August 15, p. 27.

Medina, Gloria. 2001. "Riqueza cultural de Quisqueya en Nueva York." *El Diario/La Prensa,* August 16, p. 35.

Mitchell, Christopher. 1992. "U.S. Foreign Policy and Dominican Migration to the United States." *Western Hemisphere Immigration and United States Foreign Policy,* edited by Christopher Mitchell. University Park: Pennsylvania State University Press. Pp. 89–123.

New York City Department of City Planning. 2004. *The Newest New Yorkers 2000: Immigrant New York in the New Millennium.* New York: Department of City Planning. http://www.nyc.gov/html/dcp/html/census/nny.shtml. Accessed February 2, 2006.

Ozuna, Marcelino. 2003. *Leonel, una biografía.* Santo Domingo, Dominican Republic: Llantén Editores.

Partido de la Liberación Dominicana. 2004. *Programa de gobierno, 2004–2008.* Santo Domingo, Dominican Republic: Partido de la Liberación Dominicana.

Pérez, Luis Eludis, and Cristián Rodríguez. 2001. "Inmigracion: 'Ley 245(i) naturaleza y alcances.'" *El Diario/La Prensa,* April 11, p. 8.

Presidencia de la República Dominicana. 2004. *Decreto Número 1152-04 que designa varios funcionarios en distintas dependencias del Estado.* http://www.presidencia.gov.do/frontend/amp_decretos.php?id=299. Accessed February 28, 2006.

Raful, Tony. 2002. *Política cultural del estado.* Santo Domingo, Dominican Republic: Dirección de Relaciones Públicas y Publicidad.

Rodríguez, María Elizabeth. 2005. "Dominican Home Country Project." *The Oxford Encyclopedia of Latinos and Latinas in the United States,* edited by Suzanne Oboler and Deena J. González. New York: Oxford University Press. Pp. 517–519.

Rodríguez, María Elizabeth, and Ramona Hernández. 2004. *Building Strategic Partnerships for Development: Dominican Republic—New York State.* Santo Domingo, Dominican Republic: Fundación Global Democracia y Desarrollo and CUNY Dominican Studies Institute at City College.

Rodríguez de León, F. 1998. *El furioso merengue del Norte: Una historia de la comunidad dominicana en los Estados Unidos.* New York: Sitel.

Sagás, Ernesto. 2004. "From *Ausentes* to Dual Nationals: The Incorporation of Transmigrants into Dominican Politics." *Dominican Migration: Transnational Perspectives,* edited by Ernesto Sagás and Sintia Molina. Gainesville: University Press of Florida. Pp. 53–73.

Sagás, Ernesto, and Sintia Molina, eds. 2004. *Dominican Migration: Transnational Perspectives.* Gainesville: University Press of Florida.

Sainz, Rudy A. 1990. "Dominican Ethnic Associations: Classification and Service Delivery Roles in Washington Heights." Ph.D. diss., Columbia University.

Sánchez, Wendy, and Raquel Virginia Cabrera. 2004. "Entrevista exclusiva con el Comisionado de Cultura en Estados Unidos" (October). http://espanol.groups. yahoo.com/group/abecedario/message/8262. Accessed February 3, 2006.

Sassen-Koob, Saskia. 1979. "Formal and Informal Associations: Dominicans and Colombians in New York." *International Migration Review* 13:314–332.

Suki, Lenora. 2004. *Financial Institutions and the Remittances Market in the Dominican Republic.* New York: Center on Globalization and Sustainable Development, Earth Institute at Columbia University. http://www.earthinstitute.columbia.edu/ cgsd/remittances/documents/Remittances_DR_001.pdf. Accessed January 28, 2006.

Torres-Saillant, Silvio, and Ramona Hernández. 1998. *The Dominican Americans.* Westport, Conn.: Greenwood Press.

Ventura, Miriam. 1996. "El nuevo gobierno y la cultura dominicana en NY." *El Diario/ La Prensa,* October 15, p. 16.

———. 2004. *Memorias de la transnacionalidad: Informe del Consejo Consultivo de la Casa de la Cultura Dominicana en Nueva York.* Santo Domingo, Dominican Republic: Editora Isenia Gráfica.

———. 2005. "Las variadas lecturas de esta VIII entrega de la Feria Internacional del Libro Dominicano." *Argenpress.info,* April 27. http://www.argenpress.info/ notaold.asp?num=020355. Accessed February 25, 2006.

3. Trends in Jamaican Migration: A Look at the Political, Socioeconomic, and Gender Issues

Dorothy M. Palmer

Migration has always been a topical issue as this affects each country and the way life is organized. Today, migration can be seen as a global issue that has resulted in constant media attention whether in Europe, the United States, or other parts of the world. The impact and importance, as well as the negatives associated with migration, have also prompted considerable research on this topic. One of the most recent studies conducted by the United Nations says that migration is not always negative but migrants can and have been making valuable contributions to the receiving countries (Sutherland 2006). Kofi Annan, United Nations secretary general in the report, states: "In the best cases, [migration] benefits the receiving country, the country of origin and the migrants themselves" (Hodge 2006, 1).

Migration was formerly associated with population control within a particular country and was therefore considered to be an avenue in reducing population growth (Thomas-Hope 1998). What then is migration? Migration is defined as involving a permanent change in residence, or a change in both the physical and social environs which must involve the movement across political boundaries (Namboodiri 1996; Weeks 1996). Internal migration is defined as the movement from rural to urban area or vice versa within a particular country; while international migration involves the movement across political boundaries.

Research has shown there are many reasons, both at the macro and micro levels, which have contributed to persons migrating. The theories have also looked at all the components that have contributed to this process and have attributed two main reasons for this migration process; these are called the push and pull factors (Lee 1969). Push factors pertain to one's former location and so would include certain intolerable conditions within a country that would cause a person to migrate. These would consist of intolerable taxation and climatic and social conditions, while pull factors are those that attract the immigrant to the new location and would therefore have more influence than the push factors. Pull factors would include the provision to improve one's self especially materially by acquiring an education, job, and remuneration. It is usually the pull factors that influence a person's decision making whether or not to migrate (Roberts 1974; Thomas-Hope 1992).

This paper will focus on international migration from Jamaica but will look generally at other Caribbean countries. The term "migration" will refer to international migration as defined earlier. Debates, various theories, and literature tend to focus only on the push and pull factors as the reasons influencing persons to migrate. In looking at migration from the Caribbean, however, the research has shown that although these push and pull factors are important, there are other contributing factors that propel this process and have not been covered by these traditional theories (Thomas-Hope 1992). Thomas-Hope citing Braithwaite refers to this as the "latent consciousness," which engulfs this process and which is not included in the traditional research literature.

Migration has always been present in the Caribbean and can be traced to the last two centuries. Since the abolition of slavery, the movements of the peoples from the various territories have been continuous. The literature has shown also that the migration process can be classified into different phases with the designated contributing factors associated to these phases. Thomas-Hope (1998) points out that after the abolition of slavery, a new social order was developed that showed persons with a need how to improve themselves both socially and materially and therefore enhance their own social status (189). Education was therefore seen as an important vehicle/tool to improve oneself whether by profession or occupation (191).

Background to Caribbean Migration

Migration within the Caribbean especially since the abolition of slavery may be regarded as involving different types of migrants at specific periods. Thomas-Hope (1998) identifies three major phases since the abolition of slavery that are important in this process. There is the early migration after the abolition of slavery, which involved the movements to the plantations of those sugar-producing islands undergoing expansion. These islands include Cuba, Puerto Rico, and the Dominican Republic. In addition to the expansion in the sugar-producing areas, the literature shows that towards the end of the nineteenth century, there was an expansion of the industrial operations within the region, which resulted in the employment of more persons. These operations included the Panama Canal, the railway construction in Central America, and the oil drilling and refining operations in Venezuela, Aruba, and the Netherlands Antilles of Curacao (194). The period 1911–1921 also saw an increase in the outward movement that included the trade expansion of fruits and strong communication links with Cuba and the United States, with 60 percent of the islands' exports going to the United States.

Jamaica had some 24,000 persons going to Panama, while some 121,000 persons went to Cuba. The later expansion involved the activities associated with North America and again involved the employment of migrants both seasonal and permanent persons. These operations included military bases, aluminum plants, tourism, banking, insurance, and other offshore industries (Thomas-Hope 1998, 194). Emigration to Europe and North American metropolis accelerated after the First World War and peaked in the fifties and sixties. In addition to the interregional migration, migrants from the Caribbean tended to emigrate to their respective "mother country" to which they had ties during the period of slavery. This being the case, the choice therefore would be for Jamaicans to go to Great Britain. There are many pull factors that contributed to this migration process. After the war, Europe had to rebuild and repair its basic infrastructure and therefore needed manpower, thus creating new job opportunities for immigrants. On the flip side, the depression also had an impact on the economies of these territories. Within the English-speaking area, there was the added complication of the devaluation of the British pound, which meant that imported goods would now be more expensive as these economies were dependent on getting even the basic items from the metropolitan countries. Some other pull factors included the following: language, previous relationship with the mother country, and exposure of persons who had volunteered to fight in the war, which experience would have been shared with family and friends. Roberts (1974) also cites other factors such as wage differentials, comprehensive social security system, financial assistance in case of unemployment and illness, and virtually free medical treatment. Roberts and Thomas-Hope in their analyses state however that they did not see much difference in the wages offered in the countries.

There were natural disasters such as hurricanes that affected banana, citrus, and other production. There were also the wars that affected the social and economic conditions of the country. With the decline in agricultural production and later in exports of manufactured goods, along with other factors such as growing unemployment, high cost of living, increasing external debts, reduction in public spending for social services, and high crime rate, it is estimated that some 30,000 persons migrated to the United States and the net migration to Cuba was some 22,000. Between the 1950s and the 1960s, there was a spurt of persons leaving for Great Britain, some 175,000 (Duany 2001; Roberts 1974).

There were other contributing factors including some policy changes that assisted this process. The year 1962 was an important milestone with the passing of the Commonwealth Immigration Act and with Jamaica gaining independence in that same year, and so ensured diplomatic relations with the United States of America. In 1965 there was also the passing of the United States Immigration and Nationality Act. Since 1965, a larger number of Caribbean persons have migrated to the United States (Thomas-Hope 1992).

Migration has impacted the lives of the migrants both in the country of origin and the receiving country. Thomas-Hope (2004) looks at the changes over the last three decades with regards to the destination as well as the composition of migrants. This has shown that the majority of the migrants go to the United

States and Canada, with the United Kingdom having the least. The age cohort 20 to 40 showed persons having the highest percentages in migrating, while there was also a high proportion of female migrants over males.

Social Factors

These factors will be analyzed by looking at the ways they affect the society as a whole. Social factors must therefore be seen both in terms of the out-migration country as well as the receiving country. The family is one of the institutions that has been affected by the migration process, and migration can either be beneficial to or adversely affect that institution. Research has shown that in the very early years of the migration to Great Britain, it was the norm for men, that is, the fathers and husbands, to migrate at first and then the wives, children, and in some cases other members of the extended family would follow. Canada's immigration policy tends to be sympathetic to a family being together. This system is based on a point system that emphasized education and skills. In the case of the United States, the pattern tends to be one parent, or both parents, migrate and then the children usually migrate last. Finding employment and the ability to provide for these persons is very important in the process (Thomas-Hope 1992; Duany 2001). The separation of members of the family has caused many problems for both countries. Crawford-Brown (1994) along with other Jamaican social workers use the term "barrel children" to describe a special category of children whose parents have migrated, but who depend on receiving these goods in barrels from the metropolitan countries. Emotionally however, these children are usually deprived of their parents' love, care, and protection—on the spot love—and so they themselves sometimes create other problems (1). These children sometimes stay with a grandmother, a relative, a household helper, friends, or in some cases have the older sibling looking after them. While some of these persons migrate legally, that is, have the necessary documentation, others go on a temporary basis and so they cannot sponsor any members of the family at least immediately, hence the long periods of separation.

Social Mobility is an important factor that engages the average migrant. Research has shown that migration is usually seen as a tool for upward mobility, and therefore persons would be able to achieve this goal. But as many of the migrants found out, within this new environment, this was not always the case. Thompson and Bauer (2003) document some interesting findings concerning migrants in Britain, Canada, and the United States. Some persons who migrated and had senior managerial jobs within their home country found that they had to take much less junior jobs within the new country and sometimes could not get jobs within the field that they were qualified (95). Thomas-Hope (1998) points out however that especially "among the masses" the migration is usually regarded as improving oneself materially and this would "enhance the social status" (190). The tendency was therefore to acquire the capital and this would be used to purchase the land, house, and even other disposable house-hold items and clothes.

Race and class play a critical part of the socialization process. The earlier migrants who lived in Britain were not as perturbed about the racial problems as the younger folks, especially those who were born there. The older migrants who went to Britain were accustomed within their home country's stratification system that had the whites at the top of the social ladder and blacks at the bottom (Thompson and Bauer 2003, 95). They were therefore more able to cope with the open racism whether it was at work, on the buses, at houses, or in the communities. This was not really new to them because in their home country they were accustomed to see whites treated in a particular way. Racism has shown its ugly head in many ways, such as in communities, in workplaces and schools, and even in relationships. According to Thompson and Bauer, racism in the subtle form kept the Jamaican migrants in a subordinate position (96). In America, in the early 1960s there was racial segregation in terms of public facilities and this was legal. This practice was imposed in about a third of the country, and this also involved the prohibition of mixed marriages. This also designated certain neighborhoods in the United States as black communities, although legislation was passed to address this issue.

Culture

Literature has shown that some of the migrants suffered from culture shock when they reached their new destination. One of the areas that migrants seem to be wary of is the climatic conditions (Thompson and Bauer 2003). The sharp contrast to the Jamaican sun and heat is usually blatant especially in the winter months with the fog and snow and even in the summer, especially in England, with the sun shining even though the weather is cold. Other areas include the blatant poverty among whites, the type of manual work in which they were engaged, which included scrubbing the floors and sweeping the streets. Then there were the living conditions that were so sparse, as some of these houses had no inside toilet (91). The buildings also provided some concerns especially since they seemed so old and dirty. While most of these were contributed to Britain, similar sentiments were also expressed to those living in the United States, where persons saw potholes, broken-down buildings, and poor people living rough lives. Thompson also added the emotional costs of migration and the sheer "loss and loneliness" that these migrants suffered in this new environment, which is much more impersonal than the one they had left (92). There was the role of being treated as a "nobody," and looked on as a number and a minority.

Economic Factors

Most of the countries within the Caribbean benefit economically from the flow of remittances or transfers by the migrants to their home countries.

Research has shown that the Caribbean is the "world's largest recipient of remittances, as a share of GDP" (Mishra 2006, 5). In Jamaica, remittances continue to increase each year and provide a significant contribution to the national economy as well as the individuals. Thomas-Hope (2004) points out those remittances provide a significant proportion of Jamaica's GDP. Thomas-Hope citing Samuel states that in the mid-nineties the contribution accounted for some 11.5 percent of the country's GDP. In the late nineties, when "calculated as a ratio of goods and services, remittances accounted for more than 17 %" (21). It may however be difficult to measure this accurately as there are many informal channels such as family and friends (Mishra 2006, 6). There is no doubt that some persons who migrate benefit economically and are able to provide economically more resources for the family.

Brain Drain

Some of the most educated and skilled personnel within the country migrate. The cost of this education cannot be compensated. Also the absence of these brilliant young minds is sometimes hard to compensate. An IMF document states that tertiary-level labor force (with more than twelve years of schooling) in Jamaica has been reduced by 85 percent due to emigration to OECD member countries. It must be taken into consideration that Jamaica spends more on tertiary education than primary and secondary. There is also the other side of the coin where the brain gain happens, and this relates to the value added of persons who migrate and return bringing some new skills and experience. It is very difficult to measure as stated in the literature (Thomas-Hope 2004; Mishra 2006).

Conclusion

There is a saying that migration is in the psyche of the average Caribbean person. Thomas-Hope looks at the image of migration and "the migration of one generation of Caribbean people becomes part of the image of the next. For migration is interpreted a component of the cultural environment and therefore becomes part of the image. The migrants—those still abroad and those who have returned to the Caribbean—are never completely displaced from their home society nor lost from the system" (1998). "They themselves and their migration are part of the reality for a time but remain part of the myth forever" (158).

BIBLIOGRAPHY

Anderson, Patricia Y. 1985. *Migration and Development in Jamaica.* Paper no. 2 (June). Mona, Jamaica: Institute of Social and Economic Research.

Bryce-Laporte, Roy Simon. 1985. *Caribbean Immigrations and Their Implications for the United States.* Washington, D.C.: Wilson Center.

Crawford-Brown, Claudette, and Melrose Rattray. 1994. "The 'Barrel Children' of the Caribbean: The Socio-Cultural Context of the Migrant Caribbean Family." Kingston, Jamaica: Department of Sociology and Social Work, University of the West Indies.

Duany, Jorge. 2001. "Beyond the Safety Valve: Recent Trends in Caribbean Migration." In *Caribbean Sociology: Introductory Readings,* edited by Christine Barrow and Rhoda Reddock. Kingston, Jamaica: Ian Randle. Pp. 861–876.

Hodge, Warren. 2006. "Nations Benefit from Migration, U.N. Study Says." *New York Times,* June 7. http://www.nytimes.com/world/. Accessed July 6, 2006.

Kritz, Mary M., Charles B. Keely, and Silvano M. Tomasi. 1981. *Global Trends in Migration.* Staten Island, New York: Centre for Migration Studies.

Lee, Everett S. 1969. "A Theory of Migration." In *Migration,* edited by J. A. Jackson. Cambridge: Cambridge University Press. Pp. 282–291.

Mishra, Prachi. 2006. "Emigration and Brain Drain: Evidence from the Caribbean." Working paper, International Monetary Fund.

Namboodiri, N. Krishnan. 1996. *A Primer of Population Dynamics.* New York: Plenum Press.

Palmer, Ransford. 1983. "Emigration and the Economic Decline of Jamaica." In *White Collar Migrants in the Americas and the Caribbean,* edited by Arnaud Marks and Hebe Vessuri. Leiden, Netherlands: Department of Caribbean Studies, Royal Institute of Linguistics and Anthropology. Pp. 59–72.

Pastor, Robert A. [1983]. *Caribbean Emigration and US Immigration Policy: Cross Currents.* [San German, P.R.]: Universidad Interamericana del Puerto Rico, Centro de Investigaciones Del Caribe y America Latina.

Planning Institute of Jamaica. 2005. *Economic and Social Survey.* Kingston, Jamaica: Planning Institute of Jamaica.

Roberts, George. 1974. *Recent Population Movements in Jamaica.* Kingston, Jamaica: Herald.

Roberts, George, and D. Mills. 1958. *Study of External Migration Affecting Jamaica: 1953–55.* Kingston, Jamaica: Institute of Social and Economic Research.

Senior, Clarence, and Douglas Manley. 1955. *A Report on Jamaican Migration to Great Britain.* Kingston, Jamaica: Government Printer.

Sutherland, Peter. 2006. "UN Report: Migration Is Not a One-Way Street." *International Herald Tribune,* June 7. http://www.iht.com/articles. Accessed June 7, 2006.

Thomas-Hope, Elizabeth. 1983. "Off the Island: Population Mobility among the Caribbean Middle Class." In *White Collar Migrants in the Americas and the Caribbean,* edited by Arnaud Marks and Hebe Vessuri. Leiden, Netherlands: Department of Caribbean Studies, Royal Institute of Linguistics and Anthropology. Pp. 39–58.

———. 1992. *Explanation in Caribbean Migration: Perception and the Image: Jamaica, Barbados, and St. Vincent.* London: Macmillan.

———. 1998. "Globalization and the Development of a Caribbean Migration Culture." In *Caribbean Migration: Globalised Identities,* edited by Mary Chamberlain. London; New York: Routledge. Pp. 189–199.

Thomas-Hope, Elizabeth. 2000. "Trends and Patterns of Migration to and from the Caribbean." In *International Migration and Development in the Americas.* Chile: International Organization of Migration. Pp. 58–70.

———. 2002. *Caribbean Migration.* Kingston, Jamaica: University of the West Indies Press.

———. 2004. "Migration Situation Analysis, Policy and Programme Needs for Jamaica." Report prepared for the United Nations Population Fund through the Planning Office of Jamaica. http://caribbean.unfpa.org. Accessed January 16, 2007.

Thompson, Paul, and Elaine Bauer. 2003. "Evolving Jamaican Migrant Identities: Contrasts between Britain, Canada and the USA." *Community, Work and Family* 6, no. 1:89–102.

Weeks, John R. 1996. *Population.* Belmont, Calif.: Wadsworth.

4. The Reflection of the Local and Regional Migratory Experience in the Special Collections of the Main Library of the University of the West Indies, St. Augustine

Allison Dolland
Kathleen Helenese-Paul
Yacoob Hosein

Introduction

This paper briefly examines the historical genesis of local and regional ethnic and cultural diversity with a focus on the English-speaking Caribbean and in particular Trinidad and Tobago. Within this context the paper highlights some of the special collections of the Main Library that reflect the diaspora. It is necessary at this point to state that these collections vary in that there are those which represent firstly the works/papers of descendants of migrants and secondly those collections whose content directly reflect the traditions and lived experience of the ancestors (original migrants). Areas of policy, access to collections, and directions for future development are outlined, taking into consideration the challenges faced.

The Main Library at the University of the West Indies (UWI), St. Augustine, has for decades served as a repository for documents and artifacts that depict the history and contributions of the many ethnic groups which have shaped the current socioeconomic, financial, and cultural landscape of Trinidad and Tobago and the Caribbean. It had in fact, since its inception, been one of the institutions sharing the role of a national library with the Central Library Services in Trinidad and Tobago until the opening of the National Library on March 26, 2003.

The West Indiana and Special Collections Division (WISCD) began with a fledgling array of predominantly agricultural materials acquired before 1960. At its core is material inherited from the Imperial College of Tropical Agriculture (ICTA) when the latter merged with the University College of the West Indies (as UWI was then known) in 1960 to become the Faculty of Agriculture. The WISCD collection continued to be developed through purchase; legal deposits of works published in Trinidad and Tobago; and gifts from faculty, members of the public, and the other UWI campuses. The collection has material in all formats but the special collections comprise primarily unpublished source materials such as personal papers, archival materials, rare books, and oral history tapes and transcripts, which have been derived from the library's Oral and Pictorial Records Programme (OPReP). To date, there are eighty collections that have been donated by or purchased from various citizens of Trinidad and Tobago and Caribbean personalities such as Nobel laureate Derek Walcott; renowned novelists Samuel Selvon, C. L. R. James, and Michael Anthony; and noted historian and former prime minister of the Republic of Trinidad and Tobago, Dr. Eric Williams. They span a variety of themes including music, literature, history, politics, and art.

It is important to note that along with the WISCD collections, special collections exist in national libraries and archives regionally and also reside in the depositories of first world institutions. Together they provide the region with the full picture of its colonial history. It is to be noted however that prized primary material has been lost due to the nonrecognition of their historical significance, natural disasters, lack of resources for adequate preservation, and even climatic conditions.

Colonizing the Caribbean

During the first voyage of the explorer Christopher Columbus, contact was made with the Lucayans in the Bahamas and the Taino in Cuba and the northern coast of Hispaniola. Colonists estimated that at the time of first contact the Amerindian population numbered some 40,000.[1] The Spanish, who came seeking wealth, enslaved the native population and rapidly drove them to near extinction. Although Spain claimed the entire Caribbean, they settled only the larger islands of Hispaniola, Puerto Rico, Cuba, Jamaica, and Trinidad.

Other European powers such as the French, Dutch, and British established a presence in the Caribbean after the Spanish Empire declined. England was by far the most successful of the northwestern European predators on the Spanish possessions. Trinidad came under Spanish rule when Columbus took possession of the island in 1498 on behalf of the crown of Spain, but it was not until 1532 that the island was colonized by the Spaniards. In 1783, when the Royal Cedula of Population offered large tracts of land in Trinidad on very favorable terms to Catholic settlers, the French came in droves. There were on a smaller scale some Irish, German, Italian, and English settlers. Trinidad was captured by a British naval expedition headed by Sir Ralph Abercromby in 1797 and was formally ceded to the British Crown in 1802 under the Treaty of Amiens.

The sister island of Tobago was initially isolated and unknown to Europeans for many decades after the discovery of Trinidad. As early as 1628, settlement by the Dutch began on the island in the vicinity of Plymouth on the western end of the island.[2]

The island changed hands among the Dutch, the English, and the French. In 1763, Tobago was ceded to Britain, captured by the French in 1781, and recaptured by the British in 1793. Finally, the island was ceded to Britain in 1814 by the Treaty of Paris.

Most of the primary materials concerning the early history of the region can be found in the archives of the former colonists. A few precious vestiges have remained in the region and are of critical importance in any exploration of the genesis of the region's sociohistorical development. A collection reflecting the presence of the earliest inhabitants is the Bullbrook Papers. John Bullbrook was a historian who came to Trinidad in 1913 as a petroleum geologist. He pioneered the search on the indigenous population of Trinidad, conducting extensive excavations in the Amerindian middens in various parts of the island. The collection contains correspondence with Yale University, 1941–1963; the historical society of Trinidad and Tobago, 1938–1949; and the Trinidad and Tobago Field Naturalists' Club.[3]

Among the collections held in the WISCD that explore the tapestry of daily life on a small plantation is the Young diaries, which provides a firsthand account of life on the sister island of Tobago from Sir William Young, governor of Tobago in the early-nineteenth century (1807–1815). This special collection contains his memoranda, accounts, invoices, and other documents relating to his properties. His historical, statistical, and descriptive account of the island of Tobago in his diaries provides valuable primary source material for research into the era. The works are well illustrated with watercolor sketches and maps done by Sir William Young himself. The original three volumes have been in the library's possession since the establishment of the university. A fourth volume of illustrations was purchased from a private individual in Australia in 1978. The library also has microfilm copies of three other versions of the manuscripts. The originals to these are held at the British Library, the Public Record Office, and the Royal Library at Windsor.[4]

Another diary providing authentic insights into plantation life is the Diary of Governor Ross. David Robert Ross was lieutenant governor of the British colony of Tobago in the West Indies for approximately six months in 1851. The diary covers the period January 1 to June 27, 1851. The first page of the diary contains a list of books at the government house in Tobago on June 12, 1851. This is followed by a seven-page description of Tobago with information on the following subjects: soil and rocks, rivers, climate, vegetable products, trees, coffee and tobacco, sugarcane, game, divisions, parishes, estates, and roads.

Critical to the study of the economic and social history of Trinidad and Tobago is an exploration of the Colonial Bank papers. The Colonial Bank, precursor to Barclay's Bank PLC and the present Republic Bank Limited, was established in the West Indian colonies as an effort, on the part of a group of merchants and private bankers in London, to fill the need for a banking system. Business commenced in Trinidad and other colonies (Jamaica, Barbados, British Guiana, St. Thomas) on May 15, 1837. By the end of 1837, thirteen branches and agencies had been established. The collection of letters consists of the incoming correspondence to the Colonial Bank in Trinidad from its inception in 1837 to 1885. It comprises a total of 1,848 items, the majority of which (about 57 percent) are letters from the Court of Directors in London to the manager in Trinidad. The correspondence also affords an insight into the banking needs of the sugar planters and the precarious nature of sugar production in the nineteenth century.[5]

Researchers seeking greater insight into British politics and details of the colonial legacy of the Caribbean would find the West India Committee Records of central importance. The committee was formed in the eighteenth century by a permanent association of London merchants engaged in the West Indian trade and absentee owners of West Indian estates who lived in London and its environs. It functioned as a pressure group for West Indian interests during the era of the abolition of slavery. The records include minute books of the general meetings of the Committee of Planters and Merchants together with its standing committees; minutes of the Literary Committee; minutes of the Committee of West India Merchants; and other miscellaneous records. The minute books were purchased by the Trinidad and Tobago government and deposited at the Main Library of UWI, St. Augustine.[6]

With regard to the French Creole influence, the Lopinot Family Papers, 1697–1998 comprise photocopies of original documents relating to the history of the family of Charles Joseph, Compte de Lopinot. In tracing the historical contribution of this French Creole planter to the socioeconomic landscape of the island of Trinidad, access to this special collection is critical. Charles Joseph Lopinot, sugar and cocoa planter, was born in 1738 and arrived in Trinidad in 1800 from St. Domingue. He was appointed brigadier general in the Trinidad Militia and in 1813 was also appointed to the Council of Advice. He later settled in one of the valleys of the Northern Range where, today, the village bears his name. The collection is accompanied by a brief account of the Lopinot family by Jerome F. Lopinot, a descendant of the original settler.

The life and times of another French Creole planter of note in the region is explored in the Roume de St. Laurent collection. St. Laurent was a French planter on the island of Grenada in the 1770s. He visited Trinidad and subsequently lobbied the Spanish colonial authorities resulting in the 1783 Cedula of Population, which was responsible for a wave of French immigration to Trinidad. This radically altered the cultural and linguistic landscape of the island. Vestiges of this heritage are still apparent even today. The collection consists of photocopies of three eighteenth-century manuscripts relating to the island of Tobago.

The diaries of Abbe Armand Massé, a French missionary priest, record his journey from France to Trinidad in September 1878 and detail his time and work in Trinidad. A record of his daily thoughts, the diaries shed light on a range of subjects, conditions, events, and situations in nineteenth-century Trinidad. These include descriptions of presbyteries and churches, religious feasts and ceremonies, flora and fauna, and the customs and lifestyles of the different ethnic groups on the island. Many undergraduate and graduate students refer to these diaries as source material in the course of their research on the religious history and social conditions of the island in the early-nineteenth century.[7]

Since colonization in the region ended in the mid-twentieth century, it is also important to have access to more recent accounts of the region's history, thereby ensuring that a more complete chronology of the colonial legacy is available. One collection that helps fill one gap is the Martin Adamson Papers, which explores developments in the area of education in the colony. Adamson was born in Scotland in 1901 and trained in zoology at the University of St. Andrews. On completion of his studies, he was appointed assistant in zoology to Professor D'Arcy Wentworth Thompson at St. Andrews, and they developed a lifelong friendship. In 1933 he was appointed senior lecturer and head of the Department of Entomology at ICTA. While on staff he obtained his Ph.D. degree from the University of California and was promoted to the rank of professor. He served on the staff of ICTA until his death in 1945. This collection is of interest as primary source material for the study of social conditions in Trinidad and Tobago in general and the history of ICTA, giving insights into opportunities for staff at that time, activities of particular departments, and other matters of general interest.[8]

The African Presence

In the wake of the European landings in the Americas, Africans were shipped across the Atlantic in ever growing numbers. At first the presence of the African slaves seemed incidental, merely a useful addition to local settlement and the agricultural landscape. However, it was the development of the sugar industry, first effectively shaped in Brazil, later in the Caribbean, and in the tobacco fields of the Chesapeake that Africans proved their worth to their European owners. It was a development with obvious consequences on various continents (Africa, Europe, and the Americas) and with ramifications even further afield. There evolved an amazingly complex global trade orchestrated by the European maritime powers, led by the Spaniards and Portuguese, then the Dutch, and only much later the French and the British. The fruits of slave labor (sugar, rum, rice, tobacco, and other tropical staples) reshaped European social life; the profits and material well-being from their efforts enhanced the material fortunes of the Western world. Britain abolished the slave trade in 1807. In 1817 Spain signed a treaty with Britain agreeing to abolish the slave trade in 1820, but the trade continued to the remaining Spanish colonies until 1880. In 1848 the French abolished slavery while Portugal did the same in 1869.

Even after the abolition of slavery, the former slaves were allowed little scope for maintaining their cultural identity. However, vestiges remain of their original faiths, music, language, and food, some altered through interaction with other ethnic groups. Historical artifacts related to the African experience and histories on the islands are contained in colonial records, maps, and rare books and reflect the experience of slavery from the prospective colonist. Other materials relate directly to recordings of the lived experience and are found in oral histories derived from the Oral and Pictorial Records Programme (OPReP).

One of the oldest special collections which gives a glimpse of the realities of the African presence in the region is the Grenada Plantation Reconveyance of Mortgage Document. This document is dated March 31, 1774, between Charles Sloane Cadogan (of Whitehall, Westminster) on the one hand and four other British subjects on the other. The agreement is for a loan of £20,500 to purchase from Andrew Davoran a 320-acre estate in St. George's parish, Grenada, West Indies. The document includes the names of about fifty slaves (first name only) as well as other possessions and equipment on the plantation.

Trinidad's religious and linguistic heritage is illustrated in the Christian Prayers in Yoruba collection. This collection of wooden plaques inscribed with Christian prayers in Yoruba can be traced back to a colorful Trinidadian character, a Mr. Joseph Joseph, popularly known as Mr. Zampty of Sierra Leone Village, Diego Martin, Trinidad. His maternal grandparents were from West Africa, and he developed a scholarly interest in Yoruba and taught the language at an evening school in River Estate in the late 1920s. He had learned the rudiments of wood carving from older Africans and undertook the engraving of prayers and other sentiments onto wooden plaques.[9] The six wooden plaques are inscribed with Christian prayers in the Yoruba language. Supplementing this collection, another set of tapes and accompanying transcripts, OPReP #23, provide insights into African religious heritage handed down from slavery, which remain alive and well in the region in various forms. These tapes focus on Andrew Beddoe, an Orisha priest and African drummer.

Other oral history tapes illustrate attempts by twentieth-century historians and intellectuals to reconstruct in detail, using primary sources, the African experience before and after emancipation. OPReP #46 provides access to conference presentations from the "African Past and the African Diaspora: A Symposium to Mark the 150th Anniversary of the Emancipation of Slaves."

Some of the newer collections explore the birth of black consciousness and give insight into the many aspects of the Pan-Africanist movement. One such collection is the Amy Ashwood Garvey Memorabilia. Amy was the first wife of Marcus Garvey, founder of the Universal Negro Improvement Association (UNIA). She was reported to have traveled widely throughout Jamaica, Panama, the United States, England, Liberia, Ghana, Nigeria, Trinidad and Tobago, and Las Palmas. The collection, comprising photographs, correspondence, and a long playing record, sheds light on the friendship between Amy Ashwood Garvey and Thelma Rogers of Trinidad and Tobago.[10] Another collection with such a focus is the George James Christian Papers (1868–1940).

Born in Dominica and educated in London, George James Christian was a Pan-Africanist who led the discussion on slavery and colonization at the first Pan-African Congress. He then migrated to the Gold Coast (Ghana) and in 1902 became a prominent criminal and concessions lawyer. In addition to Christian's papers, the library also owns tapes (OPReP #37) containing interviews with Ghanaian friends and relatives of Christian.

Subsequent Waves of Migration

With the emancipation of slaves in 1834 and the premature termination of the apprenticeship period in 1838, a significant proportion of ex-slaves abandoned the estates for alternative means of livelihood. Some had taken to the towns as skilled workers, others to small peasant cultivation, and those who remained recognized their bargaining power which resulted in increased wage rates in the industry. With the Caribbean islands "saddled with serious labour shortages . . . a few colonies of the region soon started to experiment with the importation of indentured labourers to keep their plantations alive."[11]

Chinese Migration to Trinidad

As early as 1802, some 23 Chinese were brought to the island of Trinidad on a trial basis for the sugar estates.[12] This was followed by the arrival of the *Fortitude* in October 1806, with 192 of an original 200 Chinese recruited in Macao and Penang and in Calcutta.[13] Initially, the government actively supported the scheme, but when their policy changed many of the early laborers attempted to repatriate or sought every available opportunity to enter into entrepreneurial pursuits. Chinese migration to the British West Indies got a fillip when it restarted in the 1850s. Between 1853 and 1884, Trinidad imported some 2,645 immigrants.[14] "When the importation of Chinese labour ceased in 1873, inter colony migration of Chinese labourers continued within the region. This resulted in a number of Chinese leaving British Guiana for Trinidad and thereby swelling their numbers in the latter colony to 5600 in 1946 and by the late 1960s they had increased to about 8400."[15]

East Indian Migration to the Caribbean

The Indian immigrants were brought to the Caribbean solely for the economic survival of the sugar industry. "About 90 percent of the immigrants came from the area of the Ganges plains: United Provinces, Oudh, Bihar, Orissa, and Central Provinces; a minority came from Bengal, the North West Provinces, and the South."[16] These laborers were recruited from their respective villages by professional recruiters who, for the most part, served the interests of many colonial powers that were heavily involved in the indentured system. The indentured laborers were contracted initially for three-year contracts and ten-year residence for the requisite requirement for the return passage to India. Later, the passage could have been commuted for a parcel of land.

The first shipment of 217 indentured laborers arrived in Trinidad on May 30, 1845, on board the *Fath Al Razak.* This stream of workers continued with minor interruptions until it was terminated in 1917. During the period about 143,900 came to Trinidad and stemmed the decline of the sugar industry by supplying a steady labor force. The descendants of the East Indian emigrants presently accounts for 38 percent of the population of Trinidad and Tobago, and they contribute significantly to the social, economic, and political development of the country.

Portuguese Migration to Trinidad and Tobago

Portuguese migration to Trinidad and Tobago took place primarily in the nineteenth century. Portuguese indentured laborers began to arrive in the Caribbean from the archipelago of the Azores in 1834, the year slavery was abolished. These Azorean laborers were the first Portuguese immigrant laborers to come to any of the West Indian territories but they were illegal immigrants. It was not until 1846 that the first group of legal Portuguese immigrants arrived in Trinidad from Madeira as contract laborers. Only one special collection provides insights into the Portuguese contribution to the historical development of the island. This collection of audiotapes (OPReP #75) represents interviews of descendants of Portuguese settlers in Trinidad and Tobago.[17] These tapes as well as documents from the WISCD thesis collection detail some of the experiences of Portuguese laborers on the island.

Some Collections Reflecting Migration

Special collections that reflect the contribution of some of the newer ethnic groups which joined the melting pot of Trinidadian and indeed Caribbean society include those that explore the Chinese presence. An early collection that explores the contributions of one of the more historically significant members of the Chinese community is the Hochoy Papers. Solomon Hochoy was born in Jamaica of Chinese parents on April 20, 1905, and arrived in Trinidad as an infant. He rose through the ranks of the civil service becoming colonial secretary in 1956. He became the first local governor of Trinidad and Tobago and later governor-general from 1962 to 1972. The collection includes documents concerning Sir Solomon Hochoy as governor from 1960, then as governor-general from 1962. Correspondence with Buckingham Palace and, to a limited extent, with Dr. Eric Williams also forms part of the collection.[18]

The Carlisle Chang Collection is one of the more recent additions to primary resources. Carlisle Chang, a local artist of renown, was born in San Juan, Trinidad and Tobago, in 1921. His father was a migrant from China and his mother, who was also of Chinese descent, was from British Guiana. The collection includes sketches of carnival costumes, numerous other sketch pads, photographs, slides, correspondence, newspaper clippings, documents relating to Carifesta V, catalogues of art exhibitions, and the medal of the Bienal de Sao

Paulo, Brazil. Deposit of the collection was as a result of a bequest from the executors of Chang's estate after his death in 2001.

Several collections explore various aspects of East Indian contributions to historical development. These include taped conference proceedings (OPReP #92), which cover presentations made on music, language, gender, and race relations in "Challenge and Change: The Indian Diaspora in Its Historical and Contemporary Contexts," a conference commemorating the 150th anniversary of the arrival of Indian indentured laborers in Trinidad. OPReP #54 consists of interviews of surviving indentured laborers and their descendants. The interviews were conducted in the Bhojpuri dialect, which was the "ethnic language" of the Indian community in Trinidad.[19]

Dennis Jules Mahabir was born in Trinidad, West Indies, in April 1920. He was the son of Jules Mahabir, the first Indo-Trinidadian magistrate, and Minnie Mahabir, founders of the Minerva Club and patrons of the *Minerva Review,* an early Indian literary magazine in Trinidad. He was editor of the *Spectator* and associate editor of the *Observer,* two Indian literary magazines in Trinidad. He also served as mayor of Port of Spain from 1957 to 1960. The Mahabir collection consists mainly of periodicals, including almost complete runs of the *Spectator, Observer,* and *Minerva Review,* and a few issues each of the *Indian, Sentinel,* and *Trinidad Presbyterian.* It also includes the manuscript of his novel *The Cutlass Is Not for Killing* (1970) and a copy of the "Report on the Carnival Riots (1881)."[20]

Another collection that explores the contribution of a notable East Indian figure in local history is the Capildeo Papers. Dr. Rudranath Capildeo, mathematician, lawyer, and politician, rose to prominence when he became a political leader of the Democratic Labour Party (DLP) in Trinidad and Tobago in 1960. As leader of the Opposition, he played a key role in the negotiations leading to the independence of Trinidad and Tobago in 1962. The collection comprises twenty-eight letters, fifteen of which were written by Capildeo himself while he was a lecturer at University College, London. This collection is central to any discourse on the political history of the island.[21]

The Middle East Connection

The Syrians and Lebanese came to the Caribbean after the 1880s not as contract labor "but migrants in search of a more prosperous and secure future than could be found in the Ottoman-dominated Middle East."[22] These migrants were mainly "from a small-landholder or tenant-farmer background, though they also included those with some educational attainment—school teachers and small businessmen."[23] These immigrants were mostly young unmarried males who started as itinerant peddlers who moved into shopkeeping, textile trading, and the import/export business.[24] Few married into the local society as most of their matrimonial partners were either arranged from their Levant homeland or from their tightly knit local and regional community.

They continued to "maintain strong links with the Middle East and perpetuate Arab customs in their family."[25] This ethnic separateness is "also carried over to their business activities; most Levantine businesses remain family and private concerns."[26] Their business and familial connections extend throughout the Caribbean and this provides them with considerable leverage for economic pursuits. The buoyant economy of Trinidad and Tobago has enabled them to successfully carve a niche in the socioeconomic fabric of the country. While there is very little primary material in the Main Library's collections on this group other than entries in colonial records, there are five Caribbean studies projects that depict the life and work of the Syrians and Lebanese in Trinidad and Tobago.[27]

The earliest Jews who came to the Caribbean were the Sephardic Jews of Spain and Portugal who fled from religious persecution. By 1916, the Jews on the island of Trinidad numbered about 20 (13 males and 7 females) who would have migrated from Curacao. All resided in the capital, Port of Spain, and their principal economic pursuits at that time were in commerce, agriculture, and the professions. Their smallness in numbers at that time militated against them from forming a Jewish community. However, their economic wealth enhanced their acceptance into the higher echelons of society, and they were able to mingle freely with the population and even intermarry.[28]

Later the island received its first influx of Jews when Germany overran Austria (the "Anschuss") in 1938. The island's lax immigration laws were soon restricted with the issuance of an order under the Immigration (Restriction) Ordinance of 1936, which was designed to stem the flow of the refugees. By February 1940, a total of 585 refugees had entered the island, 87 left, leaving 498.[29] As Martin noted, "For the first time in its history Trinidad became host to a visible, active Jewish community, complete with synagogues, Zionist and other organizations, special voluntary Jewish education for its children and an exclusive burial ground."[30]

Limited primary materials on this ethnic group are present in the Main Library's special collections. The only collection that provides insight into this part of the society is the collection Historical Notes on the Jews in Trinidad. These personal accounts, by Hans John Stecher and his family written in the 1930s, look back to the period of Jewish presence in Trinidad from about 1932 to the early war years and the Jewish emigration as a result of the annexation of Austria by the Nazis.[31]

Intra-Caribbean Migration

Migration of people between the Caribbean islands is a phenomenon that began as early as the nineteenth century. After the abolition of the British slave trade in 1807, new sources of labor had to be sought so that the agricultural economy could continue to flourish. After the Emancipation Act in 1838, it was observed by Ottley that the decade 1838 to 1848 saw an influx of labor from other Caribbean territories. According to him:

> It was not until 1843 that the first concession to obtain immigrants from Sierra Leone was granted. In the meantime, Trinidad's only salvation lay in enticing away from the shores of the other West Indian islands as many of the former slaves as possible, and in opening her traditionally open doors even wider to a motley collection of immigrants, black and white, who had heard of the reputedly good living and higher wages which residence in the country afforded.[32]

However, "in the first five years following emancipation, it was from the other West Indian islands that Trinidad drew most of its working population. . . . Despite the efforts of the several of the other islands, the labourers continued to arrive in Trinidad in their thousands year after year."[33] The island was attractive as a destination because it was a source of immediate employment since the development of the plantations and the corresponding need for labor occurred later than in other territories. The other factor was the possibility of acquiring or squatting on Crown lands as also happened in Jamaica and Guyana. It is stated: "In the 1970's the drift southwards continued . . . Trinidad relied chiefly on Grenada, St. Kitts and Nevis and sometimes Montserrat, though drawing many emigrants from other islands, while British Guiana depended heavily on Barbados."[34]

Traditionally then, Trinidad has always attracted migrants from the other West Indian territories characterized by the uneven economic development of the region. According to Basch, "Labour migration is a deeply institutionalized strategy for economic subsistence and betterment within the Caribbean."[35] Even when the sugar industry declined in the twentieth century, Trinidad continued to be a destination for migrants from neighboring territories experiencing conditions of economic stagnation.[36] Continuing into the twentieth century, Trinidad would be destined to attract immigrants from the other islands through the opening of the military bases during World War II and later through the rise of its oil industry.

Among the collections reflecting this intra-Caribbean migratory experience is the Derek Walcott Collection. Walcott, Nobel laureate for literature in 1992, is a St. Lucian poet and dramatist of international repute. He attended UWI in Mona, Jamaica, and lived for many years in Trinidad and Tobago, where he founded the Trinidad Theatre Workshop. The material comprises the illustrations and set drawings for *The Joker of Seville,* manuscripts of other plays, poems, correspondence, scrap books, and photographs, which cover the period when he was based in Trinidad and Tobago. Much of his poetry and prose up to 1981 also form part of the collection along with manuscripts for the poem *Omeros.* The collection was accepted for inclusion in UNESCO's Memory of the World Register in November 1997. It is one of the few collections that provides insights into the development of the arts in the region and facilitates the exploration of the definition of a regional self through art.[37]

The library has in its possession a collection from another renowned St. Lucian, the Earl Lewis Memorabilia. Dr. Earl Lewis, born in St. Lucia, was the brother of the late Sir Arthur Lewis, Nobel laureate in economics in 1967, and Sir Allen Lewis, the first governor-general of the island. He studied medicine at Manchester University and later specialized in psychiatry. In 1943 he joined the staff at St. Ann's Hospital, Trinidad and Tobago. He was instrumental in starting the Caribbean Federation for Mental Health and became its first president in 1959. The collection consists of correspondence with family members and colleagues, notes, and memorabilia. They shed light on Dr. Lewis's professional development, his family life and relationships, and on the social climate of the time.

One special collection that reflects the popular culture of the mid-twentieth century is the Raymond Quevedo Collection. Son of a Trinidadian mother and a Venezuelan father, Quevedo was educated at St. Mary's College in Trinidad. He later became a calypsonian, using the sobriquet Atilla the Hun. In 1946 he entered politics, was president-general of the Trinidad Labour Party, and won a seat on the Port-of-Spain City Council. He effectively merged his two roles as calypsonian and politician. The collection consists of 262 items, of which 138 are manuscripts. Included in these are manuscript copies of his book entitled *Atilla's Kaiso: A Short History of Trinidad Calypso* (1983) and short stories by him and others. Seventy-five letters written by Quevedo in various capacities are also included.[38]

The Wooding/Fraser Papers provide the researcher with insights into local jurisprudence. Sir Hugh Wooding was born of Barbadian parents in Trinidad and Tobago in 1904. He attended Queen's Royal College in Trinidad and Tobago and Middle Temple Inns of Courts and was admitted to the bar in 1927. He established an outstanding reputation in the field of civil and commercial litigation. He entered municipal politics in 1941 and became mayor of Port of Spain two years later. He was the first son of the soil to be appointed chief justice of Trinidad and Tobago (1962). Following his retirement, he served as chairman of the Constitutional Reform Commission and chancellor of UWI. Justice Aubrey Fraser was born in Barbados of Guyanese parents in 1921 and was called to the bar at Gray's Inn in 1948. He practiced law in Guyana from 1949 and joined the Supreme Court. He remained on the bench until 1962 when he was transferred to the High Court in Trinidad and Tobago and later elevated to the Court of Appeal. He worked with Sir Hugh Wooding in the latter phase of his life and the two men became great friends. Justice Fraser served as director of the Norman Manley Law School in Jamaica from 1972 to 1984. The collection mainly consists of correspondence between the two legal jurists who conferred with each other on legal and other issues. The material sheds light on various aspects of the life of both men, as well as on the social and political life in the two societies.[39]

One collection provides the researcher with information on activism in the labor movement during the first half of the twentieth century in Trinidad and Tobago. The Gaskynd Granger Papers includes a miscellany of documents: acts, booklets, bulletins, correspondence, financial statements, handwritten minutes, invitations, memos, miscellaneous forms, newspaper clippings, and reports. Granger was born in Guyana and later settled in Trinidad and Tobago. In the 1930s he became a member of the Negro Welfare Cultural and Social Association. He was one of the founders of the Public Works and Public Service Workers Trade Union that was formed in 1937 and served as a member of the union's executive. He was also a member of the National Union of Government Employees (NUGE). He was active in Tobago as a member of the Tobago Peasants and Industrial Workers Union, which was founded by A. P. T. James in 1946.[40]

Conclusion

In fulfillment of its mandate to be a leading repository of unique Caribbean materials, the WISCD has, despite difficulties, acquired some eighty special collections mainly in the disciplines of the social sciences, the humanities, and agriculture. The acquisition of many of these collections has been due to the goodwill of philanthropic donors. In addition, WISCD has resorted on occasion to the use of innovative strategies in order to secure valuable collections. These include collaborating financially with faculties for joint purchase of materials, seeking funding from international agencies, and lobbying locally and regionally to create an awareness of need to preserve their patrimony. Central to the acquisition effort has been partnering with subject experts resident at UWI campuses. Divisional librarians have been assisted by colleagues on academic staff in the evaluation and valuation of prospective acquisitions. In collaboration with an intermediary in North America, the division has more recently ventured into cyberspace using online auction houses to acquire primary materials.

Mindful of its role as the custodian of unique Caribbean resources, WISCD has over the years concentrated its efforts at enhancing access to existing resources. Researchers looking for primary source material in a variety of subjects and formats discover these resources in many different ways. Traditional methods of locating the special collections that are available at St. Augustine include the mounting of displays on their "hidden treasures," the use of printed guides, and the development of in-house electronic bibliographic databases. Various guides and indexes to the manuscripts and special collections have been published and are available for consultation via the library's website. Verbal communication about the collections is provided through frequent tours to visitors and through bibliographic instruction sessions to undergraduate and graduate-level students. Instructors of history, anthropology, and art history courses regularly schedule bibliographic instruction sessions to introduce their students to using primary sources in class projects. Analysis of use over the last two years has revealed that there has been a marked increase by local and international researchers. The division has also engaged in outreach activities in various Caribbean territories and the Americas. These have taken the form of seminars, workshops, and conference presentations aimed at sensitizing various stakeholders on the importance of preserving and safeguarding primary resources for posterity.

New information and communications technologies have created an avenue for transforming the various access points to one seamless interface where text, audio, image, and video can be accessed. The library has entered into this arena, having digitized two of its special collections: the Colonial Bank papers and the Young diaries. Recent efforts include online exhibits made available on the library's webpage.

Current challenges in the management and development of the special collections are staffing, preservation, space for proper storage, enhancement of access (indexing at the item level), the management of intellectual property rights, the challenges presented by the new technologies for digitization, and funding for the acquisition of new materials. Despite these obstacles, as a relatively small university library in a developing region, the Main Library has managed to build a valuable nucleus of special collections, many of which directly reflect authentic traditions and retentions of the original migrants. Others provide their stakeholders with fine examples of the intellectual, artistic, and cultural output of the various ethnic groups that make up the society. Yet others touch on the experiences of those nationals who migrated to all corners of the globe. These collections shed light not only on the process of reverse migration to Africa and the former colonies, but also the contributions made by nationals at home and abroad especially in the political and cultural arenas. The library has achieved much of which it can be proud. Indeed three of its special collections have been named to UNESCO's Memory of the World Register. They include the Derek Walcott Collection (1997), the Eric Williams Memorial Collection (1999), and the C. L. R. James Collection (2005). With its three nominations, the Main Library has the distinction of being surpassed only by Mexico with five nominations in the Latin America and the Caribbean zone.

With the continued commitment of its staff, the university administration, and the wider community, the Main Library will continue not only to add to the country's patrimony through it oral history programme OPReP, but also to actively solicit and purchase, where necessary, collections that will enable the Main Library to continue with its mandate to be the premier repository of unique Caribbean materials.

NOTES

1. Maximilian C. Forte, "Writing the Caribs Out: The Construction and Demystification of the 'Deserted Island' Thesis for Trinidad" (paper presented at the International Seminar on the History of the Atlantic World, 1500–1825, Cambridge, Mass., August 2004), p. 5.

2. Douglas Archibald, *Tobago "Melancholy Isle," Volume I, 1498–1771* (Port of Spain, Trinidad: Westindiana, 1987), p. 12.

3. Margaret Deanne Rouse-Jones, *Guide to Manuscripts, Special Collections and Other Research Resources for Caribbean Studies at the University of the West Indies, St. Augustine Campus Libraries* (St. Augustine, Trinidad and Tobago: University of the West Indies, 2003), p. 11.

4. Ibid., pp. 42–43, 57–58, 70.

5. Ibid., pp. 13, 102.

6. Ibid., pp. 39, 76.

7. Ibid., p. 71.

8. Ibid., pp. 9, 102.

9. Ibid., p. 22.

10. Ibid., pp. 17–18.

11. Trevor M. Millett, *The Chinese in Trinidad* (Trinidad: Inprint Caribbean Limited, 1993), p. 14.

12. Ibid., p. 17.

13. Walton Look Lai, *The Chinese in the West Indies, 1806–1995: A Documentary History* (Kingston, Jamaica: The Press, University of the West Indies, 1998), p. 22.

14. Walton Look Lai, *Indentured Labor, Caribbean Sugar: Chinese and Indian Migrants to the British West Indies, 1838–1918* (Baltimore: Johns Hopkins University Press, 1993), p. 276.

15. Millett, *Chinese in Trinidad,* p. 15.

16. Bridget Brereton, "The Experience of Indentureship: 1845–1917," in *Calcutta to Caroni: The East Indians of Trinidad,* ed. John Gaffar La Guerre (Trinidad: Longman Caribbean, 1974), p. 26.

17. Jo-Anne Ferreira, *The Portuguese of Trinidad and Tobago: Portrait of an Ethnic Minority* (St. Augustine, Trinidad and Tobago: Institute of Social and Economic Research, UWI, 1994).

18. Rouse-Jones, *Guide to Manuscripts,* p. 19.

19. Peggy R. Mohan, "Trinidad Bhojpuri: A Morphological Study" (Ph.D. diss., University of Michigan, 1978), p. 1.

20. Rouse-Jones, *Guide to Manuscripts,* pp. 25–26.

21. Ibid., pp. 12–13.

22. Trevor J. Hope, "The Impact of Immigration on Caribbean Development," in *Migration and Development in the Caribbean: The Unexplored Connection,* ed. Robert A. Pastor (London: Westview Press, 1985), p. 241.

23. Ibid., p. 242.

24. Ibid.

25. Ibid., p. 244.

26. Ibid.

27. Caribbean studies projects are final year projects of the undergraduate students of the Faculty of Humanities and Education and must be related to a Caribbean theme/topic of choice. Collectively, they constitute a rich source of information.

28. Tony Martin, "The Jews in Trinidad" (paper presented at the annual meeting of the Association of Caribbean Historians, Santo Domingo, March 1991), p. 5.

29. Ibid., p. 9.

30. Ibid.

31. Rouse-Jones, *Guide to Manuscripts,* p. 32.

32. Carlton Robert Ottley, *Notes for a Lecture on "Migration into Trinidad in the 1940's,"* publication no. 1047 (Port of Spain: Trinidad and Tobago Historical Society, 1967), p. 2.

33. Ibid., p. 1.

34. K. O. Laurence, *Immigration into the West Indies in the Nineteenth Century* ([Barbados]: Caribbean Universities Press, 1982), p. 71. Notes taken from *Parliamentary Papers 1874,* XLIV, 310–321: Blue Book Reports for 1873.

35. Kathleen Valtonen, "Bread and Tea: A Study of the Integration of Low-Income Immigrants from Other Caribbean Territories into Trinidad," quoted in *Population Movements within the English-Speaking Caribbean: An Overview,* by Linda Basch (United Nations Institute for Training and Research, 1982).

36. Ibid., p. 998.

37. Rouse-Jones, *Guide to Manuscripts,* p. 35.

38. Ibid., p. 29.

39. Ibid., p. 41. Kathleen Helenese-Paul, *Among Legal Friends: A Guide to the Papers of the Late Honourable Sir Hugh Wooding and the Late H. Aubrey Fraser* (St. Augustine, Trinidad: University of the West Indies, 1997).

40. Rouse-Jones, *Guide to Manuscripts,* p. 18.

BIBLIOGRAPHY

Allen, Susan M. "Special Collections Outside the Ivory Tower." *Library Trends* 52, no. 1 (summer 2003): 60–68.

Archibald, Douglas. *Tobago "Melancholy Isle," Volume I, 1498–1771.* Port of Spain, Trinidad: Westindiana, 1987.

Balutansky, Kathleen M. "Appreciating C.L.R. James, a Model of Modernity and Realization." *Latin American Research Review* 32, no. 2 (1997): 233–242.

Blackburn, Robin. "Anti-Slavery and the French Revolution." *History Today* 41, no. 11 (November 1991): 19–26.

Callender, Lenore. *A Guide to the Raymond Quevedo Manuscript Collection at the Main Library, the University of the West Indies, St. Augustine.* St. Augustine, Trinidad: University of the West Indies, 1993.

Center for Latin American Studies. *Migration and Caribbean Cultural Identity: Selected Papers from the Conference Celebrating the 50th Anniversary of the Center for Latin American Studies.* Occasional papers published by the Center for Latin American Studies, University of Florida, 1981.

Childs, Ronald E. "The Middle Passage Continues." *Ebony Man* 9, no. 4 (February 1994): 48–49.

Cloonan, Michèle V., and Sidney E. Berger. "The Continuing Development of Special Collections Librarianship." *Library Trends* 52, no. 1 (summer 2003): 9–13.

Crahan, Margaret E., and Franklin W. Knight, eds. *Africa and the Caribbean: The Legacies of a Link.* Baltimore: Johns Hopkins University Press, 1979.

Dabydeen, David, and Brinsley Samaroo, eds. *Across the Dark Waters: Ethnicity and Indian Identity in the Caribbean.* London: Macmillan Caribbean, 1996.

———. *India in the Caribbean.* London: Hansib/University of Warwick, 1987.

De Verteuil, Anthony. *The Corsicans in Trinidad.* Port of Spain, Trinidad: Litho Press, 2005.

———. *The De Verteuils of Trinidad.* Port of Spain, Trinidad: A. De Verteuil, 1997.

———. *The Germans of Trinidad.* Port of Spain, Trinidad: Litho Press, 1994.

Dunlap, Isaac Hunter. "Open Source Digital Image." *Management: Computers in Libraries* 25, no. 4 (April 2005): 6–48.

Encyclopædia Britannica Online. "Slavery." http://www.search.eb.com/eb/article-24159. Accessed March 8, 2006.

———. "West Indies, history of." http://www.search.eb.com/eb/article-54384. Accessed March 8, 2006.

Ferreira, Jo-Anne S. *The Portuguese of Trinidad and Tobago: Portrait of an Ethnic Minority.* St. Augustine, Trinidad and Tobago: ISER, University of the West Indies, 1994.

Forte, Maximilian C. "Writing the Caribs Out: The Construction and Demystification of the 'Deserted Island' Thesis for Trinidad." Paper presented at the International Seminar on the History of the Atlantic World, 1500–1825, Cambridge, Mass., August 2004.

Gomez, Michael A. "African Identity and Slavery in the Americas." *Radical History Review* 75 (fall 1999): 111–121.

Gosine, Mahin. *The East Indian Odyssey: Dilemmas of a Migrant People.* New York: Windsor Press, 1994.

Gosine, Mahin, Dipak Malik, and Kumar Mahabir. *The Legacy of the Indian Indenture: 150 Years of East Indians in Trinidad.* New York: Windsor Press, 1995.

Helenese-Paul, Kathleen. *Among Legal Friends: A Guide to the Papers of the Late Honourable Sir Hugh Wooding and the Late H. Aubrey Fraser.* St. Augustine, Trinidad: University of the West Indies, 1997.

Hope, Trevor J. "The Impact of Immigration on Caribbean Development." In *Migration and Development in the Caribbean: The Unexplored Connection,* edited by Robert A. Pastor. London: Westview Press, 1985. Pp. 237–261.

Johnson Jr., Pyke. "Caribbean Librarian." *Library Journal* 103, no. 4 (February 15, 1978): 432–434.

Kale, Madhavi. *Fragments of Empire: Capital, Slavery, and Indian Indentured Labor Migration in the British Caribbean.* Philadelphia: University of Pennsylvania Press, 1998.

Kiernan, James Patrick. "Caribbean Model of Memory." *Americas* 56, no. 3 (2004): 56.

La Guerre, John Gaffar. *The East Indian Today.* St. Augustine, Trinidad: UWI, [1972].

———, ed. *Calcutta to Caroni: The East Indians in Trinidad.* London: Longman Caribbean, 1974.

Look Lai, Walton. *The Chinese in the West Indies, 1806–1995: A Documentary History.* Jamaica: The Press, University of the West Indies, 1998.

Look Lai, Walton. *Indentured Labor, Caribbean Sugar: Chinese and Indian Migrants to the British West Indies, 1838–1918.* Baltimore: Johns Hopkins University Press, 1993.

Martin, Tony. *Jews in Trinidad.* Paper presented at the annual meeting of the Association of Caribbean Historians, Santo Domingo, March 1991. 24 pp.

Millet, Trevor M. *The Chinese in Trinidad.* Port of Spain, Trinidad: Inprint Caribbean Limited, 1993.

Mintz, Sidney W., and Sally Price, eds. *Caribbean Contours.* Baltimore: Johns Hopkins University Press, 1985.

Nettleford, Rex. "Migration, Transmission and Maintenance of the Intangible Heritage." *Museum International* 56, no. 1/2 (May 2004): 78–83.

Ottley, Carlton R. *Notes for a Lecture on "Migration into Trinidad in the 1840's."* Port of Spain: Trinidad and Tobago Historical Society, 1967.

Prochaska, Alice. "Special Collections in an International Perspective." *Library Trends* 52, no. 1 (summer 2003): 138–150.

Rouse-Jones, Margaret Deanne. *Guide to Manuscripts, Special Collections and Other Research Resources for Caribbean Studies at the University of the West Indies, St. Augustine.* St. Augustine, Trinidad and Tobago: University of the West Indies, 2003.

Rouse-Jones, Margaret Deanne, and Kathleen Helenese-Paul. *Spoken History: A Guide to the Material Collected by the Oral and Pictorial Records Programme (OPReP).* St. Augustine, Trinidad and Tobago: University of the West Indies, 1997.

Sabga, Joseph Abdo. *A Life Worth Remembering: Abdo Joseph Sabga (1898–1985).* Trinidad and Tobago: Zenith Services Ltd., 2000.

Salhi, Kamal. "Rethinking Francophone Culture: Africa and the Caribbean between History and Theory." *Research in African Literatures* 35, no. 1 (spring 2004): 9–29.

Samaroo, Brinsley, et al., eds. *In Celebration of 150 Years of the Indian Contribution to Trinidad and Tobago.* Vol. 2. Port of Spain, Trinidad: D. Quentrall-Thomas, 1995.

Valtonen, Kathleen. "Bread and Tea: A Study of the Integration of Low Income Immigrants from Other Caribbean Territories into Trinidad." *International Migration Review* 30, no. 4 (winter 1996): 995–1031.

Walvin, James. "A Taste of Empire, 1600–1800." *History Today* 47, no. 1 (January 1997): 11–16.

Wilson, Andrew R., ed. *The Chinese in the Caribbean.* Princeton, N.J.: M. Wiener Publishers, 2004.

Wilson, Samuel M. "Caribbean Diaspora." *Natural History* 103, no. 3 (March 1993): 54–59.

Yelvington, Kevin A. "The Anthropology of Afro-Latin America and the Caribbean: Diasporic Dimensions." *Annual Review of Anthropology* 30, no. 1 (2001): 227–260.

Cuban Diaspora

5. Cuban Rafters: Then and Now

Holly Ackerman

The motivations, significance, and geography of the Cuban rafters are more complex, powerful, and varied than was portrayed in academic and journalistic accounts in the 1990s. Single-factor explanations that initially presented the group as either exclusively politically or economically motivated were misleading. Over the course of a decade, systematic studies and testimonial literature have shown that the predominant driving force of the exodus was a felt need for freedom in political, economic, and social areas. The worldview of the rafters was at variance with the "Cuban reality," and they wanted to be free to define their own lives. Stagnation in Cuba produced an acute sense of lost time and opportunity in all spheres. And, balseros felt they knew the United States, particularly south Florida, even though most had no immediate relatives there.[1]

Unfortunately, the political/economic divide that characterized discussions in the 1990s is now giving way to another one-dimensional presentation of the rafters ten years after their arrival, characterizing the group as sympathetic, or at least tolerant, of the Cuban government, able and willing to return home, and opposed to harsh U.S. foreign policy. This new stereotype is not supported by recent research findings.

Rather than study the recent wave of rafters, some experts have dismissed them as a significant subject of inquiry either because they form a smaller wave than prior groups of Cuban refugees or because their numbers are low compared to other illegal Caribbean/Latin American migrants. They account for just 82,740 known surviving rafters outside Cuba between January 1, 1959, and June 30, 2004, a number equal to 6.9 percent of the Cuban-American population. Of these, 39,496 arrived during the 1994–1996 crisis, comprising only 3.2 percent of all Cuban Americans. However, Cuban rafters have a significance that is much larger than their absolute numbers as a result of the regionwide nature, repetition, speed, and intensity of the domestic and international crises their actions provoke. They are human sparks in a Caribbean political tinderbox.

In 1994 the various governments involved ended the exodus before the demand for exit was satiated, leaving a residual demand estimated at 250,000 persons with no other means of exit. This residuum, plus unknown numbers of the more recently disaffected, presents a continuing threat to regional stability if they are released. They present a real threat to the island's domestic stability if they are not. This frustrated reserve has fueled each round of mass sea exit from revolutionary Cuba. Looking back on Camarioca, Mariel, and the crisis of 1994, it seems obvious that another iteration of sea exodus is a possibility for which well-informed contingencies are needed.

What is more, conservative estimates suggest that at least 25 percent of rafters did not survive the trip and those who did were multiply traumatized, first through near-death experiences at sea and then in prolonged internment. It is essential that the humanitarian dimension be monitored and documented to identify the dead, improve survival rates, reduce posttraumatic stress, evolve prevention strategies, and hold governments accountable for their responses. By studying the outcomes for this most recent wave, one can clarify what does and does not work in crisis management.

A Regional Revision

Overall, the rafter exodus is most accurately described as a regional crisis affecting the entire Caribbean rather than as an event in U.S./Cuban foreign relations. Yet, during 1994, media attention focused on the United States, Cuba, the Straits of Florida, and the U.S. naval base at Guantánamo, while ignoring the rafters in other locations, most particularly sizable groups in the Bahamas and the Cayman Islands. Further study is needed to rectify this omission.

Surviving balseros who leave from the south of the island usually wash up on Cayman Brac, one of three islands comprising the small British Crown colony of the Cayman Islands. As early as 1960–1961, the *Colonial Reports of the Cayman Islands* note a "Cuban rafter crisis" when approximately 200 Cuban rafters arrived that year to be absorbed into a population of just over 10,000.

By 1993, with a total Caymanian population of 25,000, rafters were regularly transported by plane from Cayman Brac to the capital, George Town, on Grand Cayman Island where a refugee camp, known locally as "tent city," was built with an emergency grant from the European Union. Originally designed to hold 200 refugees, the camp population grew from approximately 200 in July to 1,120 in mid-August of 1994. At times the permanent population of Cayman Brac was nearly equaled by the rafters awaiting transfer to tent city. When frustrated rafters threatened to take over the town, it was not an improbable idea.

For the government of the Cayman Islands, the rafters represented the most acute humanitarian and national security crisis they had ever faced. Dozens of riot police from London and asylum officers from the United Nations High Commission on Refugees were called out to maintain order and process asylum claims respectively. Following negotiations among Caymanian officials, U.K. representatives, and the United States Department of State, tent city residents were told on December 2, 1994, that fewer than 50 of them would be granted asylum. The rest could choose from four options: returning voluntarily to Cuba; going to the U.S. "safe haven" at Guantánamo at U.S. expense; going back out to sea in repaired boats; or being forcibly repatriated to Cuba if they refused the first three options.

About a third of rafters returned to sea being towed out to open waters by Caymanian vessels. Most of the rest were airlifted to Guantánamo and eventually entered the United States through that route. About a dozen chose to demand asylum in Cayman Islands and were incarcerated, eventually being forcibly repatriated.

A small but growing stream of rafters to the Cayman Islands has continued since 1994 with a dual policy governing their fate. Those who wash ashore on Cayman Brac and avoid the attention of officials in the capital are given repaired boats and provisions and allowed to continue on their journey with most headed toward Honduras where rafters are currently given asylum. This policy is consistent with traditional Caymanian cultural practices governing assistance to distressed mariners.

Those who draw official attention are placed in Northward Prison on Grand Cayman Island until they can be involuntarily repatriated at Cuban expense. This approach is consistent with agreements negotiated among the United States, United Kingdom, and Cayman Islands in 1994 and a subsequent bilateral Memorandum of Understanding (MOU) signed between Cayman Islands and Cuba. An active public debate exists over the relative merits of the two policies with popular opinion on the side of aiding and releasing the rafters.

Those leaving from the north side of Cuba often washed up, intentionally and unintentionally, in the outer uninhabited islands of the Bahamas where they could be spotted by rescue vessels or planes and where provisions were dropped by exile rescue groups. In the early 1990s if picked up by or brought by others to Bahamian authorities, rafters were initially detained but then released and allowed to live freely in the Bahamas or to make their way to other destinations. Thousands of rafters "passed through" the Bahamas until 1996 when, according to the U.S. Committee on Refugees (USCR), the Cuban and Bahamian governments signed an MOU nearly identical to that with Cayman Islands.

USCR claims that, unlike the public U.S./Cuban agreement, neither of the secret Caymanian and Bahamian MOUs "includes any provision to screen Cuban asylum seekers to determine if they qualified as refugees nor do they include any assurances by the Cuban government that Cuba would not persecute the repatriates, nor do they include any other safeguards for those returned."

Unlike the Camarioca (1965) and Mariel (1980) boatlifts, which were unplanned but organized sea caravans leading directly from Cuba to Key West, a swell of individual rafters sends ripples in all directions, overwhelming neighboring Caribbean countries. This is the unacknowledged power and the complexity of the rafter phenomenon. It leaves Caribbean leaders facing the triple dilemma of simultaneously maintaining national security as frustrated rafters rebel against detention, safeguarding the economy where tourists and clients of offshore banks demand a placid environment, and attending to human rights and humanitarian aid when conformity with international standards only fuels further illegal entrants.

When they were denied resolution of their situation in Cayman Islands, hundreds of rafters slipped out unnoticed from the detention camp and, with long sticks in hand, placed themselves strategically in downtown George Town where cruise ships regularly disgorge tourists bringing the lifeblood of the Caymanian economy. Then the rafters called "Glass House" (the center of government) and made it clear that their situation required further review. To simplify matters in 1994, Caribbean governments found a solution for the residents of tent city, kept publicity down, and worked with Cuba and the United States to agree on a uniform policy accepted by all regional governments, but they scrapped costly human rights guarantees for future rafters.

Although affected governments have closed ranks to try to discourage rafting, the 1994 crisis showed that Cuba's domestic mechanisms for sanctioning those who demand exit were reduced. For example, during the Mariel boatlift, neighbors and coworkers could be counted upon in large numbers, both symbolically and literally, to forcefully repudiate those who registered to leave. Systematic beatings in neighborhoods, work sites, registration centers, and staging areas were the risk one ran for a chance at exit.

By 1994, those who stayed behind flocked to wish the rafters well at the shoreline with some openly bartering extra space. The Malecón riots that galvanized the crisis in 1994 were in response to government sanction of sea exits. Ordinary Cubans were not just refusing to beat the guy next door, they were protesting his arrest. In the next crisis, the Cuban government could easily face a choice between using military force to restrain the civilian population and managing the consequences of another mass release of population in a much more belligerent international context. Nonetheless, President Castro threatened another release in the summer of 2004 in response to U.S. reduction of exile visits. The cost to all governments has become sufficiently high that a proactive negotiation of the next crisis before it mushrooms would be the rational choice, though rationality has never been the guiding principle in U.S./Cuban relations.

The Rafters Now

At the time they entered the United States, rafters were bursting with the tale of their crossing or, for those who were detained, the traumas of internment and of their "North American dream." What has become of those plans and memories?

In 1994 it was relatively easy to find rafters in the halls of refugee resettlement agencies and to sample records about them in an organized way. A decade later they are scattered and a good sample is hard to find. But, a secondary analysis was conducted of those respondents to the 2004 Florida International

University poll of Cubans in Miami-Dade and Broward County, Florida, who arrived after 1990 in boats or rafts—a total of 90 persons. These data at least give information about their current political attitudes with reference to Cuba and the United States. Ironically, there is information on the political attitudes of people who, in 1994, were seeking a release from politics. In the table below, rafter responses have been compared with responses from all other Cuban Americans on key issues.

Table 1: Rafter Responses to FIU Cuba Poll Questions Compared to All Respondents

Topic	Percentage of Rafters*	Percentage of All Respondents*
Agree to send medicine	86	69
Agree to send food	81	55
Agree to support human rights groups in Cuba	93	94
Agree with exile military action	61	60
Believe in national dialogue	61	56
Feel embargo has not worked	80	76
Want to keep the embargo	57	65
Favor unrestricted travel to Cuba	61	46
Felt all voices are not being heard in Miami	78	74
The missing voice is that of stronger opposition to Castro	67	59
Would return to a democratic Cuba	40	32
People leave Cuba primarily for economic reasons	16	25
People leave Cuba because there is no freedom	52	50
People leave Cuba both for economic reasons and freedom	33	25
Involved in civic organizations in U.S.	4	13
Send money to Cuba	81	54
Florida congressional delegation is doing good job	84	85

*Percentages are rounded up to nearest whole number.

When the responses of rafters and all other respondents in the poll are compared, rafters are substantially more inclined to agree with humanitarian measures and those related to family contact: agreeing 26 percent more with sending food; 17 percent more with sending medicine; 15 percent more likely to favor unrestricted travel to Cuba; and 5 percent more in favor of a national dialogue among exiles, dissidents, and the Cuban government. Rafters are 27 percent more likely to send money to Cuba, 8 percent less likely to favor the U.S. embargo, and 8 percent more likely to return to a democratic Cuba. When it comes to explaining the exit from Cuba, they are 10 percent more likely to assert the lack of freedom or a combination of lack of freedom and economic factors than are all others.

On the other hand, they favor some very conservative measures by a wide margin with 61 percent supporting armed exile action against the Cuban government, a rate approximately equal to all others. And 67 percent believe that it is strong opposition to the Castro government that is the missing voice in Miami. They feel even more strongly about this than the rest of the Cuban community (8 percent more). They also support the very conservative Miami congressional delegation at a rate equal to all others. Although they are less supportive of the embargo than are all others, they still support it in 57 percent of cases.

Judging from the opinions of the recent arrivals in this sample, the popular presentation of them as significantly different from earlier exiles may be too simplistic. It is more accurate to say they are 15 to 30 percent more supportive of humanitarian aid to Cuba but share conservative political attitudes and solutions with earlier arrivals by an equal margin. Only 16 percent believe that people are leaving Cuba for economic reasons.

Where they are clearly different is in their strong support for open travel to and from Cuba, although, as is mentioned below, personally returning to Cuba is not an easy decision. Given that most rafters left immediate family in Cuba, it is not surprising that they want the possibility of travel open, and it raises a question about whether their support for travel is contingent upon having family in Cuba. Rather than showing solidarity or even tolerance for the Cuban government, the responses indicate that, overall, rafters share some conservative political attitudes with fellow exiles while continuing to care about the material needs of their relatives and friends in Cuba. Although rafters are contributing somewhat to liberalized attitudes in Miami, it is more likely that the increase in moderate views is due to mortality rates among the hard-liners who arrived in the early sixties. Overall, the recent arrivals are divided, with conservative views still present in significant numbers.

To expand the understanding of the rafters, sixteen persons arriving during the 1994 exodus were interviewed about their current life situation and memories of Cuba and of rafting. Their responses simply represent the informed opinions of sixteen readily identifiable individuals who participated in the crisis and cannot be generalized to the rafter population as a whole. They do, however, provide valuable description and suggest areas for further inquiry.

Among those interviewed were two women and fourteen men whose occupations in Cuba included one or more of the following: medical doctor, artist, student, university professor, airline pilot, housewife, baker, soldier, plumber, and biotechnician. In 2004 at least one of them is currently employed as a social worker, medical technician, scientific researcher, painter, small business owner, store clerk, artist, housewife, auto mechanic, building manager, chauffeur, and truck driver.

At time of arrival, four were single and all others were married. Six of the sixteen have studied either in technical or vocational schools or at local colleges and universities since their arrival with one receiving a college degree and several others receiving technical certifications. Eight of the sixteen have become fluent in English. Another five "manage" English in their jobs but prefer living primarily in Spanish and do not consider themselves fluent. Three make no effort to speak English and have jobs and living situations where it is not necessary to speak English. Current ages range from twenty-two to sixty-two.

Rafters were asked if they still think about their experience at sea. Traumatic memories remain for most balseros, and it is more difficult to discuss in 2004 than at arrival. A typical response came from a rafter from Havana and his wife who ended up in Guantánamo on their second attempt to leave the country. The first time they were apprehended at gunpoint by the frontier guard, and the man was awaiting trial on *salida illegal del país*. He reasoned that he had to leave before his trial date or he would be incarcerated. The story is related hesitantly, in hushed tones and with evident pain. In 1994 these stories came quickly, urgently, and in a loud voice. They were recent events that might be forgotten if not revealed. Today they are traumas that will not heal.

The second exit would take place outside of Havana and the couple had to wait a week without funds in a rural area to rendezvous with sixteen other people who were going with them. They hid in a wooded area near a farm and used animal troughs for drinking and bathing. Eventually bug bites covered them, they had no food, and they were suffering from exposure when one of the farm dogs discovered them and barked incessantly until farm residents came. They were lucky that the farmers shared food with them and did not give them away.

Once at sea for two days the raft took on water, rising hour by hour. They reached a point where repairs were no longer possible, and they had only a few more hours before the boat sank entirely. At first panic broke out. Some rafters had been seasick from the start, and they were the first to hallucinate. One man wanted to go back but no one knew which direction was north or south and the raft was worthless.

Finally silence came over the group as people waited for death with a calm resignation. The rafter was praying for his three stepchildren. Their father had died while on military duty in Africa and now, he thought, they would lose their mother and him as well. He regretted having caused them this second loss and wished he had not brought his wife along. As he prayed for them, a buzzing sound drew his attention and the group was sighted by Hermanos al Rescate, eventually being picked up by the U.S. Coast Guard and taken to Guantánamo.

One rafter related his worst moment and said his memories of it come less and less frequently now but that he still wakes up with nightmares about the trip. "One guy was delusional and hallucinating. He thought I was a chivato working for Fidel and he kept trying to throw me out of the boat. We all feared him and, at times, I thought the others were going to let him throw me overboard. I squatted in a corner by myself."

Thirteen of the rafters experienced detention at Guantánamo. Surprisingly, although they felt initially desperate, overall, they are philosophical about the experience. Repeatedly, balseros said of Guantánamo, "Me hizo independiente. Me hizo hombre." Other comments included, "My freedom began right there in Guantánamo when we protested our conditions. It was chaos at first but we built a society there." Another said, "It was a way to sort us out, to weed us out. For us it was a time to get ready for the United States."

But it is freedom that is the main theme that runs from the escape planning through camps in Guantánamo, Bahamas, and Cayman Islands and into life in the United States. It is a word heard over and over again by interviewers. One rafter said:

> Quien gano su libertad caballero en su balsa, seguirá balsero mientras viva. Ser balsero es una experiencia única, un renacer espiritual, social, material. Es una metamorfosis irreversible. . . . Memorias hay muchas, pero la mayor es el sentimiento de plenitud espiritual cuando amaneces en medio del mar, sin costa a la vista. Te sientes por primera vez LIBRE.

Another rafter, reflecting on his years in the United States, first commented, "No one has stopped me on the street to look at my ID, no one comes to my house to tell me what to do. I feel free. I am treated like an adult." Another rafter talked of a search conducted by the military in his tent in Guantánamo. They were looking for contraband. As he stood outside the tent, he felt that he had returned to Cuba and he was in a state of deep anxiety. He expected his things to be examined and to be arrested because of the socially critical nature of the drawings he had made of camp life. But the soldiers only searched the areas where contraband had been suspected, and all his artwork was in tact. No repudiation of its content followed. The sharp contrast of his expectation of censure and resolution of the search left him with an indelible impression of what freedom meant.

Another said, "I can go to a restaurant anywhere and take my family, the same with the beaches. When I first arrived I went once to a restaurant and Jorge Mas Canosa was there. It shocked me. The big shots and the little people could just walk into the same place and both would be seated. We didn't have to leave when he came in." Freedom was the number one spontaneous topic and it is freedom not politics that continues to occupy the balseros. There was almost no discussion of political systems, political participation, and the mechanisms of democracy, but a constant reference to being able to think, talk, and travel freely.

In the United States—Work and Uncertainties

Balseros now have a decade of work behind them, and they understand the uncertainties of individual freedom. Typical comments in response to a question about the best and worst aspects of American life included the following: "The U.S. is three things . . . work, work and work." Another said, "I worry most about unemployment. Other people live with this uncertainty and I tell myself that I can too but what would happen if I lost my job? This worries me. I'm not going to lose my job . . . but you worry." A third remarked, "It was hard to learn that you must pay for everything."

One rafter, preoccupied with healthcare, said:

> I'll tell you what my North American dream wasn't. The U.S. has an ineffi-
> cient system of healthcare. In Cuba it was efficient. Here it is "metalizado" (o
> sea basado en dinero). I worry that I'll get sick and I have no health insurance.
> Why is this that you have no healthcare here? It is wrong to make women beg
> for money to get their children an operation. The U.S. should look to Europe
> a little more.

Another remarked, "We knew when we came that we would be behind and we have to save for retirement. Retirement is my big worry . . . that and the fear that my children will be Americanized and move away from us."

By contrast, a rafter told of recreating his Cuban life in Miami. He sees all the same friends and has brought his family. He finds that material things mean less and that he devotes himself exclusively to leisure activities with his family and friends when not working. "In Cuba materials things meant so much more and you were occupied with them all the time . . . getting food, finding shoes. Here, the things are there if you want them. I can just be with my friends on the weekend. I don't have to be looking for material things all the time."

Return Visits to Cuba

When asked about travel to Cuba, these sixteen balseros were evenly divided between those who had and had not returned. Talking about the complexity of return travel, one rafter said, "Frankly, I'm afraid. And, I don't want to ask permission. I don't want that feeling of helplessness again. I'd rather not go." A father of two young children born in the United States said:

> I only have so much money and time. I can't do everything. We just get one
> vacation. I took the whole family to Cuba three years ago but they don't want
> to go back. The kids say "Oh no, not Cuba." It's hot, there's no air condition-
> ing, everything is falling down. It's dirty. My wife and I can see how it was.
> We understand it . . . but you can't make kids understand. It's not Disneyland.
> Cuba isn't Disneyland. Doesn't come close.

Another rafter related a complex tale of the circumstances of his leaving. A former pilot, he abandoned his plane in the Cayman Islands and rafted from there to the United States. When he applied to bring first his children and then siblings and parents, he was told each time that he must pay almost ten thousand extra dollars to cover the cost the Cuban government incurred in going to pick up the plane he abandoned. The second time the "surcharge" was assessed, he complained and was told the cost would be applied for each relative because of his traitorous conduct. He said, "I have to bring them out. I can't go back. No telling what they would do to me."

Several of those who have not returned raised similar fears. If they had stolen supplies or equipment for their rafts or had an especially zealous Committee for the Defense of the Revolution or came from small towns where there was heightened visibility in public life, they feared what might happen if they returned. These rafters give testimony to Juan Antonio Blanco's point, made recently in *Encuentro en la Red,* that "the government in Havana makes multiple use of its migration policy." New arrivals limit themselves and are limited by the Cuban government both in their decision to try to visit and in the conduct of their new life, by the assumption that a highly individually nuanced censure will follow based on preexisting and present antigovernment behavior. Refusing to return is equated with political action by these former rafters. Conversely, the "mano de Fidel" still modifies behavior of those who want to visit.

Conclusions

By 1994 uncontrolled release was a time-honored pattern for dealing with pent-up demand for exit in Cuba, but one that was increasingly intolerable to the United States. Internment of tens of thousands of rafters was the result. The regional crisis caused by rafters was collectively resolved by the U.S. and Caribbean leaders through secret agreements that made continued rafting increasingly dangerous and less likely to succeed. New forms of individual exit and/or incidents of mass release will need to be "invented" before ordinary Cubans can leave in any numbers. What is clear from the data at hand is that the population is diverse and not as easily categorized as has been presented to date.

NOTE

1. For an extended bibliography of works on the subject, see Holly Ackerman, "The Cuban Rafter Phenomenon: A Selected Bibliography," http://balseros.miami.edu/Mainnavigation.htm.

THE CUBAN RAFTER PHENOMENON:
A SELECTED BIBLIOGRAPHY

Content of the Bibliography

A primary selection criterion for inclusion in this bibliography was the extent to which each item treated the subject of rafting. All or a very substantial portion of the work needed to be dedicated to some aspect of the post-1959 rafter phenomenon. Excluded were many otherwise worthy academic publications, particularly texts and overviews of U.S./Cuban relations, that include a few paragraphs giving a very general description of the 1994 crisis and offering speculation about what caused it without providing supporting data.

Second, the material needed to be based in direct experience or, for nonparticipant authors, to be well-grounded theoretically and methodologically. In the first grouping, testimonies of rafters, service providers and, in smaller numbers, officials/policymakers were selected regardless of their perspective or the quality of their prose. Basically, any participant in events who has published has been included. The reason for this was simply to give readers exposure to detailed description by the rafters themselves and to draw attention to hard-to-find materials that researchers might otherwise be unable to locate. Naturally, most of these accounts are in Spanish. Testimonial accounts written by a rafter or social services provider who worked directly with rafters are marked with an asterisk (*).

Academic treatments needed to be more rigorous, presenting strong methodological grounding and analysis. This second criterion was tempered by an effort to be comprehensive and to include a variety of theories and perspectives. The formats included are non-fiction books, scholarly journal articles, dissertations, video/film, selected archives, government publications, occasional papers, reports, and proceedings.

Journalistic production on this subject is so extensive that it was impossible to gather and evaluate this category in the time available for this bibliography. The same is true of the extensive literature on the case of rafter Elián González. With the exception of the film category, fiction is not included. These materials will be added over time.

Like the rest of the website, this bibliography is a living thing. Readers are encouraged to submit citations that may have been overlooked to holly.ackerman@duke.edu. The author will also annotate and update the bibliography at intervals.

Books

Abella, Rosa M., and Dolores F. Rovirosa. 1999. *Febrero 24, 1996 Derribo de dos avionetas: Bibliografía.* Miami, Fla.: Cuban Heritage Collection, University of Miami.

Ackerman, Holly, and Juan M. Clark. 1995. *The Cuban Balseros: Voyage of Uncertainty.* Miami, Fla.: Policy Center of the Cuban American National Council.

Antón, Alex, and Roger E. Hernández. 2002. *Cubans in America: A Vibrant History of a People in Exile.* New York: Kensington Books.

*Arbelo, William. 1989. *Más allá de mis fuerzas.* Miami, Fla.: Ediciones Universal.

Bardach, Ann L. 2002. *Cuba Confidential: Love and Vengeance in Miami and Havana.* New York: Random House.

*Casañas Martín, Wilfredo. 2000. *La gran verdad de una desilusión.* Madrid: Edición personal.

Castro, Max J. 1999. *Free Markets, Open Societies, Closed Borders?: Trends in International Migration and Immigration Policy in the Americas.* Coral Gables, Fla.: North-South Center Press.

Centro de Estudios de Alternativas Políticas, ed. 1996. *Anuario CEAP: Emigración Cubana.* Havana: CEAP.

Clark, Juan M. 1990. *Cuba, mito y realidad: Testimonios de un pueblo.* Miami, Fla.: Saeta Ediciones.

*Concepción, Julio Antonio. 1993. *Odyssey or Calvary?* Miami, Fla.: Nadir Publishing.

Cruz, Nilo. 2004. *A Bicycle Country.* New York: Dramatists Play Service.

de Acha, Eduardo. 1995. *La inocencia de los balseros.* Miami, Fla.: Ediciones Universal.

De la Campa, Román. 2000. *Cuba on My Mind: Journeys to a Severed Nation.* New York: Verso.

*Díaz, Tomás. 1994. *Balseros en Guantánamo: Su historia y su testimonio.* Miami, Fla.: Nuevos Horizontes Internacionales.

Díaz Mantilla, Daniel. 1996. *Las palmeras domésticas.* La Habana: Casa Editora Abril.

Fernández, Alfredo A. 2000. *Adrift: The Cuban Raft People.* Houston, Tex.: Arte Público Press.

*Fibla, Alberto. 1996. *Barbarie: Hundimiento del remolcador "13 de marzo."* Miami, Fla.: Rodes Print.

García, Maria C. 1996. *Havana USA: Cuban Exiles and Cuban Americans in South Florida, 1959–1994.* Berkeley: University of California Press.

Gay, Kathlyn. 2000. *Leaving Cuba: From Operation Pedro Pan to Elian.* Brookfield, Conn.: Twenty-First Century Books.

Gonzáles Valdéz, Alberto D. 1999. *Las noventa millas interminables.* Puerto Rico: s.n.

Grenier, Guillermo J., and Lisandro Pérez. 2003. *The Legacy of Exile: Cubans in the United States.* Boston: Allyn and Bacon.

Hernández Díaz, Alejandro, and Dick Cluster. 1998. *The Cuban Mile.* Pittsburgh, Pa.: Latin American Literary Review Press.

Herrera, Andrea O. 2001. *Remembering Cuba: Legacy of a Diaspora.* Austin: University of Texas Press.

LeoGrande, William M. 1995. *The United States and Cuba after the Cold War: The 1994 Refugee Crisis.* Washington, D.C.: Institute for the Study of Diplomacy, School of Foreign Service, Georgetown University.

López Blanch, Hedelberto. 1998. *La emigración cubana en Estados Unidos: Descorriendo mamparas.* La Habana: Editorial SI-MAR.

*Lorenzo, Omar. 1995. *Reflexiones prohibidas.* George Town, Grand Cayman, Cayman Islands: Casa de Cultura.

Martínez, Milagros. 1996. *Los balseros cubanos: Un estudio a partir de las salidas ilegales.* La Habana: Editorial de Ciencias Sociales.

Mason, T. K. 1984. *Across the Cactus Curtain: The Story of Guantánamo Bay.* New York: Dodd Mead.

Masud-Piloto, Felix R. 1996. *From Welcomed Exiles to Illegal Immigrants: Cuban Migration to the U.S., 1959–1995.* Lanham, Md.: Rowman and Littlefield.

*Morales, Roberto. 2004. *65 Horas con la muerte.* Miami, Fla.: Minitman Press.

Morgado, Marcia, and Juan Abreu. 1993. *Rafts.* Miami, Fla.: LOMA Publishers.

Ochoa, Ernesto. 1995. *Balseros.* Coral Gables, Fla.: North-South Center, University of Miami, Iberian Studies Institute.

Ortega, Luís. 1998. *Cubanos en Miami.* La Habana: Editorial de Ciencias Sociales.

*Perera González, Domingo M. 1998. *Fraternidad entre alambradas: Guantánamo 1994–95.* Miami, Fla.: Ediciones Plaza d'Praha.

*Perera González, Domingo M., and Jorge Portuondo Jorge. 2001. *Encierro, incertidumbre y sexo.* Miami, Fla.: Spin Quality Printing.

*Puentes, Enel F. 1996. *Guantánamo Bay '94: Dos caras de la misma moneda.* Miami, Fla.: Ediciones Plaza D'Praha.

Ricardo Luis, Roger. 1994. *Guantánamo: The Bay of Discord.* New York: Ocean Press.

*Rodríguez, Marisol S. 1997. *Guantánamo el último paso hacia la libertad.* Miami, Fla.: D'Fana Editions.

Rodríguez Chávez, Ernesto. 1997. *Emigración cubana actual.* La Habana: Editorial de Ciencias Sociales.

Rothe, Eugenio M. 2004. "Post-Traumatic Stress Symptoms in Cuban Children and Adolescents during and after Refugee Camp Confinement." In *Trends in Posttraumatic Stress Disorder Research,* edited by Thomas A. Corales. Hauppauge, N.Y.: Nova Science Publishers.

Soderlund, Walter C., R. C. Nelson, and E. D. Briggs. 2003. *Mass Media and Foreign Policy: Post-Cold War Crises in the Caribbean.* Westport, Conn.: Praeger.

Stepick, Alex, and Max J. Castro. 2003. *This Land Is Our Land: Immigrants and Power in Miami.* Berkeley: University of California Press.

Tobar, Héctor. 2005. *Translation Nation: Defining a New American Identity in the Spanish-Speaking United States.* New York: Riverhead Books.

Triff, Soren. 2001. *Cultura sin miedo: Antología de la revista "Catálogo de letras" 1994–1999.* Miami, Fla.: Catálogo de Letras.

*Valdés, Zoé. 1995. Preface to *En fin, el mar: Cartas de los balseros cubanos.* Palma de Mallorca, España: Bitzoc.

*Vázquez Fernández, Carmen. 1999. *Balseros cubanos.* Madrid, España: Editorial Betania.

Zapater, Fernando A. 2003. *Cuentos cortos y poemas de un balsero.* Philadelphia: Xlibris.

Dissertations

Ackerman, Holly. 1996. "Mass Migration, Nonviolent Social Action, and the Cuban Raft Exodus, 1959–1994: An Analysis of Citizen Motivation and International Politics." Ph.D. diss., University of Miami.

Álvarez, Sandra Dalis. 2001. "Getting a Head Start on Assimilation: An Analysis of Cuban American Women in a Head Start Program." Ph.D. diss., Kansas State University.

Clark, Juan M. 1976. "The Exodus from Revolutionary Cuba (1959–1974): A Sociological Analysis." Ph.D. diss., University of Florida, Gainesville.

Greenhill, Kelly. 2003. "People Pressure: Strategic Engineered Migration as an Instrument of Statecraft and the Rise of the Human Rights Regime." Ph.D. diss., Massachusetts Institute of Technology.

Henken, Theodore A. 1998. "Cuban and Mexican Migration to the United States: Refugee Flows and Labor Migration in the Modern World System." Master's thesis, Tulane University.

Lima, Maritza. 1997. "Day Treatment Program for Cuban Rafter Refugee Children-Focus: Treatment for Posttraumatic Stress Disorder and Prevention of Acculturation Stress." Psy.D. diss., Caribbean Center for Advanced Studies, Miami Institute of Psychology.

Miller, Gretchen. 2003. "A Cuban Refugee Raft Memorial Museum." Master's thesis, University of Florida, School of Architecture.

Neske, Robert. 1999. "Assumption of Adequacy: Operation Safe Haven: A Chaplain's View." Master's thesis, U.S. Army Command and Staff College, Ft. Leavenworth, Kans. http://cgsc.cdmhost.com/cgi-bin/showfile.exe?CISOROOT=/p4013coll2&CISOPTR=636.

Simantirakis, Christina. 2000. "The Cuban Shoot-Down of Two United States-Registered Civil Aircraft on 24 February 1996: Study of a New Case of Use of Weapons against Civil Aircraft." Ph.D. diss., McGill University.

Timmel, Jill L. 2001. "Creativity and Acculturation: Psychological and Cultural Effects on the Divergent Thinking of Cuban Preadolescent Immigrants Entering the United States." Ph.D. diss., Cornell University.

Vicente, Andrea Cristine. 2004. "The Cuban-U.S. Transnational Relationship: The Impact of Recent Migration on Cuban and Cuban-American Society." Master's thesis, Florida State University. http://etd.lib.fsu.edu/theses/available/etd-11042004-143801/.

Films and Videos

Anton, Alex, and Joe Cardona. 1996. *Adios Patria? El Exodo Cubano.* 80 mins. Miami, Fla.: Malecon Films.

Bosch, Charles, and Josep Domenech. 2002. *Balseros.* 120 mins. Barcelona: Lauren Films. VHS and DVD.

Dystra, Jorge. 2003. *En fin el mar.* 102 mins. Spanish with English subtitles. Film.

Gilpin, Margaret, and Luis F. Bernaza. 1994. *Estado del Tiempo/Changing tides.* 34 mins. Spanish with English subtitles. VHS.

Hogar de Transito. s.n. *En busca de la libertad: Hogar de transito para los refugiados cubanos.* 27 mins. VHS.

Journeyman Pictures, Inc. 1998. *A New Cuban Crisis.* 37 mins. VHS.

Leff, Neil M., Mario Ortiz, and Norton Rodríguez. 2001. *Libertad.* 110 mins. Miami, Fla.: Bougainvillea Films. Video and DVD.

Lopez, Carmen. 2003. *Black & Blue: A Rafter's Journey.* 59 mins. Film.

Oller, Rafael. 1995. *American Purgatory: 90 Days behind the Wire at Guantánamo USNB.* 90 mins. VHS.

Rodriguez, Norton, and others. 2001. *Libertad.* 110 mins. Miami, Fla.: Bougainvilla Films.

Government Reports and Publications

Ackerman, Holly. 2006. *Cuba: Potential Refugee Crisis? An Assessment.* Writenet report commissioned by the United Nations High Commissioner for Refugees, Emergency and Security Services, June 2006. http://www.unhcr.org/home/RSDCOI/44eb2fd44.pdf.

Allen, Arthur A. 1996. *The Leeway of Cuban Refugee Rafts and a Commercial Fishing Vehicle.* Springfield, Va.: U.S. Coast Guard Office of Research and Development.

Potocky-Tripodi, Miriam. 2002. *Needs Assessment of Cuban and Haitian Refugees, Entrants, and Parolees in South Florida.* Contract #LK054, Refugee Services, Florida Department of Children and Families and the Institute for Public Opinion Research, Florida International University. Miami, Fla.

Reynolds, Nicholas E. 2003. *A Skillful Show of Strength: U.S. Marines in the Caribbean, 1991–1996.* Washington, D.C.: History and Museums Division, Headquarters, U.S. Marine Corps.

State of Florida, HRS:OSRA. 1994. *1994: The Status of Florida's Refugee/Entrant Population, Entrants: Florida's Unique Population.*

United States. 1994. "The President's News Conference, August 19, 1994." *Weekly Compilation of Presidential Documents* 30 (August 22): 1682–1690.

———. 1996. "Joint Statement on Normalization of Migration, Building on the Agreement of September 9, 1994." *International Legal Materials* 35 (March): 327–330.

———. 1996. "Joint Statement with the Republic of Cuba on Normalization of Migration, May 2, 1995." *Weekly Compilation of Presidential Documents* 31 (May 8): 752–753.

United States. Congress. House. Committee on International Relations. Subcommittee on the Western Hemisphere. 1995. *The Cuban March 13th Tugboat Incident: Hearing before the Subcommittee on the Western Hemisphere of the Committee on International Relations, House of Representatives,* 104th Cong., 1st sess., January 25, 1995. Washington, D.C.: GPO.

———. 1996. *The Clinton Administration's Reversal of U.S. Immigration Policy toward Cuba: Hearing before the Subcommittee on the Western Hemisphere of the Committee on International Relations, House of Representatives,* 104th Cong., 1st sess., May 18, 1995. Washington, D.C.: GPO.

United States. Congress. Senate. Committee on Armed Services. 1994. *Situation in Cuba: Hearing before the Committee on Armed Services, United States Senate,* 103rd Cong., 2nd sess., August 25, 1994. Washington, D.C.: GPO.

United States Coast Guard. "Alien Migrant Interdiction Statistics." http://www.uscg.mil/hq/g-o/g-opl/amio/AMIO.htm.

United States General Accounting Office. 1995. *Cuba: U.S. Response to the 1994 Cuban Migration Crisis: Report to Congressional Requesters.* Washington, D.C.: Gaithersburg, Md.

Journal Articles

Ackerman, Holly. 1996. "The Balsero Phenomenon, 1991–1994." *Cuban Studies* 26:169.

——. 1996/1997. "Protesta social en la Cuba actual: Los balseros de 1994." *Encuentro de la cultura cubana* 3 (winter): 125.

——. 2005. "Los balseros: Antes y ahora." *Encuentro de la cultura cubana* 36 (spring): 131.

——, guest ed. 2005. "The Cuban Balsero Crisis Ten Years Later." *Latino Studies* 3, no. 3 (November): 372–428.

Aja Díaz, Antonio. 2000. "La emigración de Cuba en los años noventa." *Cuban Studies* 30:1.

Andrews, Thomas C., and others. 1997. "Self-Mutilation and Malingering among Cuban Migrants Detained at Guantánamo Bay." *The New England Journal of Medicine* 336, no. 17 (April 24).

Blanco, Juan A. 2004. "Emigrantes, desterrados, exiliados e opositores: La excepcionalidad de la política migratória cubana." *Encuentro en la red,* May 17 and 23.

Bonnin, Rodolfo, and Chris Brown. 2002. "The Cuban Diaspora: A Comparative Analysis of the Search for Meaning among Recent Cuban Exiles and Cuban Americans." *Hispanic Journal of Behavioral Sciences* 24, no. 4:465.

Brenner, Philip, and P. Kornbluh. 1995. "Clinton's Cuba Calculus." *NACLA Report on the Americas* 29, no. 2:33.

Campisi, Elizabeth. 2005. "Guantánamo: Safe Haven or Traumatic Interlude? The Cuban Balsero Crisis Ten Years Later." *Latino Studies* 3, no. 3 (November): 372.

Colomer, Josep. 2000. "Exit, Voice, and Hostility in Cuba." *International Migration Review* 34, no. 2:423.

del Valle, Patricia, Adriana G. McEachern, and Maria Q. Sabina. 1999. "Using Drawings and Writings in a Group Counselling Experience with Cuban Rafter Children, 'Los Balseritos.'" *Guidance and Counseling* 14, no. 4:20.

Falcoff, M. 1995. "The Other Cuba." *National Review* XLVII, no. 10 (June 12): 34–38, 43.

Fowler, Victor. 2002. "A Traveler's Album: Variations on Cubanidad." *Boundary 2* 29, no. 3:105–119.

Greenhill, Kelly. 2002. "Engineered Migration and the Use of Refugees as Political Weapons: A Case Study of the 1994 Cuban Balseros Crisis." *International Migration* 40, no. 4:39.

Henken, Ted. 2005. "Balseros, boteros y el bombo: Persistencia de un trato migratorio especial." *Encuentro de la cultura cubana* 36 (spring): 142.

Howe, James C. 1994. "Coast Guard Rescues of Cuban Migrants." *North-South: The Magazine of the Americas* 4, no. 2 (September/October): 48.

Hughes, Joyce. 1999. "Flight from Cuba." *California Western Law Review* 39 (fall).

Little, Cheryl. 1999. "InterGroup Coalitions and Immigration Politics: The Haitian Experience in Florida." *University of Miami Law Review* 53, no. 4:717.

Lyons, David. 1994. "Asylum Rule Change Decried." *National Law Journal* 17 (September 5): A6.

Masud-Piloto, Félix. 2005. "Bienvenidos a Guantánamo: Una perspective histórica." *Encuentro de la cultura cubana* 36 (spring): 121.

McCready, Siobhan. 1994. "The Science of Saving Rafters." *Sea Frontiers* 40, no. 6 (December): 14.

Nackerud, Larry, Alyson Springer, and others. "The End of Cuban Contradiction in U.S. Refugee Policy." *International Migration Review* 33, no. 1:176.

Palmer, Gary W. 1997. "Guarding the Coast: Alien Migrant Interdiction Operations at Sea." *Connecticut Law Review* 29:1565.

Pérez, Marta. 1997. "The Varela Centers: An Immigrant Education Program in Response to Cuban Guantánamo Bay Crisis." *Migration World Magazine* 25, no. 3:23.

Pitts, W. D. 1995. "A Guantánamo Diary—Operation Sea Signal." *JFQ* (autumn): 114.

Rieff, David. 1995. "From Exiles to Immigrants." *Foreign Affairs* 74:76.

Rosendahl, Bruce. 1994. "Awaiting Rafters." *Sea Frontiers* 40, no. 6:8.

Rosendahl, Bruce R., and Thomas N. Lee. 1993. "Roulette in the Straits of Florida." *Sea Frontiers* 39, no. 3 (May/June): 8.

Rothe, E. M., H. Castillo, and others. 1998. "Sintomatología post-traumática en niños y adolescentes balseros Cubanos: Una synopsis de tres estudios." *Monografías de Psiquiatria* 10, no. 1:18.

Rothe, Eugenio M., Hector Castillo-Matos, Kim Brinson, and John Lewis. 2000. "La Odisea de los balseros cubanos." *Medico Interamericano* 19, no. 12:578.

Rothe, Eugenio M., Hector Castillo-Matos, and Ruben Busquets. 1996. "Posttraumatic Stress Symptoms in Cuban Adolescent Refugees during Camp Confinement." *Annals of the American Society for Adolescent Psychiatry* 26.

Rothe, Eugenio M., John Lewis, Hector Castillo-Matos, and others. 2002. "Posttraumatic Stress Disorder among Cuban Children and Adolescents after Release from a Refugee Camp." *Psychiatric Services* 55, no. 8:970.

Rumbaut, Ruben G. 1976. "The Family in Exile: Cuban Expatriates in the United States." *The American Journal of Psychiatry* 133, no. 4:395.

Sartori, Maria E. 2001. "The Cuban Migration Dilemma: An Examination of the United States' Policy of Temporary Protection in Offshore Safe Havens." *Georgetown Immigration Law Journal* 15, no. 1:319.

Solomon, B. 1994. "Clinton's Fast Break on Cuba." *National Journal* 26, no. 36:2044.

Suarez, Virgil. 2000. "The Cultura of Leaving: Balsero Dreams." *Hopscotch: A Cultural Review* 2, no. 2:2–13.

Turner, Elisa. 1991. "Mythic Presence." *ARTnews* 90, no. 10:20.

Vanderbush, Walt, and Patrick J. Haney. 1999. "Policy Toward Cuba in the Clinton Administration." *Political Science Quarterly* 114, no. 3:387.

Vicent, Mauricio. 1994. "Éxodo y exilio para los balseros desde Cuba, con dolor." *Cronica centroamericana* 341 (September): 58.

Occasional Papers, Reports, and Proceedings

Amnesty International. 1994. "Cuban 'Rafters'—Pawns of Two Governments." http://www.amnestyusa.org/countries/usa/document.do?id=7916C7D99ECA804080 2569A600605620. Accessed May 24, 2004.

Castro, Max J. 1995. "Cuba: The Continuing Crisis." *North-South Agenda Papers,* no. 13. Coral Gables, Fla.: Dante B. Fascell North-South Center, University of Miami.

———. 2002. "The New Cuban Immigration in Context." *North-South Agenda Papers,* no. 58. Coral Gables, Fla.: Dante B. Fascell North-South Center, University of Miami.

Center for Migration Studies. 1984. *In Defense of the Alien: Proceedings of the Annual National Legal Conference on Immigration and Refugee Policy.* New York: Center for Migration Studies.

Clark, Juan M. 1977. *Why? The Cuban Exodus: Background, Evolution and Impact in U. S. A.* Miami, Fla.: Union of Cubans in Exile.

Human Rights Watch/Americas. 1994. *Cuba: Repression, the Exodus of August 1994, and the U.S. Response.* 18.

Mesa-Lago, Carmelo. 1995. "Cuba's Raft Exodus of 1994: Causes, Settlement, Effects, and Future." *North-South Agenda Papers,* no. 12. Coral Gables, Fla.: Dante B. Fascell North-South Center, University of Miami.

Quintana, Míriam, comp. 1995. *Migración cubana: Crisis de los balseros en el verano de 1994.* Ciudad de La Habana, Cuba: Centro de Estudios sobre América, Sección de Información Científica.

Solomon, William S. 1995. *Covering Cuba: The Balseros Crisis, August–September, 1994.* Washington, D.C.: Association for Education in Journalism and Mass Communication.

U.S. Committee for Refugees. 1996. "Following Controversial Repatriation, the Bahamas Permits Cuban Boat People to Apply for Asylum." *Refugee Reports* 17:5.

Selected Archives

Newspapers from the Refugee Camp at Guantánamo 1994–1996:

El Balsero—One digital copy is available of the first issue at the Cuban Heritage Collection, University of Miami Libraries.

El Bravo—A total of five issues were distributed. All five are available at the Cuban Heritage Collection, University of Miami Libraries.

el éxodo—Twenty-five editions were published between November 20, 1994, and September 10, 1995. All original manuscripts are held at the Cuban Heritage Collection, University of Miami Libraries.

El Futuro—Original manuscripts available at the Cuban Heritage Collection, University of Miami Libraries.

Que Pasa?—A weekly, bilingual paper edited by the U.S. Military Information Support Team (MIST) for circulation to the rafters. The Cuban Heritage Collection has many issues.

6. Escritores cubanos en Europa: Guillermo Cabrera Infante en Londres y Zoé Valdés en París

Rafael E. Tarragó

Al tomar el poder en Cuba en 1959 el Movimento 26 de Julio bajo la dirección del Dr. Fidel Castro Ruz, pocas personas abandonaron la isla por razones políticas. Entre los escritores y artistas el único de renombre en hacerlo fue el poeta Gastón Baquero, editor en el periódico *El Diario de la Marina,* quien había mantenido relaciones con el gobierno del general Fulgencio Batista, del que fue sucesor el gobierno revolucionario del Dr. Castro. A medida que el gobierno revolucionario se fue radicalizando entre 1959 y 1961 el número de emigrantes (personas desilusionadas o afectadas negativamente por esa radicalización) aumentó y casi todos se iban para los Estados Unidos de América, pero el número de escritores y artistas que abandonó Cuba entre 1959 y 1961 no aumentó en la misma proporción que el de cubanos en otras profesiones.

En 1961 tuvo lugar una disputa entre funcionarios del ICAIC (Instituto Cubano de Artes e Industrias Cinematograficas) y la redacción de la revista *Lunes de Revolución* en relación con el cortometraje *PM,* dirigido/producido por Sabá Cabrera, la cual terminó en una reunión de las partes en disputa y numerosos intelectuales con el dirigente del gobierno revolucionario [el entonces Primer Ministro] Dr. Fidel Castro Ruz. La disputa entre el ICAIC y *Lunes* se basaba en la decisión del primero de no permitir la proyección pública de *PM* y su incautación, por considerar este cortometraje derrogatorio del pueblo cubano, y la contención del segundo que *PM* meramente proyectaba la vida nocturna habanera y en nada insultaba al pueblo cubano ni ofendía al gobierno revolucionario.

La reunión de Fidel Castro con los intelectuales concluyó con un discurso conocido después como "Palabras a los intelectuales", en el cual este dijo que con la Revolución todo, pero sin la Revolución nada era permitido.[1] Después de este discurso del Dr. Catro la proyección pública de *PM* fue prohibida y la revista *Lunes de Revolución* fue clausurada. Este evento provocó el abandono de la isla por muchos intelectuales y escritores y artistas temerosos de verse silenciados. Gran parte de estos se fueron para Europa. Guillermo Cabrera Infante, de la redacción de *Lunes de Revolución,* fue uno de ellos.[2]

Entre 1973 y 1990 el número de intelectuales, escritores y artistas cubanos que salían de la isla disminuyó considerablemente por razones varias, pero cuando el gobierno cubano permitió en 1994 la salida de Cuba con la posibilidad de volver muchos escritores y artistas comenzaron a salir en jiras y para dictar cursos o hacer estudios avanzados en el exterior y se radicaron fuera de de la isla, aunque volvían a Cuba a visitar a familiares y amigos. La mayor parte de estos cubanos se estableció en Europa o en Latinoamérica. Algunos decidieron no volver a la isla y entre estos se encuentra la novelista Zoé Valdés.[3]

Este trabajo incluye una bibliografía selecta de lo que se ha escrito sobre Guillermo Cabrera Infante (1929–2005) y Zoé Valdés (n. 1959) como emigrantes por razones políticas. No están incluidos escritos de ellos o sobre ellos como literatos solamente—material maravilloso para otra bibliografía—sino aquellos en que ellos expresan implícita o explícitamente su descontento con el gobierno revolucionario cubano y donde se comenta su obra o se les hace preguntas sobre la situación política en Cuba y se habla de ellos como exiliados. Además de libros y artículos de revistas académicas incluye entrevistas y artículos de revistas de actualidades y diarios.

Guillermo Cabrera Infante, un cubano en Londres

Guillermo Cabrera Infante nació en la ciudad de Gibara, en el norte de la region oriental de Cuba, dentro de lo que hoy es la Provincia de Holguín, en el seno de una familia de obreros de convicciones políticas radicales. Sus padres fueron miembros fundadores del Partido Cumunista en Gibara. Se mudó a La Habana con su familia siendo niño y allí comenzó a trabajar en *Hoy,* el periódico del Partido Comunista Cubano. Cabrera infante participó en actividades contra el gobierno de Fulgencio Batista entre 1953 y 1958 y cuando entró a formar parte de la Redacción de la revista *Lunes de Revolución* en 1959 era un ferviente admirador del Movimiento 26 de Julio.[4]

En los años 1950 Cabrera Infante comenzó a escribir críticas de cine para la revista *Carteles* bajo el seudónimo G. Cain (pronunciado como Caine en inglés), pero su primer libro fue una colección de relatos, *Así en la paz como en la guerra,* publicada en 1960, en la cual revela compenetración con los ideales revolucionarios del momento. Como miembro de la Redacción de *Lunes de Revolución* mostró una gran curiosidad por saber lo que pasaba en el mundo de las ideas fuera de Cuba, pero su conflicto con el gobierno revolucionario cubano comenzó con la disputa entre el ICAIC y *Lunes* por *PM.* No aceptar la decisión de Fidel Castro en sus "Palabras a los intelectuales" puso a Cabrera Infante en conflicto con el gobierno cubano. Después de la clausura de *Lunes* fue enviado como diplomático a la embajada cubana en Bruselas, pero en 1965 salió de Cuba para nunca más volver. Poco despues se estableció en Londres con su segunda esposa, Miriam Gómez, y sus dos hijas y en esa ciudad murió en 2005.

En una entrevista que le hizo en 1970 Rita Guibert Cabrera Infante dijo que Londres lo escogió a el y no él a Londres. Explica esto diciendo que en Madrid no se sentía gusto, que en los Estados Unidos no podía entrar a no ser que se declarara refugiado político, que París nunca le gustó por más de un fin de semana y que en Londres le habían hecho una oferta de trabajo.[5] Tal parece que en realidad las cosas fueron más complicadas, pero el hecho es que los primeros años de Cabrera Infante en Londres fueron plagados por la falta de trabajo y el ostracismo. En esa época la mayor parte de los intelectuales europeos compartía la creencia expresada en el título del libro de Hernando Calvo y Katlijn Declercq, *The Cuban Exile Movement. Dissidents or Mercenaries?* Para ellos el criticar a Fidel Castro equivalía a ser un agente del gobierno de los Estados Unidos de América y Cabrera Infante no ganó amigos en Londres cuando publicó sus razones para abandonar Cuba en el número del 30 de julio de 1968 de la revista argentina *Primera Plana.*[6] Tres años después de las declaraciones de Cabrera Infante en *Primera Plana,* que le valieron acusaciones de ser un traidor a su patria y calumniador del gobierno revolucionario cubano, así como su expulsión de la Unión Nacional de Escritores y Artistas de Cuba, estalló el Caso Padilla. Cuando el encarcelamiento y pública autocrítica del poeta cubano Heberto Padilla en 1971 (reminiscente de la Rusia de José Stalin) provocó el repudio del gobierno revolucionario cubano por algunos de sus antiguos admiradores en Europa y Latinoamérica Cabrera Infante pudo sentirse vindicado.

Después de trabajar escribiendo guiones para películas y de vivir muchas veces de préstamos de amigos, Cabrera Infante consiguió estabilidad económica y éxito literario con la publicación de la novela *Tres tristes tigres* en 1967. Su éxito quedó establecido en 1979 con la publicación de *La Habana para un Infante difunto.* En 1997 se convirtió en un consagrado de las letras al recibir el Premio Cervantes, y cuando murió en 2005 su obra era universalmente reconocida, pero todavía es un autor prohibido en Cuba por haber sido un crítico constante y abierto del gobierno revolucionario. En 1992 publicó una compilación de artículos titulada *Mea Cuba* en la que sobresalen los artículos políticos y en entrevistas y artículos para periódicos y revistas nunca perdió la oportunidad de criticar el dogmatismo y la intolerancia del gobierno del Dr. Fidel Castro en Cuba. Pero quizás lo más subversivo que escribió contra el gobierno revolucionario cubano fue sus novelas *Tres tristes tigres* y *La Habana para un Infante difunto,* en las cuales rinde homenaje a La Habana de noche denigrada por el programa ideológico de ese gobierno en 1959. La Habana de *PM,* para la cual no había lugar dentro de la Revolución.

Zoé Valdés, una cubana en París

Zoe Valdes nació en La Habana en 1959, en el Año de la Revolución. En sus primeros años trabajó para la UNESCO y en la embajada cubana en París y fue asistenta del director de *Revista de Cine Cubano.* En 1985 recibió en Cuba el premio Carlos Ortiz por *Todo para una sombra* y en 1986 recibió el premio Roque Dalton por *Respuesta para vivir.* En los 1990s sacó de Cuba copias del manuscrito de su novela *La nada cotidiana,* la cual fue publicada en francés antes de ser publicada en español en España en 1996. Salió de Cuba en 1995 invitada a dictar en París un curso sobre el escritor y héroe de la independencia de Cuba de España José Martí (1853–1895) y nunca regresó a la isla.[7]

El exilio en París de Zoé Valdés en 1995 fue diferente a lo que el exilio en Londres fue para Cabrera Infante en 1965. La visión de un Fidel Castro infalible y perfecto ya era cuestionada por los intelectuales europeos y ya no condenaban a todos los disidentes cubanos inmediatamente como agentes de los Estados Unidos de América. Entre 1960 y 1990 el gobierno cubano se hizo sentir en el exterior a traves de sus portavoces, tanto cubanos como extranjeros, para impedir que los escritores y artistas cubanos exiliados en Europa (y aún en los Estados Unidos de América) pudieran desarrollar sus carreras, pero para 1990 las cosas comenzaron a cambiar, en parte por los eventos en Europa Central y en Europa Oriental que desacreditaron a la Unión Soviética y a sus aliados.[8] Además, Zoé Valdés encontró en París a escritores y artistas cubanos desilusionados con el gobierno de La Habana, como Eduardo Manet, Severo Sarduy y Nivaria Tejera. Valdés vive hoy en día en un París donde en 2001 se le concedió asilo político a Ileana de la Guardia—hija de un oficial del ejército Revolucionario de Cuba condenado por narcotráfico y actividades contrarrevolucionarias en 1989—y donde en 2003 la organización Reporters Sans Frontières organizó en el Theatre du Rond-Point, en la Avenida de los Campos Elíseos, una reunión de escritores y artistas en protesta por la suppresión violenta de los disidentes en Cuba.[9]

Las novelas de Zoé Valdés son eróticas y pueden llamarse feministas, porque en ellas el sexo es un arma femenina para liberarse de la opresión de los hombres. Pero desde *La nada cotidiana* en 1995 hasta *El pie de mi padre* en 2002 sus novelas son políticas. En *La nada cotidiana* escribe sobre la joven llamada Patria, nacida el 1 de mayo de 1959, quien es nombrada así por su padre, un revolucionario fervoroso. *Te di la vida entera* (1996) es otra historia de desilusión en la cual las mujeres son maltratadas por los hombres y donde un hombre visto en un principio como un libertador resulta ser un opresor abusivo. Los autores cubanos radicados en Francia desde la época de "Palabras a los intelectuales" (como Manet, Sarduy y Tejera) no criticaban públicamente al gobierno revolucionario cubano, pero Zoé Valdés ha sido diferente y su ejemplo ha tenido seguidores desde 1995. Un gran número de escritores y artistas cubanos ha abandonado Cuba en los últimos diez años y desde Europa (como José Triana) o México (como Eliseo Alberto) condenan abiertamente el dogmatismo y la intolerancia del gobierno del Dr. Castro en Cuba.[10]

Conclusiones

En las novelas de Zoé Valdés aparece la problemática de la brusca ruptura causada por el exilio. Como en las novelas de Cabrera Infante, La Habana es parte integrante de sus novelas, excepto que Cabrera Infante escribe sobre una Habana vibrante antes de la radicalización del gobierno revolucionario y ella escribe sobre una La Habana reprimida y deprimente donde los personajes viven una vida diaria marcada por la apatía. Su feminismo se expresa en un rechazo del estado, porque en un régimen socialista como el cubano el estado toma el lugar del marido y el padre en un régimen patriarcal. En *Te di la vida entera* (1996) Cuca Martínez se sacrifica por el indigno Juan Pérez y su hija María Regla se sacrifica por la Revolución, y ambas son víctimas de la entrega total.[11]

Cabrera Infante critica indirectamente al gobierno revolucionario en sus novelas alabando a La Habana ruidosa y dinámica que el gobierno revolucionario reprimió. En los ensayos políticos en *Mea Cuba* (donde se reproducen sus declaraciones del 30 de Julio de1968 en *Primera Plana* y el artículo "Mordidas del Caimán Barbudo"—publicado originalmente en inglés en el número de 4–17 de junio de 1981 del periódico *London Review of Books*), en artículos y en sus entrevistas lo critica duramente y abiertamente. Una excepción es la serie de artículos sobre escenas y personalidades londinesas publicados por el periódico español *El País* ("Icosaedros"), donde critica al gobierno del Dr. Castro indirectamente con sus alabanzas a Inglaterra por virtudes políticas inexistentes en Cuba como la tolerancia y la libertad de escoger. Carlos Cuadra ha comparado estos artículos de Londres a las *Cartas Inglesas* que Voltaire escribió como críticas indirectas de los vicios y defectos del gobierno y la sociedad del rey Luis XV en Francia.[12]

Cabrera Infante salió de Cuba y se estableció en Londres en una época en la cual los intelectuales de Occidente apoyaban incondicionalmente al gobierno revolucionario cubano y veían en todo cubano que lo criticaba un agente subversivo de los Estados Unidos de América. Cuando Zoé Valdés llegó a París en esa ciudad ya se habían establecido muchos cubanos desilusionados con el gobierno revolucionario cubano y entre los intelectuales franceses el marxismo leninismo ya no era un credo infallible e indiscutible. Sería interesante investigar por qué Londres no fue escogido como lugar de exilio por más cubanos después de 1961. También sería interesante identificar a los autores y artistas cubanos que salieron de la isla después de 1961 y se establecieron en París y hacer un inventario de sus obras publicadas fuera de Cuba.

En este trabajo bibliográfico he compilado lo que se ha escrito en un contexto político sobre Guillermo Cabrera Infante y Zoé Valdés, dos escritores cubanos exiliados en Europa. Espero que sea útil a los investigadores interesados en la vida y obra de estos, así como a aquellos interesados en los cubanos exiliados en esos países.

NOTAS

1. Véase Fidel Castro Ruz, *Palabras a los intelectuales* (La Habana: Ediciones del Consejo Nacional de Cultura, 1961).

2. Véase Jacobo Machover, *La memoria frente al poder. Escritores cubanos del exilio: Cabrera Infante, Severo Sarduy, Reinaldo Arenas* (Valencia: Universitat de Valencia, 2001).

3. Véase Priscilla Gac-Artigas, "La memoria fragmentada en la novelística de Zoé Valdés", en *Reflexiones: Ensayos sobre escritoras hispanoamericanas contemporáneas,* vol. 2, ed. Priscilla Gac-Artigas (New Jersey: Ediciones Nuevo Espacio, 2002), pp. 315–342.

4. Raymond D. Souza, *Guillermo Cabrera Infante. Two Islands, Many Worlds* (Austin: University of Texas Press, 1996), pp. 37–38.

5. Rita Guibert, *Seven Voices. Seven Latin American Writers Talk to Rita Guibert,* trad. al inglés por Frances Partridge (Nueva York: Alfred A. Knopf, 1973), pp. 397–398.

6. Véase Hernando Calvo y Kathlijn Declercq, *The Cuban Exile Movement. Dissidents or Mercenaries?* (Nueva York: Ocean Press, 2000); Alfred MacAdam, "Guillermo Cabrera Infante", en *The Paris Review: Confesiones de escritores. Escritores Latinoamericanos* (Buenos Aires: El Ateneo, 1996), pp. 72–73.

7. Véase D. H. Figueredo, "Valdés, Zoé", en *Encyclopedia of Caribbean Literature,* vol. 2, ed. D. H. Figueredo (Westport, Conn.: Greenwood Press, 2006), pp. 795–796.

8. Véase Ileana Fuentes, "¿Exiliados o traidores? El alcance extrainsular de la política cultural cubana, 1960–1990", en *Creación y Exilio. Memorias del I Encuentro Internacional Cuba en la Distancia,* ed. Fabio Murrieta (Madrid: Editorial Hispano-Cubana, 2002), pp. 251–256.

9. Alain Hertoghe, "Rencontre avec Ileana de la Guardia", *La Croix,* marzo 31, 2001, p. 8; Bernard Durau, "Cuba-Soirée anti-Castro à Paris", *L'Humanité,* septiembre 30, 2003, sección *International.*

10. Véase Nanne Timmer, "Experiencia y representación en *La nada cotidiana* de Zoé Valdés", en *Creación y Exilio,* pp. 125–131; Andres Oppenheimer, "Cubans Are New Stars of Literary World", *The Toronto Star,* abril 4, 1998, p. M19.

11. Gac-Artigas, "La memoria fragmentada", pp. 317–325.

12. Carlos Cuadra, "'Icosaedros': The English Letters", en *Guillermo Cabrera Infante: Assays, Essays, and Other Arts,* ed. Ardis L. Nelson (Nueva York: Twayne Publishers, 1999), pp. 39–92.

BIBLIOGRAFÍA

Libros y artículos sobre los escritores cubanos exiliados

Calvo, Hernando, y Katlijn Declercq. *The Cuban Exile Movement. Dissidents or Mercenaries?* Nueva York: Ocean Press, 2000.

Durau, Bernard. "Cuba—Soirée anti-Castro à Paris". *L'Humanité,* septiembre 30, 2003, sección *International.*

Fornet, Ambrosio. "La diáspora cubana y sus contextos". *Casa de las Américas* 41, no. 222 (enero–marzo 2001): 22–29.

Fuentes, Ileana. "¿Exiliados o traidores? El alcance extra-insular de la política cultural cubana, 1960–1990". En *Creación y Exilio. Memorias del I Encuentro Internacional Con Cuba en la Distancia,* editado por Fabio Murrieta. Madrid: Editorial Hispano-Cubana, 2002. Pp. 251–256.

Hertoghe, Alain. "Rencontre avec Ileana de la Guardia". *La Croix,* marzo 31, 2001, p. 8.

Machover, Jacobo. *La memoria frente al poder. Escritores cubanos del exilio: Guillermo Cabrera Infante, Severo Sarduy, Reinaldo Arenas.* Valencia: Universitat de Valencia, 2001.

Maratos, Daniel C., y Marnesba D. Hill. *Escritores de la diáspora cubana. Manual Bibliográfica.* Metuchen, N.J.: Scarecrow Press, 1986.

Oppenheimer, Andres. "Cubans Are New Stars of Literary World". *The Toronto Star,* abril 4, 1998, p. M19.

Vázquez Díaz, René, comp. *Bipolaridad de la cultura cubana. Ponencias del Primer Encuentro de Escritores de Dentro y Fuera de Cuba.* Estocolmo: Olaf Palme International Center, 1994.

Selección de libros y artículos sobre Guillermo Cabrera Infante

Anhalt, Nedda G. de. "*Mea Cuba:* The 'Proust-Valia' of History". En *Guillermo Cabrera Infante: Assays, Essays, and Other Arts,* editado por Ardis L. Nelson. Nueva York: Twayne Publishers, 1999. Pp. 188–209.

Cuadra, Carlos. "'Icosaedros': The English Letters". En *Guillermo Cabrera Infante: Assays, Essays, and Other Arts,* editado por Ardis L. Nelson. Nueva York: Twayne Publishers, 1999. Pp. 39–52.

Guibert, Rita. "Guillermo Cabrera Infante, Londres, 5–12 de octubre de 1970". En *Seven Voices. Seven Latin American Writers Talk to Rita Guibert,* trad. al inglés de Frances Partridge, introducción por Emir Rodríguez Monegal. Nueva York: Alfred A. Knopf, 1973. Pp. 341–436.

Hernández, Roger E. "Cabrera Infante, Guillermo". En *Encyclopedia of Caribbean Literature,* vol. 1, editado por D. H. Figueredo. Westport, Conn.: Greenwood Press, 2006. Pp. 123–125.

MacAdam, Alfred. "Guillermo Cabrera Infante, entrevistado en 1982". *The Paris Review: Confesiones de escritores. Escritores latinoamericanos,* prólogo de Noé Jitrick. Buenos Aires: El Ateneo, 1996. Pp. 61–93.

Souza, Raymond D. *Guillermo Cabrera Infante. Two Islands, Many Worlds.* Austin: University of Texas Press, 1996.

Tyler, Christian. "Private View: Infidelity of a Cuban Exile". *The Financial Times,* noviembre 19, 1994.

Ulloa, Justo C., y Leonor A. Ulloa. "*Mea Cuba:* Critical Readings from Exile". En *Guillermo Cabrera Infante: Assays, Essays, and Other Arts,* editado por Ardis L. Nelson. Nueva York: Twayne Publishers, 1999. Pp. 140–155.

Selección de obras de Guillermo Cabrera Infante

"Bites from the Bearded Crocodile". *London Review of Books* 3, no. 10 (junio 4–17, 1981): 3–8.

La Habana para un Infante difunto. Barcelona: Seix Barral, 1979.

Mea Cuba. Barcelona: Plaza y Janes, 1992.

"Mordidas del Caimán Barbudo". *Quimera* (Barcelona) 39–40 (julio–agosto 1984): 66–82.

Tres tristes tigres. Barcelona: Seix Barral, 1967.

Selección de artículos sobre Zoé Valdés

Cordero, María de Jesús. "La construcción de la identidad femenina y nacional en *La hija del embajador*". En *Reflexiones: Ensayos sobre escritoras hispanoameri-canas contemporáneas,* vol. 2, editado por Priscilla Gac-Artigas. New Jersey: Ediciones Nuevo Espacio, Colección Académica, 2002. Pp. 327–342.

Cortanze, Gerard de. "Zoé Valdès; La Havane entre rire et larmes". *Le Figaro,* septiembre 4, 1997, sección *Litterature Etrangère.*

Figueredo, D. H. "Valdés, Zoé". En *Encyclopedia of Caribbean Literature,* vol. 2, editado por D. H. Figueredo. Westport, Conn.: Greenwood Press, 2006. Pp. 795–796.

Gac-Artigas, Priscilla. "La memoria fragmentada en la novelística de Zoé Valdés". En *Reflexiones: Ensayos sobre escritoras hispanoamericanas contemporáneas,* vol. 2, editado por Priscilla Gac-Artigas. New Jersey: Ediciones Nuevo Espacio, Colección Académica, 2002. Pp. 317–325.

Grangeray, Emilie. "Voyage dans le temps". *Le Monde des Livres,* noviembre 24, 2000.

Herzberg, Nathaniel. "Zoé Valdès et la France, du Festival de Cannes a la prefecture de Police". *Le Monde,* mayo 30, 1998.

Latil, Sophie. "ARTE Un documentaire sur l'ecrivain cubain; La douleur de Zoé Valdès". *Le Figaro,* enero 14, 2000.

Orsenna, Erik. "Volcanique Havane". *Le Monde des Livres,* octubre 17, 1997.

Timmer, Nanne. "Experiencia y representación en *La nada cotidiana* de Zoé Valdés". En *Creación y Exilio. Memorias del I Encuentro Con Cuba en la Distancia,* editado por Fabio Murrieta. Madrid: Editorial Hispano-Cubana, 2002. Pp. 125–131.

Selección de libros de Zoé Valdés

Café Nostalgia. Barcelona: Planeta, 1999.

La hija del embajador. Barcelona: Emecé, 1997.

Milagro en Miami. Barcelona: Planeta, 2001.

La nada cotidiana. Barcelona: Emecé, 1995.

El pié de mi padre. Barcelona: Planeta, 2002.

Querido primer novio. Barcelona: Planeta, 1999.

Te di la vida entera. Barcelona: Planeta, 1996.

7. Cuba en Alemania: situación socio-demográfica y bibliográfica

Ulrike Mühlschlegel

Cuba está de moda en Alemania: El ex-canciller Gerhard Schröder fumaba puros de la marca Cohiba; los jóvenes beben mojitos en los bares y restaurantes cubanos y después se van a bailar salsa a los clubes, mientras que sus padres acuden a los conciertos de los miembros del Buena Vista Social Club. Las camisetas con el retrato del Che nunca se pasaron de moda y ahora incluso vuelven los afiches con la famosa fotografía que Alberto Korda hizo del Che. Pero en este texto no se hablará de la recepción de la cultura cubana en Alemania ni de las relaciones políticas y diplomáticas. Se hablará, más bien, de los cubanos que vivieron y viven en Alemania.[1]

En 1978, la República Democrática de Alemania (RDA o Alemania Oriental) y Cuba firman un Acuerdo Bilateral sobre Cualificación Sectorial y Empleo de Trabajadores.[2] En esta época, Cuba tenía problemas para garantizar el pleno empleo de su población: se estima que sobraban entre 100,000 y 150,000 trabajadores en el país. Los contratos de trabajo para los cubanos en Alemania se firman entre Cubatécnica—la institución cubana responsable de la coordinación, la realización y del cumplimiento de los contratos—y la institución responsable en la RDA, que es el Departamento de trabajadores extranjeros, pertenenciente a la Secretaría de Estado de Salarios y trabajo, dependiente del Ministerio del mismo nombre.[3] En la RDA no sólo hay obreros provenientes de Cuba, sino también otros grupos de trabajadores extranjeros: de Argelia, Angola, Vietnam y de países europeos vecinos como Polonia y Hungría.

Entre 1980 y 1984, el número de cubanos que viene cada año a Alemania Oriental es de 6,000. Entre 1984 y 1988 son 12,000 cubanos por año, o sea, que las cifras se duplican. De los trabajadores sólo 16%–20% son mujeres, porque los cubanos trabajan en sectores que requieren mucha fuerza física, como la producción de neumáticos, la industria química, la industria metalúrgica o también el sector forestal.[4]

Los cubanos que vienen con el acuerdo bilateral a Alemania Oriental debían tener entre 18 y 35 años y ser solteros. Sin embargo, las estadísticas muestran que el promedio de edad era de 29 años y hubo hasta personas de 40 años.[5] Vienen unas pocas parejas casadas, otras se casan durante su estancia en la RDA.

Los trabajadores contratados vienen por 4 años, aunque hay excepciones: pueden regresar antes por motivos personales o familiares urgentes. En otros pocos casos se quedan por más tiempo, porque la empresa en Alemania Oriental lo requiere. Los trabajadores no reciben un permiso de residencia permanente, sino un documento de identidad temporal de la RDA. Sus pasaportes cubanos se depositan en las fábricas o compañías donde trabajan. Viven en residencias para trabajadores (Arbeiterwohnheime) y, con el permiso de las autoridades, pueden viajar a otros países socialistas. También se organizan viajes colectivos a países de Europa del este, donde existen reglamentos estrictos para los viajes a Cuba.

La visita de colegas alemanes a las residencia de trabajadores es sumamente difícil. Deben entregar sus documentos de identidad a los guardias o porteros y tienen que registrarse en listas.[6] Los cubanos, por su parte, tienen sus propios pequeños gimnasios, bibliotecas y salas para fiestas y reuniones. Así, los contactos con los alemanes se reducen a un nivel mínimo que es, precisamente, lo que desean las autoridades de ambos países. Como resultado de esta política se dio un número muy bajo de matrimonios binacionales.

Antes del viaje a Alemania Oriental, los trabajadores contratados asisten a cursos preparatorios en Cuba. Allí reciben informaciones sobre el país, la cultura y sus futuros lugares de trabajo. Los grupos son acompañados por traductores, que también se quedan en la RDA por 4 o más años. Cada grupo de trabajadores tiene un capataz y cada comarca[7] tiene un encargado para los trabajadores cubanos.

Además de los trabajadores, hay otros grupos de cubanos en Alemania Oriental. Entre ellos figuran estudiantes e investigadores cubanos, que estudian y trabajan sobre todo en las universidades de Berlín, Iena, Rostock y Leipzig, pero su número es mucho más bajo que el de los trabajadores contratados. Existen cooperaciones en el area de los Medios de Comunicación: Las emisoras de radio y de televisión mantienen un intercambio de técnicos, que se basa en el Acuerdo de Intercambio Cultural entre Cuba y Alemania Oriental firmado en 1961. Lo más llamativo son, probablemente, las innumerables delegaciones del Gobierno, del Partido Comunista, de los sindicatos y de las organizaciones juveniles que de Cuba vienen a visitar la Alemania Oriental. Muchas veces, sus miembros, pasan varios meses en la RDA donde asisten a cursos de Marxismo-Leninismo en academias de orientación ideológica. Tanto entre los estudiantes cubanos como entre las delegaciones, Alemania Oriental es el país preferido entre todos los países socialistas, lo que se debe a su nivel de vida relativamente alto y a las comodidades de la vida cotidiana. Los estudiantes y algunas de las delegaciones se financian con becas del Gobierno, del Partido, de los sindicatos o de las organizaciones juveniles.

En Cuba, el término Alemania era idéntico al de Alemania Oriental. Las relaciones políticas con Alemania Occidental, lógicamente no eran estrechas, y el número de cubanos allí se mantenía muy bajo. La Alemania reunificada cancela todos los tratados internacionales de la RDA, entre ellos también los acuerdos sobre el intercambio de investigadores, de estudiantes y de trabajadores. Así en 1989, el año de la caída del muro, hay aproximadamente 9,000 trabajadores cubanos en Alemania Oriental. Un año después, en 1990, año de la reunificación de Alemania, quedan tan sólo 2,800.[8]

Hoy en día, no tenemos cifras fiables sobre el número de cubanos residentes en Alemania. Se estima que son alrededor de 8,000, entre ellos muchas más mujeres que hombres. Esto es un fenómeno recurrente en la emigración procedente de Latinoamérica: En 2004 viven 60,915 mujeres latinoamericanas en Alemania, pero sólo 29,980 hombres.[9] Las mujeres cubanas vienen a Alemania como esposas o como miembros de familias residentes en Alemania, o entran con visado de turista. Si deciden quedarse más allá de los tres meses (la duración máxima de sus visados), muchas de ellas deciden entonces incorporarse a la economía sumergida: realizando trabajos domésticos como limpieza de casas o cuidado de niños. Otras trabajan en la prostitución, lo cual no es específico de las mujeres cubanas, sino que se trata de una problemática común en parte de las mujeres que entran al país sin un permiso de residencia. Se estima que el 60% de las mujeres que trabajan en la prostitución tienen nacionalidad extranjera. Una acción policial en 1990 registró 121 prostitutas latinoamericanas en Frankfurt, de ellas 77 sin documentos legales.[10]

Otro grupo destacado de cubanos en Alemania son los artistas, entre ellos destacan los músicos, bailarines y pintores. Si bien algunos cubanos adquieren la nacionalidad alemana a través del matrimonio con una nacional, en general, se puede decir que muchos cubanos tienen problemas con su estatus inseguro en Alemania y carecen de un permiso de residencia permanente. Por ello, es difícil de determinar su número, siendo éste en todo caso bastante bajo y, hoy en día, los cubanos pasan casi desapercibidos en la vida diaria alemana.

¿Cuál es el estado actual de la bibliografía sobre los cubanos en Alemania? En este área se destacan los trabajos de Sandra Gruner-Domić sobre los trabajadores extranjeros cubanos en la Alemania Oriental, además, existen unos pocos estudios afines al esta temática. En este momento (2005) dos tesis—una de doctorado y otra de cátedra—sobre los cubanos en la RDA que se hallan fase de preparación. Sin embargo, cabe resaltar que la situación actual de los cubanos en la Alemania reunificada está muy poco estudiada. A un nivel más general, existen trabajos sobre los inmigrantes latinoaméricanos en general y en especial, sobre las mujeres de igual procedencia en Alemania. Estos estudios se centran sobre todo en la situación legal de las mujeres y en su inserción en el mercado laboral.

La bibliografía general sobre Cuba y las relaciones entre ésta y Alemania es muy extensa, debido a la gran importancia que los estudios cubanos tienen en las áreas de Literatura, Lingüística, Ciencias Políticas, Historia, Geografía e Historia Natural en Alemania. Hasta el momento, lamentablemente, carecemos de una recopilación bibliográfica de dichos trabajos.

NOTAS

1. Agradezco al Dr. Hubertus Büschel (Berlín) sus valiosos comentarios e indicaciones bibliográficas sobre el tema.

2. En alemán: *Regierungsabkommen über die Qualifizierung bei gleichzeitiger Beschäftigung.*

3. En alemán: *Ministerium für Arbeit und Löhne der DDR/ Staatssekretariat für Arbeit und Löhne, Abteilung Ausländische Arbeitskräfte (MfAL/SAL-AAK).*

4. Sandra Gruner-Domić, *Kubanische Arbeitsmigration in die DDR 1978–1989. Das Arbeitskräfteabkommen Kuba - DDR und dessen Realisierung* (Berlin: Institut für Sozialforschung, 1997), p. 7.

5. Gruner-Domić, *Kubanische Arbeitsmigration.* Allí se encuentran datos estadísticos y sociales muy detallados.

6. Gruner-Domić, *Kubanische Arbeitsmigration,* p. 37.

7. En alemán: *Bezirk;* una entidad administrativa y territorial, del tamaño entre un municipio y un departamento.

8. Gruner-Domić, *Kubanische Arbeitsmigration,* p. 37.

9. Sandra Gruner-Domić, *Latinas in Deutschland. Eine ethnologische Studie zu Migration, Fremdheit und Identität* (Münster: Waxmann, 2005); Julia Paz de la Torre, "Lateinamerikanische Immigrantinnen und ihrer Integration in den deutschen Dienstleistungssektor", en *Traumwelt, Migration und Arbeit,* ed. Aktionsgemeinschaft Solidarische Welt (Berlin, 2004), pp. 37–43.

10. Paz de la Torre, "Lateinamerikanische Immigrantinnen".

BIBLIOGRAFÍA

Gruner-Domić, Sandra. *Abriss zur Geschichte der Arbeitskräftemigration in der DDR. Die bilateralen Verträge zur Beschäftigung ausländischer Arbeiter (1961– 1989).* Berlin: Institut für Sozialforschung, 1998.

———. "Beschäftigung statt Ausbildung. Ausländische Arbeiter und Arbeiterinnen in der DDR (1961–1989)". En *50 Jahre Bundesrepublik, 50 Jahre Einwanderung: Nachkriegsgeschichte als Migrationsgeschichte,* editado por Jan Motte, Rainer Ohliger, y Anne von Oswald. Frankfurt am Main; New York: Campus, 1999. Pp. 215–240. [English version: "Employing better than giving a formation. Foreign workers in F.R.G. (1961–1989)", *Migrance* 17–18 (2001).]

———. "Zur Geschichte der Arbeitskräftemigration in die DDR. Die bilateralen Verträge zur Beschäftigung ausländischer Arbeiter (1961–1989)". *Internationale wissenschaftliche Korrespondenz zur Geschichte der deutschen Arbeiterbewegung* 32, no. 2 (1996): 204–230.

———. *Kubanische Arbeitsmigration in die DDR 1978–1989. Das Arbeitskräfteabkommen Kuba - DDR und dessen Realisierung.* Berlin: Institut für Sozialforschung, 1997.

———. "Lateinamerikanische Immigrantinnen in Deutschland vor und nach 1989. Entwicklung, Formen und Motive einer Migration in zwei Gesellschaften". *Archiv für Sozialgeschichte* 42 (2002).

———. *Latinas in Deutschland. Eine ethnologische Studie zu Migration, Fremdheit und Identität.* Münster: Waxmann, 2005.

Krämer, Raimund. "Archäologische Grabungen in einer verschwundenen Diplomatie. Zu den Beziehungen der DDR mit Lateinamerika". En *Deutschland, Lateinamerika: Geschichte, Gegenwart und Perspektiven*, editado por Manfred Mols y Christoph Wagner. Frankfurt am Main: Vervuert, 1994. Pp. 79–100.

————. "Das verschmähte Erbe". *Zeitschrift für Kulturaustausch* (1999:2). http://cms.ifa.de/index.php?id=kraemer0. Consultado en el Internet mayo 15, 2006.

Krüger-Potratz, Marianne. *Anderssein gab es nicht: Ausländer und Minderheiten in der DDR*. Münster: Waxmann, 1991.

Kuck, Dennis. "Für den sozialistischen Aufbau ihrer Heimat? Ausländische Vertragsarbeitskräfte in der DDR". En *Fremde und Fremd-Sein in der DDR: Zu historischen Ursachen der Fremdenfeindlichkeit in Ostdeutschland*, editado por Jan C. Behrends, Thomas Lindenberger, y Patrice G. Poutrus. Berlin: Metropol, 2003. Pp. 271–281.

Ohne Papiere (número temático de la revista ila 250 [2001]).

Paz de la Torre, Julia. "Lateinamerikanische Immigrantinnen und ihrer Integration in den deutschen Dienstleistungssektor". En *Traumwelt, Migration und Arbeit*, editado por Aktionsgemeinschaft Solidarische Welt. Berlin, 2004. Pp. 37–43.

Schäfter, Elke, y Susanne Schultz. "Putzen, was sonst? Latina in Berlin: bezahlte Hausarbeit für Migrantinnen". *Lateinamerika: Analysen und Berichte* 23 (1999): 97–110.

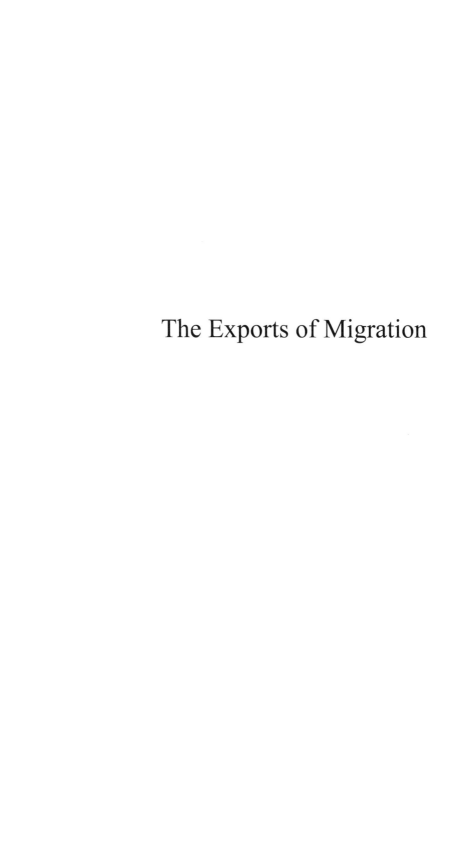

The Exports of Migration

8. *Maladie sans frontières:* The Latin American Cholera Pandemic of 1991–1995

David Block

After nearly a century's absence from the Western Hemisphere, cholera struck Peru in 1991. Within four months every Peruvian department reported incidences of the disease, and before the year was out, epidemic cholera had reached as far south as central Chile and as far north as southern Mexico. The year 1991 marked the beginning of a contagion that would eventually touch every Latin American country except Uruguay, cause 11,000 deaths, and establish endemic cholera in parts of the region. This paper examines cholera's relentless spread across national borders and the international response before turning to the well-documented Peruvian case to consider the impact of epidemic disease on social and political dynamics.

Cholera is an ancient malady. A description of cholera-like symptoms appears in a Sanskrit manuscript dating to 500 B.C., and the early history of the disease centers on Asia. In the nineteenth century, cholera played an important role in the development of epidemiology when the English physician John Snow mapped the residences of cholera patients to show their clustering around a public water pump in central London that was polluted by sewage. This early application of the principles of GIS established water as cholera's principal vector and called attention to the need to prevent commingling of potable and waste waters.

The onset of mass transportation systems in the nineteenth century transformed cholera from a localized disease to a widely dispersed one. The first multiregional contagion, which lasted from 1817 to 1823, was associated with the Turko-Persian War and spread through much of the Middle East. A second pandemic, associated with the aforementioned Dr. Snow and with the death of Henry James's father, began in Russia in 1829 and migrated westward. It reached New York in 1832 and subsequently spread along the eastern seaboard and Gulf Coast of the United States. The devastation caused by these and four subsequent pandemics in the nineteenth century was instrumental in the construction of urban water and sewage systems around the globe and in the establishment of a worldwide surveillance system for cholera and plague in 1896.[1] Five decades without large-scale outbreaks led to a belief that cholera would not recur in pandemic form. However, in 1961, a new cholera strain, labeled El Tor for the Egyptian quarantine camp where it was first identified, launched from the Celebes. Thirty years later, the resulting seventh pandemic reached the Pacific Coast of South America.

Cholera afflicts its victims with uncontrollable episodes of diarrhea and vomiting that quickly disrupt fluid balances and, if untreated, can cause acute dehydration, shock, renal failure, and death. In the developed world, cholera cases seldom reach the critical stage. Periodic outbreaks of the illness, such as those documented on the U.S. Gulf Coast in 1973, are treated with fluid replacement and the application of antibiotics; cholera is a bacterium. In the developing world, cholera's consequences are much more pernicious and longer-lived. The African phase of the seventh pandemic produced more than 45,000 cases and nearly 3,500 deaths.[2]

Cholera is a classic crowd infection. It afflicts only humans and passes from host to host through ingestion of human body wastes. Thus, cholera's optimum habitat is a city with poor sanitation, for example, nineteenth-century London or twentieth-century Lima. But, though it thrives in an urban setting, the disease exacts its highest death toll in the countryside, where access to medical care is unreliable. Thus, poor urban sanitation correlates with high cholera incidence; poor access to medical care correlates with high mortality.

A crazy quilt of international health organizations tracks epidemic disease and organizes resources for combating them. The World Health Organization (WHO), headquartered in Geneva, the Atlanta-based Centers for Disease Control (CDC), and the Pan American Health Organization (PAHO), in Washington, all monitored the seventh cholera pandemic in Latin America. Discussions of the difficulties of their overlapping missions and of the sources that these organizations compile will appear later in this paper. Information on the WHO website tracks the thirty-year movement of the El Tor strain around the globe. From 1961 and its outbreak in Indonesia, the pandemic reached Bangladesh in 1963, neighboring India in the next year, the USSR, Iran, and Iraq between 1965 and 1966, and West Africa—where it had not appeared in more than a century—in 1970.[3] At each interval, health experts expressed hope that the pandemic had been contained, and each time they were wrong.

Upon reaching South America, cholera spread rapidly from the Peruvian coast as outlined by the isobars in map 1.

With dreadful speed, cholera moved up the Pacific Coast to Ecuador and Colombia, across the Darien Gap to Panama and into northern Central America and southern Mexico. Cholera has long been associated with the sea; its pandemics move along the world's coastlines before they travel to the interior. However, since many human hosts carry cholera without exhibiting its symptoms, neither screening nor quarantine will prevent its movement from one human population to another. The highly publicized case of Aerolineas Argentinas flight 386, which arrived in Los Angeles with dozens of sick passengers on February 14, 1992, underlines the effectiveness of jet aircraft as international cholera delivery systems.[4]

Map 1. Spread of Cholera Epidemic in Latin America, 1991–1992. "Medical Geography and Cholera in Perú." http://www.colorado.edu/geography/gcraft/warmup/cholera/cholera.html.

As was documented for several Peruvian cities, cholera normally spreads within a locale through its water system. In Trujillo, a combination of broken and illegally tapped pipes, sporadic water pressure, and inadequate chlorination delivered cholera right to the residential tap.[5] Transmission is not limited to drinking water, however. Other means documented in the first year of the pandemic include the following: garden vegetables irrigated with raw sewage in Chile, contaminated shellfish in Ecuador, and carrying contaminated seafood in travelers' luggage for consumption in the United States.

The initial introduction of cholera to Peru has taken on the status of an urban legend. Initial reports blamed the pumping of infected bilge from a Chinese freighter taking on fish meal at the port of Chimbote. Another account cited effects from atmospheric changes wrought by the oil well fires of the first Gulf War. It seems most likely that the cholera bacterium developed in plankton off the Peruvian coast and passed to humans through consumption of fish or shellfish. Cholera control has been complicated by discoveries from recent research on the life cycle of the bacteria that cause it. Once thought incapable of life outside a human host for more than a few hours, cholera has been shown to survive for extended periods in a state of dormancy. Warm, salty water proves especially hospitable to maintaining cholera, and its bacteria have been isolated in fish, shellfish, and plankton.[6] This discovery has inserted cholera into the debate over possible effects of global warming. An increase in water temperatures, especially in areas affected by El Niño currents, may prolong the life expectancy of cholera and extend its range.

The following time series (fig. 1), compiled from data reported by PAHO, shows cholera cases in six Latin American republics in the years 1991–1997.

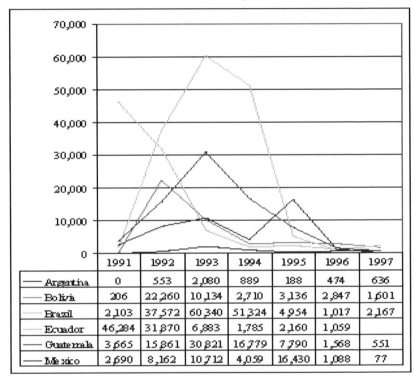

	1991	1992	1993	1994	1995	1996	1997
Argentina	0	553	2,080	889	188	474	636
Bolivia	206	22,260	10,134	2,710	3,136	2,847	1,601
Brazil	2,103	37,572	60,340	51,324	4,954	1,017	2,167
Ecuador	46,284	31,870	6,883	1,785	2,160	1,059	
Guatemala	3,665	15,861	30,821	16,779	7,790	1,568	551
Mexico	2,690	8,162	10,712	4,059	16,430	1,088	77

Fig. 1. Cholera Cases Reported from Six Latin American Countries, 1991–1997. *Health in the Americas,* vol. 1 (Washington, D.C.: Pan American Health Organization, 1998), pp. 128–129.

The figure illustrates several modalities of contagion. Cholera spread from its Peruvian epicenter in a series of waves. Ecuador, part of the first wave, reported its highest incidences in 1991; Guayaquil alone counted over 10,000 cases before the end of February. Thereafter, Ecuadorian cases declined markedly and incessantly. In 1992 a second wave of cholera peaked in Bolivia, and, again, the trend line forms a single, sharp peak. Brazil's first cases appeared in April 1991, but the Brazilian outbreak was confined to western Amazonia until 1993, when it spread to the northeast, claiming more than 60,000 victims and causing 670 deaths. Mexico and Central America reported cholera as early as June and July of 1991. However, contagions there peaked two years later. Guatemala reported 30,000 cases in 1993 and the subsequent, uninterrupted decline that characterized the regional trajectory. Mexico recorded a different trajectory. After reducing cholera cases by 60 percent between 1993 and 1994, Mexico experienced a resurgence in 1995, suggesting that the disease had established an endemic presence in the southeast coastal region of the country. Argentina represents a case of low rates of infection, one shared with Chile, Costa Rica, and Venezuela.

Not surprisingly, those countries that reported the fewest cholera cases were those with the best-developed public health programs. Epidemiological studies of the seventh pandemic have suggested several possible correlations between those afflicted and social indicators. In the Andes, cholera incidence correlated most significantly with infant mortality and, negatively, with maternal illiteracy.[7] Mexican studies identify a combination of urbanization, poverty, and environment as offering the highest level of explanatory power.[8] While the specifics of the Andean and Mexican cases may well reflect significant regional nuances, both studies show cholera's close association with poverty.

Peru bore the brunt of the seventh pandemic. The magnitude of the contagion, shown in figure 2, made Peru the world's leader in cholera cases in the first three years after 1991. Peru's 2,077 cholera-related deaths in 1991 and its 4,602 mortalities between 1991 and 1997 also set world standards.[9] The Peruvian data most closely resemble those from Ecuador shown in figure 1, with an overwhelming number of cases reported at the outset of the epidemic followed by a pronounced descent in the following years. However, as reflected in the different scales of the two graphs, Peru experienced a contagion ten times the size of Ecuador's and more than five times that of Brazil. A country of 22 million people registered 656,956 cholera cases in the first seven years of the decade, 322,562 in 1991 alone.

As staggering as they are in their aggregate, these statistics only begin to describe the effects of cholera in Peru. PAHO estimates that the national economy suffered losses exceeding $150,000,000, when exports, fisheries, tourism, and "certain other activities" are considered.[10] Raw statistics also hide how unevenly cholera afflicted the Peruvian people. Reports gathered by the Ministerio de Salud for the first six months of 1991 present rates of infection and death, morbidity and mortality in the dry idiom of public health, for Peru's twenty-five departments. Resorting these data to conform to Peru's major eco-geographic regions shows some remarkable regional variances.

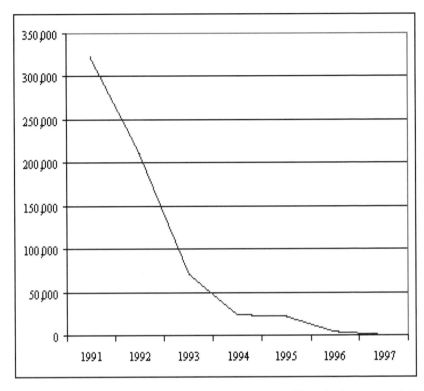

Fig. 2. Peruvian Cholera Cases Reported, 1991–1997. *Health in the Americas,* vol. 1 (Washington, D.C.: Pan American Health Organization, 1998), p. 128.

The coastal region, which includes more than half of the country's population, three of its four largest cities, and most of the country's major hospitals, reported 83 percent of the nation's cholera cases and 41 percent of its cholera-related deaths. The highlands and Amazonian regions, with smaller populations and fewer hospitals than the coast, reported correspondingly fewer cholera cases and cholera-related deaths. However, the coastal mortality rate, less than half of one percent, is much lower than that of either the highlands or the Peruvian Amazon (see table 1). These statistics clearly show that the further Peruvians lived from the coast, the less likely they were to contract cholera but, if infected, they were more likely to die from it. An oral history of the epidemic, collected in the Cajamarca countryside, describes living conditions bereft of sanitation systems, far removed from medical care, and without sources of news from outside the immediate locale.[11] These accounts resonate dreadfully with those chronicled by the Peruvian Commission on Truth and Reconciliation, whose final report underscores the horrible price that campesinos paid during the violence of the 1980s and 1990s.[12]

Table 1: Population and Cholera Statistics for Peru

Region	Population	Cholera Cases	Cholera Deaths	Mortality Rate (deaths/cases)
Coast	12,540,000 (57%)	181,646 (83%)	861 (41%)	0.47
Highlands	7,480,000 (34%)	21,519 (9.8%)	567 (27%)	2.60
Amazon	1,198,000 (9%)	15,523 (7.1%)	649 (31%)	4.18

Sources: Cholera statistics from Carlos Reyna and Antonio Zapata, *Crónica sobre el cólera en el Perú* (Lima: DESCO, 1991), p. 109; population statistics from "Censos" tab of homepage of Instituto Nacional de Estadística e Información, http://www.inei.gob.pe/home.htm.

Cholera reached Peru as the country endured a period of great social and economic upheaval. Alan García's presidency (1985–1990) bankrupted the treasury, saddled the nation with quadruple-digit levels of inflation, and alienated international investors. After his election in 1990, Alberto Fujimori implemented a set of neoliberal economic policies, dubbed "Fujishock," intended to end hyperinflation and make Peru eligible for financial assistance from the International Monetary Fund. By effectively raising prices and holding wages in check, Fujishock dramatically reduced living standards for the poor and simultaneously weakened social programs. At the same time many armed rebellions threatened to topple the established social and political order. Shining Path was only the most notorious of several guerrilla groups active at the time. In the face of these exigencies, the country's health system was deemed expendable. Government healthcare expenditures for 1991 represented less than 25 percent of what they had been a decade earlier.[13] Peru was ripe for a public health disaster in 1991, and decisions made by the Fujimori regime magnified the crisis.

In retrospect, the six weeks, beginning on the first of February 1991, determined the extent and impact of the cholera epidemic in Peru. Table 2 offers an outline for the discussion that follows.

Peru's first cholera cases—there are several claimants to the dubious honor—occurred in late January of 1991 and were officially confirmed on February 4. Carlos Vidal, the minister of health and a former officer in the Pan American Health Organization, organized an initial response based on transparency—reporting the outbreak to PAHO and to the Peruvian press—and public warnings against the consumption of unboiled water and uncooked seafood. At Vidal's urging the government declared a 120-day health emergency in the second week of February and allocated $4,000,000 to combat the cholera outbreak. However, these were the only examples of the national government taking decisive action to combat the epidemic.[14]

Table 2: Chronology of the Cholera Epidemic in Peru,
February 1–March 18, 1991

Week	Cholera Extension	Events
1 (Feb. 1–7)	North Coast of Peru	Confirmation of cholera by Ministry of Health; 20 cholera-related deaths in Chimbote and Chancay
2 (Feb. 8–15)	Lima	Ministry of Health notifies PAHO of cholera; first sustained reports in Peruvian press; Peru declares health emergency; first export restrictions imposed
3 (Feb. 16–23)	entire Peruvian coast, Ecuadorian coast	First report by CDC; Europe imposes ban on food imports
4 (Feb. 24– Mar. 2)	Peruvian highlands	Ministry of Health exhausts its emergency budget; Fujimori eats ceviche before cameras in Pisco
5 (Mar. 3–10)	Peruvian Amazon	Ecuador expands export controls; Fujimori eats ceviche in Chimbote
6 (Mar. 11–18)	Colombia, all Peruvian departments, except Cuzco	Minister of Health resigns

Having already committed themselves to an economic austere program, Fujimori and his ministers were loath to depart from IMF targets and refused to allocate additional funds or to lobby aggressively for international aid. Increasingly stringent sanctions on Peruvian exports and the resulting complaints from influential industrialists and labor unions reinforced the regime's neoliberal predilections. While never confronting Vidal or disavowing his policies, Fujimori began a public campaign against his minister of health. The president chose seafood as his weapon. On February 24, Fujimori and members of his retinue appeared before television cameras eating ceviche in the southern coastal city of Pisco. A week later, he repeated the gesture in Chimbote, one of the areas most severely affected by cholera. In both cases, the president delivered a homily on what one commentator called the "high patriotic virtues" of Peruvian fish.[15] Thus by word and deed the Peruvian president undercut his health minister's position and discarded his sound medical advice. Although Vidal remained at his post until March 17, he was unable to muster support for a vigorous campaign against a disease that had reached epidemic proportions.

To the extent that it is reflected in the press, popular opinion supported Fujimori's actions. Cholera, always associated with poverty, became synonymous with ignorance, disgrace, and filth. "COLERA La Maldición de la Mugre" reads the headline of an account in the February 11th edition of *Caretas*. Faced with the insult of slander added to injury, many cholera patients refused to acknowledge that they had contracted cholera, even when interviewed in their hospital beds. Peruvians' embarrassment at the arrival of cholera to their country is reflected in a letter to the editor in a subsequent issue of the magazine that accuses journalists who reported on the disease of irresponsibility.[16] *Caretas'* editors appended a response, defending its reporters, to the reader's complaint, but cholera reporting largely vanished from the Peruvian press with Vidal's resignation a month later. Despite its disappearance from the government's agenda and from the news, cholera refused to follow suit. It would kill nearly 3,000 Peruvians in 1991.[17]

Cholera cases in Latin America have not assumed major proportions since 1995. As a result, international health officials have declared an end of the seventh pandemic and moved on to attend other concerns. However, the cholera epidemic identified several indelible issues. Accounts of the Peruvian experience demonstrate the inherent conflict between trade and public health, a WTO vs. WHO. Reporting the cholera outbreak to international health authorities had tangible, and immediate, economic consequences. Even the most conservative estimates of lost revenues and opportunity costs to the Peruvian economy exceed $150,000,000. With the stakes so high, there is great temptation to hide information until an epidemic is well established. Think of the Chinese reaction to SARS. Also the tendency of trading partners to impose restrictions on imports that were in no way affected by disease caused undue hardship to the Peruvian economy and will not encourage future disclosures.[18]

Clear in all of the studies of the pandemic is the relationship between cholera and poverty. Access to potable water, to health services, and to public health information is critical to preventing and containing the disease. Adequate nutrition, shelter, and literacy provide disease resistance along with a higher quality of life, in general. Peruvian disinvestments in sanitation and healthcare documented in this paper were mirrored, if not matched, by other Latin American countries in the last decade of the 1900s. Estimates made in the 1990s place the cost of restoring the health infrastructure to even the levels of the 1970s at $200 billion.[19] Seen in this light, treating the disease becomes more cost effective than preventing it, if one only discounts the terrible human suffering.

The international donor community did not distinguish itself in responding to the cholera pandemic in Latin America. With estimates of the possible size of the disaster—one international health official prophesied 40,000 deaths—and the amount needed to merely treat the stricken ($42 million), Peru received less than $20 million, much of that from the EEC and NGOs.[20] Some research has attributed the lukewarm response to the magnitude of the problem and to donors' preference for relieving natural disasters rather than health emergencies that have no clear end in sight. However, Cuba immediately dispatched a mission of physicians and epidemiologists to Lima. This response, an example of what has been labeled Cuba's "health diplomacy," stood in marked contrast to that of the developed world and enhanced Cuban prestige and influence in Peru.

Disasters, of all stripes, have a way of exposing inequalities that lie hidden in a society. In his resignation from the health ministry, Carlos Vidal attributed part of the lack of government enthusiasm for his position to the fact that "the rich do not catch cholera."[21] Access to potable water in Peru, like living on the high ground in New Orleans, is a function of wealth. Disasters also expose the relationship between governors and the governed. The social implications of neoliberalist economics prescribes a loose compact, making individuals largely responsible for their own welfare. A resident from a squatter settlement in Chosica provides eloquent analysis with her simple words:

> La obligación de parar las enfermedades, sería acá en salud, tendrían la obligación de apoyar, de ayudar, pero hoy en día no se encuentra nada de apoyo. En cuanto a la mejora de vida que el gobierno mismo dice que defiende, creo que existe una ley que dice que nosotros tenemos derecho a tener una buena vida, que cada peruano tiene derecho a vivir bien, sin embargo no tenemos, asi que si uno quiere vivir bien cada una tiene que ver la manera de mejorar su vida, por su cuenta. (Testimony of Deidamia Bautista of Chosica in *Cólera, la version de los afectados,* p. 58)

The Peruvian experience could have been lifted from the pages of Henrik Ibsen's *An Enemy of the People,* with Carlos Vidal in the role of the idealistic Dr. Stockmann playing opposite Fujimori's cynical Burgomeister. In Peru, it was neoliberalism channeled through government policy that encouraged, or at least did not discourage, a discourse on cholera that promoted personal hygiene rather than building a solid health infrastructure. The government and the press focused on the importance of hand washing rather than on the need for clean water and squandered the opportunity to address the underlying causes of disease. More unfortunate, still, the international community watched the drama from the audience.

Coda: Sources for Researching the Seventh Cholera Pandemic in Latin America

The seventh pandemic has yet to enter the Latin American studies canon. Searching *HAPI* and the *Handbook of Latin American Studies* with subject and keyword strategies connecting "cholera" (or "colera") with Peru produce scanty results, the most useful of which is Marcos Cueto's *El regreso de las epidémias: Salud y sociedad en el Perú del siglo XX* (1997), recently translated as *The Return of Epidemics* (2001). Applying the same strategies to online library catalogs adds three additional monographs to the list, cited in the text as *Cólera,* Reyna's *Crónica,* and Panisset's *International Health Statecraft.*

To examine the pandemic in any depth requires delving into medical and scientific literature, which is better indexed but more rarely held by Latin American collections. International health agencies, WHO, CDC, and PAHO compile two basic sources of information: health alerts and statistics on morbidity and mortality. Establishing an accurate chronology of cholera's outbreak in Peru and its spread across the hemisphere is best constructed using two services, *Morbidity and Mortality Weekly Report,* published by the CDC and WHO's *Weekly Epidemiological Record.* These two organizations share information and their published data will, theoretically, replicate. In Latin America, the first link in the international health reporting chain is PAHO, in Washington, D.C. PAHO relies on CDC and WHO for rapid reporting but publishes a useful compendium *Health in the Americas* (1998–)—formerly, *Health Conditions in the Americas* (1961–1994)—and its companion publication, *Health Statistics from the Americas* (1991–).

To date the most fertile sources for investigating the pandemic are referenced in PubMed. Here appear article titles and abstracts, some of them remarkably informative in themselves, to studies done in public health and epidemiology. This literature adds information on cholera—its origins, impact in various regions of Latin America, lessons for health professionals, and government policy analysis—that fleshes out the health statistics provided by international agencies.

Although they currently stand alone—at least to my knowledge—digital materials developed by the Geographer's Craft Project offer a promise for how the World Wide Web can simultaneously enhance research and teaching. *Medical Geography and Cholera in Peru*[22] contains a good orientation and beginning bibliography as well as files, such as the map reproduced in this paper, no longer resident on the servers where they first appeared.

Peruvian periodical and current events reporting from Lima provide a number of insights, but poorly reflect the cholera epidemic as a crisis. The short news cycles decried by many analysts and competition from other events, such as the discovery of the videotape of Sendero Luminoso leaders "partying down," certainly reduced local coverage. And cholera's unfortunate reflection on the Peruvian nation itself added incentive for the press to move on to something else. Those accounts resulting from Peruvian investigators reference a number of regional newspapers and periodicals that future researchers would gainfully examine.

Despite the presence of a great deal of relevant information, the definitive study of the seventh cholera pandemic in Latin America remains to be written. And it may never be written in Latin America itself.

NOTES

1. Richard A. Cash and Vasant Narasimhan, "Impediments to Global Surveillance of Infectious Diseases: Consequences of Open Reporting in a Global Economy," *Bulletin of the World Health Organization* 78, no. 11 (2000): 1358.

2. Rita R. Colwell, "Global Climate and Infectious Disease: The Cholera Paradigm," *Science* 274, no. 5295 (December 1996): 2026.

3. World Health Organization, *Cholera,* http://www.who.int/mediacentre/factsheets/fs107/en/index.html (accessed April 4, 2006).

4. Nathaniel C. Nash, "Latin Nations Feud over Cholera Outbreak," *New York Times,* March 10, 1992, http://query.nytimes.com/gst/fullpage.html?res=9E0CE0DB1730F933A25750C 0A964958260&sec=health (accessed April 4, 2006).

5. Daniel Swederlow and others, "Waterborne Transmissions of Epidemic Cholera in Trujillo, Peru: Lessons for a Continent at Risk," *The Lancet* (July 4, 1992): 28–29.

6. Cowell, "Global Climate," p. 2027.

7. Marta-Louie Akers and others, "Are There National Risk Factors for Epidemic Cholera?" *International Journal of Epidemiology* 27 (1998): 332.

8. René J. Borroto and Ramón Martinez-Piedra, "Geographical Patterns of Cholera in Mexico, 1991–1996," *International Journal of Epidemiology* 29 (2000): 768.

9. *Health in the Americas,* vol. 1 (Washington, D.C.: Pan American Health Organization, 1998), p. 128.

10. *Health in the Americas,* p. 126. Estimates of economic loss became something of a political football. PAHO would later increase its estimate to $400,000,000 and some industrial advocates cited even larger numbers, one as high as $700,000,000. Ulysses Panisset, who has carefully studied the politics of the Peruvian epidemic, favors an estimate of $170,000,000. Ulysses B. Panisset, *International Health Statecraft* (Landham, Md.: University Press of America, 2000), pp. 172–173.

11. *Cólera, la versión de los afectados* ([Lima]: PREDES, 1991), pp. 11–19.

12. The report of the commission is at http://www.cverdad.org.pe/ingles/ifinal/index.php.

13. Marcos Cueto, *The Return of Epidemics: Health and Society in Peru during the Twentieth Century* (Burlington, Vt.: Ashgate Publishing, 2001), p. 109.

14. Cueto, *Return of Epidemics,* pp. 113–120.

15. Carlos Reyna and Antonio Zapata, *Crónica sobre el cólera en el Perú* (Lima: DESCO, 1991), p. 80.

16. Letter from Aldo Chirella O., *Caretas,* March 4, 1991, p. 1.

17. In a shameless revision of history, Alberto Fujimori points to public health advances as one of the major accomplishments of his presidency. See his website, "Desde Tokyo," www. fujimorialberto.com.

18. Cash and Narasimhan, "Impediments to Global Surveillance," p. 1364.

19. R. I. Glass and others, "Epidemic Cholera in the Americas," *Science* 256, no. 5063 (June 12, 1992): 1525.

20. Panisset, *International Health Statecraft,* p. 168.

21. Cueto, *Return of Epidemics,* p. 122.

22. See http://www.colorado.edu/geography/gcraft/warmup/cholera/cholera.html.

WORKS CITED

Akers, Marta-Louie, and others. "Are There National Risk Factors for Epidemic Cholera?" *International Journal of Epidemiology* 27 (1998): 330–334.

Borroto, René J., and Ramón Martinez-Piedra. "Geographical Patterns of Cholera in Mexico, 1991–1996." *International Journal of Epidemiology* 29 (2000): 764–772.

Cash, Richard A., and Vasant Narasimhan. "Impediments to Global Surveillance of Infectious Diseases: Consequences of Open Reporting in a Global Economy." *Bulletin of the World Health Organization* 78, no. 11 (2000): 1358–1367.

Cholera. World Health Organization. http://www.who.int/mediacentre/factsheets/fs107/en/index.html. Accessed April 4, 2006.

Cólera, la versión de los afectados. [Lima]: PREDES, 1991.

Colwell, Rita R. "Global Climate and Infectious Disease: The Cholera Paradigm." *Science* 274, no. 5295 (December 1996): 2025–2031.

Cueto, Marcos. *The Return of Epidemics: Health and Society in Peru during the Twentieth Century.* Burlington, Vt.: Ashgate Publishing, 2001.

Glass, R. I., and others. "Epidemic Cholera in the Americas." *Science* 256, no. 5063 (June 12, 1992): 1524–1525.

Health in the Americas. 2 vols. Washington, D.C.: Pan American Health Organization, 1998.

"Medical Geography and Cholera in Perú." http://www.colorado.edu/geography/gcraft/warmup/cholera/cholera.html. Accessed April 4, 2006.

Nash, Nathaniel C. "Latin Nations Feud over Cholera Outbreak." *New York Times,* March 10, 1992. http://query.nytimes.com/gst/fullpage.html?res=9E0CE0DB1730F933A25750C0A964958260&sec=health. Accessed April 4, 2006.

Panisset, Ulysses B. *International Health Statecraft.* Landham, Md.: University Press of America, 2000.

Reyna, Carlos, and Antonio Zapata. *Crónica sobre el cólera en el Perú.* Lima: DESCO, 1991.

Swederlow, Daniel, and others. "Waterborne Transmissions of Epidemic Cholera in Trujillo, Peru: Lessons for a Continent at Risk." *The Lancet* (July 4, 1992): 28–32.

9. Dubious Exports: U.S. Gangs in Latin America, a Bibliographic Survey

Gabrielle M. Toth

This paper treats the important and intriguing tale of how the members, structures, and social threats of U.S. gang activity have been exported to Latin America, Central America in particular, and its impact in the United States. Critics agree this exportation of gangs and their violence to Latin America was not done intentionally yet its consequences are being felt acutely in both post–civil war Central America and post 9/11 United States.

The complexities of gang life also impact a bibliographer's world as well. Finding resources and literature on gang migration from the United States to Latin America and back again can be a laborious undertaking. While gangs in general have long been the focus of academic study, the study of U.S.-to-Latin America gang migration, in its most earnest and deadly form, has only occurred in recent years. Perhaps for this reason, searches of the criminal justice literature do not reveal much. What do turn up are accounts from more pragmatic sources, such as police trade publication accounts of what is happening on the ground. NGOs and politicized journalists at both ends of the spectrum are also writing on the topic. Some very sophisticated and illuminating work is coming out of unexpected academic quarters, such as communications and geography departments. One can only imagine which other disciplines' practitioners may dive into the work of examining these U.S.-created, Latin-based gangs in all their complexity and consequence.

But first, one should look at how there came to be Latino gangs in the United States and how these gangs ended up replicating themselves in Central America. In 1988 *U.S. News and World Report* ran a cover story on ethnic gangs and organized crime, including groups in the United States that originated in Central America.[1] Today, two of the most notorious such gangs are the Mara Salvatrucha, or MS-13, and the Mara 18, or M-18. Though some police suggest that such gangs were formed in El Salvador in the 1970s or earlier, most suggest that these gangs arose in Los Angeles in the early 1980s.[2] This would coincide with research studies in El Salvador which show that gangs were not present there before the armed conflict. "Rather, the war caused an exodus to the north, and young Salvadorans came into contact with gangs that already existed in places like Central and Southern Los Angeles, California," according to an OAS information specialist.[3]

What brought these young migrants to Los Angeles? What made them migrants, that is? Violence in their homelands, among other reasons. Some say that during the late 1980s, refugees of the Farabundo Marti Front for National Liberation formed what is now known as Mara Salvatrucha.[4] El Salvador's twelve-year civil war drove more than a million refugees from the country.[5] Thousands saw their families murdered and were forced to flee.[6] El Salvador, Guatemala, and Nicaragua all found a tentative peace.

Conservatives, according to U.S. political rubrics, trace Central American gangs to people "displaced by Central American civil wars in the 1980s and to illegals who have been deported from the U.S. and then returned."[7] Commentators on the left point out that U.S. involvement in Central America played a part. According to Michael Hogan:

> American intervention in Central America in the 1980s to support corrupt, militarist regimes and destroy popular resistance created millions of refugees, many of them children. Thousands of these ended up on the streets of Los Angeles, Miami, Chicago, and other American cities. Often without a father figure, inured to violence from years of warfare, distrustful of authority, they joined street gangs already in existence, or formed those of their own.[8]

This U.S. gang problem became Central America's gang problem after the mid-1990s due to two key events: the 1992 riots in Los Angeles over the acquittal of police alleged to have beaten Rodney King, and new immigration laws in 1996. During these riots, nearly 1,000 Salvadoran youths were rounded up by INS agents and were deported to El Salvador.[9] "As the anti-immigrant backlash deepened and public attitudes toward juvenile offenders became more punitive, the INS launched the Violent Gang Task Force, targeting immigrants with criminal records for deportation to their countries of origin."[10] California put forth strict new anti-gang laws. Prosecutors charged young gang members as adults, and "three-strikes and you're out" legislations dramatically increased jail times for third-time offenders.[11]

In 1996 such attitudes found their way into federal immigration law. The Illegal Immigration Reform and Immigrant Responsibility Act allowed for noncitizens sentenced to a year or more in prison to be deported to their countries of origin. Foreign-born Americans, too, could be stripped of their citizenship and expelled. The number of deportable crimes increased and included such crimes as drunk driving and petty theft. In 1998 some 56,000 were deported to Central America and the Caribbean.[12]

From 2000 to 2004, "an estimated 20,000 young Central American criminals, whose families had settled in the slums of Los Angeles in the 1980s after fleeing civil wars at home, were deported to countries they barely knew. Many of the deportees were native English speakers who had arrived in the United States as toddlers but had never bothered to secure legal residency or citizenship."[13]

What would prove even more troubling for Central America was that not only were they getting tens of thousands of criminals sent "home" to them, but the nations had no knowledge of what they were getting, since "the new U.S. immigration rules banned U.S. officials from disclosing the criminal backgrounds of the deportees."[14] These deportations have helped the United States lower its crime rates. In January 2006 the *Economist* reported that Kevin Kozak of the Immigration and Customs Enforcement (ICE) Agency said that 30 percent of gang members picked up by his agency in the United States are arrested and charged with crimes; but the other 70 percent are deported. "There is no alternative; they are in the United States illegally, but evidence does not exist to prosecute them for any specific crime."[15]

Back in 1998 a UNICEF study highlighted the role of U.S. gangs in the creation of Central American ones. "The report says the gang subculture was brought to El Salvador by boomerang emigrants deported from the U.S. after becoming involved in gangs in low-income neighborhoods of large U.S. cities."[16]

What are the effects of this immigration on Central America? One, clearly, is an increase in crime. "Officials in El Salvador say they cannot ask the United States to stop the deportations, but nor can they cope with them on any large scale."[17]

The U.S. penitentiary system is like a finishing school for gang members, and then they are deported. Once they arrive in places like Honduras, they go to work. Or, as researcher Andrew Papachristos notes, "With little or no connection to their new homes, deported gang members typically face a simple choice: either find a way to return to the United States or seek protection from local gang members."[18] Numbers are hard to get, but estimates put the number of active gang members in Central America and Mexico in excess of 100,000. In El Salvador, population 6.7 million, there are more than 10,000 core gang members, and fifteen municipalities either have been or are controlled by gangs. In Honduras, population 6.9 million, the number of gang members may be more than 40,000. Gangs overwhelmed local governments, which were unaware of the problem they had been sent.[19]

In Nicaragua, presidential candidates could not campaign without a safe-conduct bribe to gangs in many neighborhoods. One needs similar safe-conducts to shop in many of the open-air markets of Guatemala and El Salvador. Peace accords in Central America, which brought about the withdrawal of U.S. advisors and contra mercenaries, have left behind ammunition, grenades, land mines, and automatic rifles, all to be had at low, low prices.[20]

It should be clear that some of the factors that propelled Central American youth into gang membership once they reached the United States effectively kept them involved even after they were deported. If, when they arrived in places like Los Angeles, they felt alienated from a foreign culture, had grown up amidst violence, and had few educational or job prospects, the same held true once they returned to Central America.

This question of identity is key. These youths effectively belong nowhere and are wanted nowhere. They were illegals in the United States, and they are misfits in their so-called home countries. Or, as scholar Elana Zilberg puts it, places like El Salvador are now "host to a new social formation built on this puzzling relationship between space and identity. Deported Salvadoran immigrant gang youth—banished from the United States after spending the better part of their young lives in this country—are returned 'home' to a place where, in their memory, they have never been."[21]

One young El Salvadoran's story Zilberg considers illustrates how dangerous these ruptured identities can be. Gato belonged to one gang from where he grew up in Los Angeles, was deported to El Salvador, and found himself living in what had been his old neighborhood but was now rival gang territory. Another deported gang member described himself as being Salvadoran living in America living a Chicano lifestyle. These young, uneducated, unemployed and maybe unemployable youths are more cosmopolitan than anything.[22]

So these youths return home and, with nothing better to do or with no viable alternatives, begin doing what they do best—regrouping and, often, returning to criminal activity. But this gang identity is a dangerous one not only for their states, but for themselves. With their wild tattoos covering their bodies, gang members wear their identities openly and make an easy target for Central American law enforcement, whether they are actually involved in illegal activity or not. Gang members are open to the threat of "social cleansing." In Honduras such extrajudicial measures have resulted in the deaths of over 2,000 youths since 1998.[23] Their crime? Being suspected of holding gang membership. In 2006 the *Economist* reported: "According to Salvadoran police officials, any *marero* with tattoos must have murdered someone in an initiation rite."[24] Casa Alianza, an advocate for street children, has documented that sometimes police, sometimes vigilantes, shoot gang members on sight.[25] Such activities would be troubling anywhere, but are especially so in nations trying to leave corruption and human rights abuses behind.

In 2002 Honduras enacted a series of "zero tolerance" laws such as one allowing the government to imprison people for up to twelve years merely on suspicion of gang membership—sometimes determined merely by the presence of tattoos on their bodies.[26] "Equally worrisome to the regime's reluctant disarmament is the role taken on by military and state police forces in the crackdown on youth gangs in Guatemala, El Salvador and Honduras."[27] Some are concerned that Central American countries may be near to taking a step backward toward the "repressive top-down police practices" of the recent past.[28]

As for the people of Central America, they give strong support to just such measures. It is not difficult to understand why. In 2004, Guatemalan President

Berger admitted he had been unable to curb a wave of violence. As such, he deployed 4,000 soldiers and elite police commandos onto the streets of the capital in July 2004. In El Salvador, President Tony Saca launched operation "Super Heavy Hand" in 2004, which in its first two weeks rounded up 800 suspected gang members.[29]

While these zero-tolerance and heavy-handed laws have had widespread support, they have also had unintended consequences. Within a year of enacting tough anti-gang laws in Honduras, that nation's prison system swelled to 200 percent beyond capacity.[30] Prison riots in April 2003 and May 2004 ensued.[31] One such prison riot in Guatemala left 31 dead.[32] Back in Honduras, the Mara Salvatrucha based in Tegucigalpa believed security forces were to blame for a May 17, 2004, prison fire that killed 105 of its gang members.[33] Guards reportedly did not open the cellblock for two hours after the fire began. In retaliation for these crackdowns, gang members responded with acts like the December 2004 bus massacre in Honduras that left 28 people dead.[34]

Interestingly, some of these heavy-handed approaches to gang activity were also exported from the United States, namely, from New York Mayor Rudy Giuliani's model. There has been some retreat, however, as, like in the United States, Latin American officials realize that the efficacy of many of these anti-gang measures have never been studied and they, in fact, appear to not work.[35] "We cannot arrest ourselves out of the gang problem," said one Latin American police official to the *Economist* in January 2006. According to the *Economist,* Guatemala and Honduras have not yet caught on, but Honduras may have—the election of Manuel Zelaya in November, it says, is a good sign, as Zelaya was "less prone to get-tough rhetoric than his opponent."[36]

And now these policies are not working for the United States, either, as the deported sometimes return and bring their gang activity back with them. This return has made U.S. law enforcement take notice, especially in the wake of the events of September 11, 2001.

In the summer of 2003, a young Latina's nearly beheaded body was found in rural Virginia, where she had been sent as part of the witness protection program. She was allegedly associated with Mara Salvatrucha in northern Virginia, near Washington, D.C., a place where Salvadoran immigrants are plentiful.[37] Now the Virginia attorney general has made gangs a priority, the U.S. government is finding the money for anti-gang task forces, and the FBI, as of 2005, has set up a National Gang Task Force to "centralize and coordinate the national collection of intelligence on gangs."[38] The MS-13 National Gang Task Force coordinated the capture, in Texas, of a key MS-13 figure believed to be responsible for the Honduran bus massacre of December 2004.[39] Some, like U.S. Representative Dan Burton, a Republican from Indiana, were concerned that increased violent activity will destabilize the democratic and economic progress in the Western Hemisphere. He noted in a March 2005 press release that "many experts warned that this violence leads to increasing illegal immigration, drug smuggling and trafficking in persons and weapons to the United States."[40]

To some, the specter of an al-Qaeda-led, Central American–based attack looms large. There is no hard evidence of such a possibility, and the FBI keeps struggling to convince Americans that an alleged meeting between an al-Qaeda operative and Salvatrucha members in Honduras in 2003 is pure myth. A recent Republican candidate for governor of Virginia made much of that meeting in his stump speech against crime.[41]

Most observers all along the political spectrum believe that a matchup between al-Qaeda and Central American gangs is highly unlikely, as each group is pretty much closed off to outsiders and probably finds the other abhorrent. Nonetheless, twenty years ago a Chicago gang, the El Rukns, met with Moamar Quadafi and, for $2.5 million, were willing to make attacks against specified U.S. targets.[42]

What both the United States and Central America can fear is greater American involvement in Central America, which the gang problem clearly demands. Few would argue against the idea that the United States is absolutely necessary in this struggle, if not only because it has played a hand in the problem's creation but because it has the resources needed to tackle it.

Central American governments have budgets ravaged by years of civil war and, ironically, police and similar forces gutted by the necessities of saving money, throwing out corrupt officials, and simply shrinking the size of forces once the wars concluded. This necessary undertaking to promote human rights has left these nations more vulnerable to gang violence.

From Washington's point of view, these challenges are an opportunity and a threat. Joint initiatives, training programs, and the like to combat gangs could help to keep the region on the side of the United States, rather than Venezuela, and would be palatable to a populace clearly interested in strong measures to get rid of gangs. But the United States must go slowly, lest it be perceived "as a funder of a military force designed to subdue the Central American population."[43]

Though there are a number of issues I have not touched on—the spread of gang culture and youth culture in the forms of mode of dress and taste in music and slang, the appropriation and misappropriation by gang wannabes of gang symbolism, the role of free trade in offering both problems and solutions—it should be clear that the migration of gang activity presents a complex study in what globalization has wrought.

NOTES

1. J. Seamonds and S. Minerbrook, "Ethnic Gangs and Organized Crime," *U.S. News and World Report* 104, no. 2 (January 18, 1988): 29.

2. "Out of the Underworld," *Economist,* January 7, 2006, pp. 23–26.

3. Ampara Trujillo, "Cutting to the Core of the Gang Crisis," trans. Kathy A. Ogle, *Americas* 57, no. 6 (November/December 2005): 56–57.

4. Tony Vaquera and David W. Bailey, "Latin Gang in the Americas: Los Mara Salvatrucha," *Crime and Justice International* 20, no. 83 (November/December 2004): 4.

5. Fe Montaigne, "Deporting America's Gang Culture: Photographer Donna DeCesare Puts a Human Face on One of the United States' Most Shameful Exports," *Mother Jones* 24, no. 4 (July/August 1999): 44.

6. Kari Lydersen, "Grim News in Central America: Wave of Gang Violence Grows," *Resource Center of the Americas,* January 29, 2004, http://www.americas.org/item_12 (accessed February 21, 2006).

7. Michael Hogan, "Dismantling the Central American Gangs and Recovering a Lost Generation," *MR Zine,* January 21, 2006, http://mrzine.monthlyreview.org/hogan210106.html (accessed February 21, 2006).

8. Ibid.

9. "Latin American Youth: Anger and Disenchantment on the Margins," *NACLA Report on the Americas* 32, no. 1 (July/August 1998): 20.

10. Ibid.

11. Ana Arana, "How the Street Gangs Took Central America," *Foreign Affairs* 84, no. 3 (May/June 2005): 98–110.

12. Montaigne, "Deporting America's Gang Culture."

13. Arana, "How the Street Gangs."

14. Ibid.

15. "Out of the Underworld," pp. 23–26.

16. Catherine Elton, "From San Salvador's Streets to a Study Program," *Christian Science Monitor,* April 19, 2001, p. 7.

17. "Out of the Underworld," pp. 23–26.

18. Andrew V. Papachristos, "Gang World," *Foreign Policy* (March/April 2005): 49–55.

19. Adam Wolfe, "Central American Street Gangs Enter Geopolitics," *Power and Interest News Report,* August 26, 2005, http://www.isn.ethz.ch/news/sw/details.cfm?ID=12615 (accessed February 21, 2006).

20. Hogan, "Dismantling the Central American Gangs."

21. Elana Zilberg, "Fools Banished from the Kingdom: Remapping Geographies of Gang Violence between the Americas (Los Angeles and San Salvador)," *American Quarterly* 56, no. 3 (September 2004): 759–779.

22. Zilberg, "Fools Banished from the Kingdom."

23. Tim Rogers, "Central America's Uneasy Disarmament," *NACLA Report on the Americas* 39, no. 1 (July/August 2005): 12–14.

24. "Out of the Underworld," pp. 23–26.

25. Lydersen, "Grim News in Central America."

26. Arana, "How the Street Gangs," pp. 98–110.

27. Rogers, "Central America's Uneasy Disarmament," pp. 12–14.

28. Ibid.

29. Ibid.

30. Lydersen, "Grim News in Central America."

31. Arana, "How the Street Gangs," pp. 98–110.

32. Wolfe, "Central American Street Gangs."

33. Tom Hayden, "Latest Honduran Prison Massacre: 'Homies Were Burning Alive,'" *Prison Legal News* 16, no. 1 (January 2005): 8.

34. Ibid.

35. Ibid.

36. "Out of the Underworld," pp. 23–26.

37. "Virginia Farming Communities Create Task Forces to Combat Latino Gangs," *Organized Crime Digest* 25, no. 17 (December 10, 2004): 1.

38. Statement of Chris Swecker, Assistant Director, Criminal Investigation Division, Federal Bureau of Investigation Before the Subcommittee on the Western Hemisphere, House International Relations Committee, April 20, 2005, http://www.fbi.gov/congress/congress05/swecker042005.htm (accessed February 21, 2006).

39. Ibid.

40. "Gangs and Crime in Latin America: Burton Schedules Wednesday Hearing to Examine Threat of Gangs and Increasing Crime Rates in Western Hemisphere," U.S. House of Representatives, Committee on International Relations, Henry J. Hyde, Chairman (March 16, 2005).

41. "Out of the Underworld," pp. 23–26.

42. Papachristos, "Gang World," pp. 49–55.

43. Wolfe, "Central American Street Gangs."

BIBLIOGRAPHY

Allender, David M. "Gangs in Middle America: Are They a Threat?" *FBI Law Enforcement Bulletin* 70, no. 12 (December 2001): 1–15.

Arana, Ana. "How the Street Gangs Took Central America." *Foreign Affairs* 84, no. 3 (May/June 2005): 98–110.

Ballve, Teo. ". . . YA! Youth Activism." *NACLA Report on the Americas* 38, no. 5 (March/April 2005).

"Beyond the Mafia: Organized Crime in the Americas." *Crime and Justice International* 14, no. 20 (September 1998): 30.

Binford, Leigh. "A Failure of Normalization: Transnational Migration, Crime, and Popular Justice in the Contemporary Neoliberal Mexican Social Formation." *Social Justice* 26, no. 3 (fall 1999): 123–144.

"Bringing It All Back Home." *Economist,* May 22, 2004, pp. 31–32.

Campo-Flores, Arian, and others. "The Most Dangerous Gang in America." *Newsweek* 145, no. 13 (March 28, 2005): 22–25.

Daschle, Tom. "Challenges to U.S. Leadership 'Will Only Grow.'" *Miami Herald,* February 7, 2006. http://www.miami.com.mld.miamiherald/news/opinion/. Accessed February 21, 2006.

Dowdney, Luke. "Neither War nor Peace: International Comparisons of Children and Armed Violence." http://www.coav.org.br/publique/cgi/cgilua.exe/sys/start.htm?sid=104&UserActiveTemplate=_en. Accessed February 21, 2006.

"El Salvador Gang Member: I'm No Terrorist." *Miami Herald,* February 24, 2005. Posted at Resource Center of the Americas. http://www.americas.org/item_ 18122. Accessed February 21, 2006.

Elton, Catherine. "From San Salvador's Streets to a Study Program." *Christian Science Monitor,* April 19, 2001, p. 7.

"The Encounter on Globalization, Migration, and Militarization: 'A Dialogue between NGOs'; NGOs of the Border Encuetro." *Social Justice* 28, no. 2 (summer 2001): 113–131.

"Gangs and Crime in Latin America: Burton Schedules Wednesday Hearing to Examine Threat of Gangs and Increasing Crime Rates in Western Hemisphere." U.S. House of Representatives. Committee on International Relations. Henry J. Hyde, Chairman. March 16, 2005.

"Gangs Plague Central America." *Wall Street Journal, Eastern Edition,* December 11, 2003, p. A14.

Garland, Sarah. "Central America: Anti-Gang Agreement." *NACLA Report on the Americas* 37, no. 5 (March/April 2004): 1.

Hayden, Tom. "Latest Honduran Prison Massacre: 'Homies Were Burning Alive.'" *Prison Legal News* 16, no. 1 (January 2005): 8.

Hogan, Michael. "Dismantling the Central American Gangs and Recovering a Lost Generation." *MR Zine,* January 21, 2006. http://mrzine.monthlyreview.org/hogan210106.html. Accessed February 21, 2006.

Homies Unidos website. http://www.homiesunidos.org/. Accessed March 16, 2006.

Johnson, Stephen, and David B. Muhlhausen. "North American Transnational Youth Gangs: Breaking the Chain of Violence." *Executive Summary Backgrounder,* no. 1834 (March 21, 2005). www.heritage.org/research/urbanissues/bg1834.cfm. Accessed February 21, 2006.

———. "North American Transnational Youth Gangs: Breaking the Chain of Violence." *Royal Canadian Mounted Police Gazette* 67, no. 4 (2005). http://www.gazette.rcmp.grc.gc.ca. Accessed February 21, 2006.

———. "North American Transnational Youth Gangs: Breaking the Chain of Violence." *Trends in Organized Crime* 9, no. 1 (fall 2005): 38–54.

Knox, George W. "Addressing and Testing the Gang Migration Issue: A Summary of Recent Findings." In *Gangs: A Criminal Justice Approach,* edited by J. Mitchell Miller and Jeffrey P. Rush. Highland Heights, Ky.: Academy of Criminal Justice Sciences, 1996.

LaFranchi, Howard. "Latest U.S. Export: Youth Gang Culture to Central America." *Christian Science Monitor,* November 5, 1996, p. 1.

"Latin American Youth: Anger and Disenchantment on the Margins." *NACLA Report on the Americas* 32, no. 1 (July/August 1998): 20.

Lydersen, Kari. "Grim News in Central America: Wave of Gang Violence Grows." *Resource Center of the Americas,* January 29, 2004. http://www.americas.org/item_12. Accessed February 21, 2006.

Maxson, Cheryl. "Civil Gang Injunctions: The Ambiguous Case of the National Migration of a Gang Enforcement Strategy." In *American Youth Gangs at the Millennium,* by Finn-Aage Esbensen, Stephen G. Tibbetts, and Larry Gaines. Long Grove, Ill.: Waveland Press, 2004.

Maxson, Cheryl, and Malcolm W. Klein. *Street Gangs Migration in the United States.* http://www.streetgangs.com/migration/sgmig96.html. Accessed February 21, 2006.

Maxson, Cheryl Lee. *Gang Members on the Move.* Washington, D.C.: U.S. Department of Justice, Office of Justice Programs, Office of Juvenile Justice and Delinquency Prevention, 1998.

MoLoney, Anastasia. "Vigilante Heaven." *New Internationalist* 376 (March 2005): 22–24.

Montaigne, Fe. "Deporting America's Gang Culture: Photographer Donna DeCesare Puts a Human Face on One of the United States' Most Shameful Exports." *Mother Jones* 24, no. 4 (July/August 1999): 44–52.

Moser, Caroline, and Bernice van Bronkhorst. "Youth Violence in Latin America and the Caribbean: Costs, Causes, and Interventions." *LCR Sustainable Development Working Paper No. 3, Urban Peace Program Series.* World Bank, Latin America and Caribbean Region, Environmentally and Socially Sustainable Development SMU, August 1999. http://go.worldbank.org/2U20EGAFJ0. Accessed February 21, 2006.

"New Jersey Gangs Are More Greatly Diverse." *Organized Crime Digest* 24, no. 8 (May 2, 2003): 2.

"New York: Southwest Migrants Bring Gang Warfare." *Crime Control Digest* 35, no. 31 (August 3, 2001): 6.

"Out of the Underworld." *Economist,* January 7, 2006, pp. 23–26.

Pan American Health Organization. "Gang Violence Requires a Preventive Approach." *PAHO Today: The Newsletter of the Pan American Health Organization.* http://www.paho.org/English/DD/PIN/ptoday03_apr05.htm. Accessed February 21, 2006.

Papachristos, Andrew V. "Gang World." *Foreign Policy* (March/April 2005): 49–55.

———. "State-Sponsored Gang Migration" (February 26, 2005). http://davidholiday.com/weblog/2005/02/state-sponsored-gang-migration.html. Accessed February 22, 2006.

Rodgers, Dennis. "Globalization and Development Seen from Below." *Revista Envio* 272 (March 2004). http://www.envio.org.ni/articulo.php?id=2153. Accessed February 21, 2006.

Rogers, Tim. "Central America's Uneasy Disarmament." *NACLA Report on the Americas* 39, no. 1 (July/August 2005): 12–14.

———. "Central America Takes Harder Line against Gangs." *Christian Science Monitor,* July 6, 2004, p. 7.

Rotella, Sebastian. *Twilight on the Line: Underworlds and Politics at the U.S.-Mexico Border.* New York: Norton, 1998.

Salomon, Leticia, Julieta Castellanos, and Mirna Flores. *La delincuencia juvenil: Los menores infractores en Honduras.* Tegucigalpa: Centro de Documentatcion de Honduras, 1999.

Scott, Cathy. "Unwittingly, California Exports Gang Violence." *Christian Science Monitor,* December 13, 2001, p. 2.

Seamonds, J., and S. Minerbrook. "Ethnic Gangs and Organized Crime." *U.S. News and World Report* 104, no. 2 (January 18, 1988): 29.

Sheldon, Randall G., Sharon K. Tracy, and William B. Brown. *Youth Gangs in American Society.* 3d ed. Belmont, Calif.: Thomson/Wadsworth, 2004.

Skolnick, Jerome H., Ricky Blumenthal, and Theodore Correl. "Gang Organization and Migration." In *Gangs: The Origins and Impact of Contemporary Youth Gangs in the United States,* edited by Scott Cummings and Daniel J. Monti. Albany: State University of New York Press, 1993.

Smutt, Marcela, and Jenny Lissette E. Miranda. *El fenómeno de las pandillas en El Salvador.* San Salvador: UNICEF; FLASCO Programa El Salvador, 1998.

Statement of Chris Swecker, Assistant Director, Criminal Investigation Division, Federal Bureau of Investigation Before the Subcommittee on the Western Hemisphere, House International Relations Committee, April 20, 2005. http://www.fbi.gov/congress/congress05/swecker042005.htm. Accessed February 21, 2006.

Sullivan, Mark. "Latin America: Terrorism Issues." In *CRS Report for Congress: Received through the CRS Web.* Congressional Research Service, Library of Congress, March 29, 2005. Accessed February 21, 2006.

Thompson, Ginger. "Shuffling between Nations, Latino Gangs Confound the Law." *New York Times,* September 26, 2004, p. 1.

Trujillo, Ampara. "Cutting to the Core of the Gang Crisis." Translated by Kathy A. Ogle. *Americas* 57, no. 6 (November/December 2005): 56–57.

U.S. Congress. Letter to his Excellency Ricardo Maduro [of Honduras on Appropriate Responses to the American Youth Gang Phenomeon], August 15, 2005.

Valdez, Al. "Gangs: Migration or Imitation?" *Police* 22, no. 1 (January 1998): 48.

———. "The Highways and Byways of Crime." *Police* 23, no. 2 (February 1999): 44–47.

———. "Street-Wise Veteran Gives Sage Advice." *Police* 24, no. 6 (June 2000): 66–68.

Vaquera, Tony, and David W. Bailey. "Latin Gang in the Americas: Los Mara Salvatrucha." *Crime and Justice International* 20, no. 83 (November/December 2004): 4–10.

Vazsonyi, Alexander T. "Migration, Culture Conflict, and Crime." *International Criminal Justice Review* 13 (2003): 202–204.

Vigil, James Diego. "Learning from Gangs: The Mexican American Experience." *ERIC Clearinghouse on Rural Education and Small Schools.* Charleston, W.Va., 1997. http://www.ericdigests.org/1997-4/gangs.htm. Accessed February 21, 2006.

"Violent Gangs Spread Largely through Migration of Families." *Crime Control Digest* 32, no. 17 (April 25, 1997): 1. Also published in *Juvenile Justice Digest* 25, no. 9 (May 15, 1997): 3.

"Virginia Farming Communities Create Task Forces to Combat Latino Gangs." *Organized Crime Digest* 25, no. 17 (December 10, 2004): 1–3.

Washington Office on Latin America. "Gang Violence in Central America" (October 17, 2005). http://www.wola.org/gangs/gangs.htm. Accessed February 21, 2006.

———. Memo by Geoff Thale. "International Assistance in Responding to Youth Gang Violence in Central America," September 30, 2005. http://www.wola.org/media/international_coop_memo.pdf. Accessed February 21, 2006.

———. Memo by Geoff Thale and Clara Rodriguez, WOLA, and Margaret Popkin, Due Process of Law Foundation. "Youth Gangs in Central America," February 22, 2005. http://www.wola.org/media/dplf_wola_background_memo_feb23%5B1%5D.pdf. Accessed February 21, 2006.

———. "Voices from the Field: Local Initiatives and New Research on Central American Youth Gang Violence." Full report on conference by Erin Scheik. February 23, 2003. http://www.wola.org/gangs/conference_page_more_info.htm. Accessed February 21, 2006.

Winton, Alisa. "Youth, Gangs and Violence: Analyzing the Social and Spatial Mobility of Young People in Guatemala City." *Children's Geographies* 3, no. 2 (August 2005): 167–184.

Wolfe, Adam. "Central American Street Gangs Enter Geopolitics." *Power and Interest News Report,* August 26, 2005. http://www.isn.ethz.ch/news/sw/details.cfm?ID=12615. Accessed February 21, 2006.

Zilberg, Elana. "Fools Banished from the Kingdom: Remapping Geographies of Gang Violence between the Americas (Los Angeles and San Salvador)." *American Quarterly* 56, no. 3 (September 2004): 759–779.

———. "From Riots to Rampart: A Spatial Cultural Politics of Salvadoran Migration to and from Los Angeles." Ph.D. diss., University of Texas at Austin, 2002.

———. "Transnationalism by Force: Youth, Migration and Violence between the Americas." http://translocal-flows.ssrc.org/english/zilberg/. Accessed March 16, 2006.

Migration: The Mexican Experience

10. El Colegio de México: legado del exilio español

Micaela Chávez Villa
Víctor J. Cid Carmona

Antecedentes

Al abandonar el trono Alfonso XIII, se proclamó la Segunda República Española con Niceto Alcalá Zamora en la presidencia y Manuel Azaña como Primer Ministro; pronto implementaron una serie de medidas de corte liberal como la separación de la iglesia y el Estado, la libertad de cultos y la ley de congregaciones religiosas, todas ellas con un objetivo: la limitación de la influencia del clero en la vida pública. Desde el inicio de la Segunda República y hasta 1936 el gobierno enfrentó diferencias políticas, sociales, regionales y religiosas que dificultaron su eficacia; los tres problemas principales que obstaculizaban la unidad republicana fueron el nacionalismo regional, el radicalismo popular y la continua influencia—y oposición—de la iglesia, el ejército y la aristocracia.[1]

La difícil situación culminó con el inicio de la Guerra Civil Española, el pretexto para el estallido del conflicto armado fue el asesinato del dirigente conservador Calvo Sotelo el 13 de julio de 1936, el 18 del mismo mes surgió el golpe de estado de diversos sectores militares que tuvo como punto de partida el Marruecos español, estos grupos constituyeron el llamado Movimiento Nacional y tuvieron como dirigente al general Francisco Franco Bahamonde.

Durante los tres años que duró la guerra los republicanos fueron perdiendo terreno debido a fricciones internas que no les permitieron formar un frente común para defender la República.[2]

El gobierno republicano itinerante que tuvo como sedes Madrid, Valencia y Barcelona se derrumba ante la entrada del ejército nacionalista el 26 de enero de 1939 en Barcelona. Manuel Azaña renuncia el 27 de febrero y huye a Francia, dejando así de funcionar el gobierno republicano; finalmente el 1º de abril Francisco Franco proclama el término de la guerra civil.[3]

Los republicanos españoles que habían salido de España con motivo de la pérdida de la guerra se ven obligados a tomar una decisión determinante en septiembre del mismo año 1939, al declararse la Segunda Guerra Mundial.

Tal circunstancia dividirá al exilio en dos grandes grupos. En primer lugar, el de aquellos que habían luchado durante la Guerra Civil y que la consideraban una guerra contra el totalitarismo, el fascismo y en favor de la democracia y la libertad. Para ellos el final de la guerra española no era el final de su contienda y se enrolan en la resistencia francesa, luchando al lado de los soldados franceses.

El segundo grupo—la mayoría—decidió marcharse a América; entre ellos los que se sentían comprometidos con la cultura y para quienes la guerra no era solamente la resistencia militar, sino que tenía dimensiones mundiales, en las que la cultura estaba involucrada. De forma que se produjo un masivo exilio de tipo cultural a los países de Iberoamérica. México, Estados Unidos, Argentina, Venezuela, Colombia y Chile recibieron el mayor número de exiliados, pero México los aventajó a todos.[4]

El viaje a México

El primer contingente de españoles que por la Guerra Civil tuvieron que dejar su patria y venir a México, estuvo integrado por un grupo de cerca de 500 niños que a bordo del *Mexique,* de origen francés, fletado por encargo del presidente Cárdenas, viajaron desde Francia a México, desembarcando en Veracruz el 7 de junio de 1937.[5]

El segundo gran contingente de refugiados que arribó a México lo hizo en el barco *Sinaia,* que zarpó del puerto francés de Séte, al sur de Marsella, el 25 de mayo de 1939. A bordo, se encontraba un enviado especial del periódico El Nacional, quien entrevistó a la señora Susana Gamboa, quien traía una misión oficial de la delegación de México en París. El refiere las actividades llevadas a cabo durante el viaje, que consistieron en la organización de conferencias (junto con los intelectuales que se encontraban a bordo), sobre diferentes aspectos de la vida mexicana: geografía, historia, política, cultura, etc. Además de realizarse la selección de los refugiados por grupos profesionales con el objeto de reintegrarlos a sus labores; se construyó un fichero profesional en el que se encontraban los antecedentes, actividades y grado de conocimientos técnicos de cada uno de los refugiados, que sería útil en la distribución de los trabajadores en las distintas regiones del país.

Se organizaron pláticas entre españoles que ejercían la misma actividad o profesión para compartir conocimientos; y de manera especial debe mencionarse la impresión mimeografiada del periódico titulado *Sinaia* que mantuvo al grupo informado de los acontecimientos de Europa y América. En el número publicado el 12 de junio se lee "es este el último número de Sinaia, periódico de a bordo, inspirado en el sentimiento firme de la unidad antifachista, en la voluntad indomable de reconquistar la patria escarnecida, en el designio tenaz de apoyar y defender la construcción revolucionaria de México, país hermano".[6]

Después de casi veinte días de travesía, el 13 de junio llegan al puerto de Veracruz, la gran mayoría partió hacia distintos estados de la república y otros, principalmente los que eran intelectuales o profesionistas, llegaron a la capital;

casi en su totalidad se avecindaron en el centro, además de situarse en colonias como: Roma, Cuauhtémoc, Juárez y San Rafael.[7]

En los meses que siguieron a la llegada del *Sinaia,* arribó al puerto de Veracruz, el 7 de julio de 1939, el barco *Ipanema* con 508 trabajadores, entre los que se encontraban abogados, arquitectos, escultores, choferes, electricistas, escritores, periodistas, editores, hoteleros, profesores, médicos y militares; entre otros; además de mujeres y niños;[8] el 27 de julio, arribó el *Mexique* y posteriormente otras embarcaciones.

Los llegados a la ciudad de México contaron con la ayuda del Servicio de Emigración de la República Española (SERE) que los auxilió con 3 pesos diarios por persona. Posteriormente se instaló la Junta de Auxilio a los Refugiados Españoles (JARE), con la misma intención. Además, ambos organismos facilitaron capital para invertir en diversos negocios y establecieron centros de asistencia médica, colegios, industrias y explotaciones agrícolas. Algunos otros exiliados recibieron ayuda económica de parientes, amigos o paisanos, miembros de la colonia española residente en México.[9]

Quiénes fueron los exiliados

Las ocupaciones de los exiliados que llegaron a México se consignan en la tabla 1.[10]

Tabla 1: Exiliados españoles en México

	Campesinos	Obreros	Oficinistas	Intelectuales	Tecnicos	Varios
Sinaia	118	276	83	267	84	29
Ipanema	72	167	81	134	33	28
Mexique	260	387	79	135		155
Grupo I				818		
Grupo II	3	38		127		112
Grupo III		8		48		57
Grupo IV	14	61		134		146
Totales	467	937	243	1,663	117	527

Encabezan la lista los exiliados que viajaron en los barcos, *Sinaia, Ipanema* y *Mexique;* los grupos I al IV obtuvieron visados de México y viajaron ya con ayuda del SERE y del JARE, ya sufragando el precio del billete con fondos propios. Es de llamar la atención el número de intelectuales, 1,663, frente al de campesinos, 467, cuando éstos, por decisión del general Cárdenas, deberían constituir el grueso del exilio.

Los españoles recién llegados podían obtener la nacionalidad mexicana en 48 horas y el libre ejercicio de una profesión se lograba con la simple presentación de un documento justificativo que acreditara tener los estudios indispensables.[11]

Los exiliados españoles procedían de las siguientes instituciones: Junta para Ampliación de Estudios, Institución Libre de Enseñanza, Centro de Estudios Históricos, Residencia de Estudiantes y del Instituto-Escuela. Se trataba de españoles progresistas que compartían los ideales de la Revolución, a los que se les llamó "refugiados". A su llegada a México se les concedió la nacionalidad mexicana, se les ofrecieron puestos de trabajo y se crearon incluso instituciones adecuadas para su plena integración laboral y académica, la más destacada de ellas, la Casa de España en México,[12] fundada en 1940.

El origen de la Casa de España en México

Sobre la idea de traer a México a los republicanos españoles cabe mencionar el recuerdo de Daniel Cosío Villegas, que en 1936 fungía como encargado de la legación mexicana en Portugal y se mantenía al tanto de lo ocurrido en el vecino país, particularmente sobre la suerte de profesores e intelectuales:

> Se me ocurrió escribirle a Luis Montes de Oca pintándole esta situación y sugiriéndole que hablara con el presidente Cárdenas para proponerle que el gobierno de México invitara a un grupo limitado de esos intelectuales a trasladarse a México y proseguir en nuestro país sus actividades normales mientras la república se sobreponía a los sublevados franquistas. . . . Montes de Oca hizo la gestión y pronto me comunicó que estaba autorizado por el presidente Cárdenas para trasladarme a Valencia y hacer las negociaciones necesarias con las autoridades republicanas, que ya habían abandonado Madrid.[13]

Entre enero y julio de 1937 Cosío Villegas se dedicó a elaborar listas de invitados a partir de informes del Instituto de Cooperación Intelectual de París y de la Junta de Ampliación de Estudios de Londres, así como considerando las sugerencias de Gabriela Mistral y Alfonso Reyes. Las gestiones para recibir en México a los intelectuales fueron satisfechas un año después; así, el 20 de agosto de 1938 apareció el decreto de creación de la Casa de España que decía:

> El señor presidente de la República dispuso que se invitara, previo el conocimiento y la conformidad del Gobierno de la República Española, a un grupo de profesores e intelectuales españoles para que vinieran a México a proseguir los trabajos docentes y de investigación que han debido interrumpir por la guerra.[14]

Para cumplir con sus fines, la Casa de España fue dirigida y gobernada por un patronato, que nombró el jefe del Estado, general Cárdenas, y que estuvo constituido por los señores Alfonso Reyes (presidente), Eduardo Villaseñor, Gustavo Baz y Enrique Arreguín (vocales) y Daniel Cosío Villegas (secretario). Con los gastos del nuevo instituto cargó por completo el Gobierno Mexicano del cual dependía, con adscripción especial y directa a la Presidencia de la República.

Las autoridades de la Casa se plantearon varias posibilidades de colaboración de los intelectuales incorporados a la Casa. Mientras determinaban con claridad las acciones a seguir, establecieron un sistema flexible; en razón de ello, dejaron que los españoles, conforme a su vocación y aptitud, desarrollaran sus actividades con entera libertad. Luego de explorar, considerar y examinar las posibilidades de colaboración, se decidieron como más convenientes dos de ellas, a saber, la de formar con sus componentes un centro de altos estudios y la de comisionarlos a las universidades o planteles similares para reforzar sus cuerpos profesionales. Se adoptó, en definitiva, una solución mixta. Los admitidos como miembros dieron cursos y conferencias en la Casa y en los referidos planteles y se dedicaron a la investigación o a la preparación de obras de arte o de literatura.

El patronato clasificó a los miembros de la casa en residentes, honorarios, especiales y becados. Residentes eran los contratados y remunerados de un modo regular (hoy los llamaríamos de tiempo completo). Honorarios, los que por no estar vinculados permanentemente a la institución, no recibían remuneración alguna, o sólo podían obtenerla en el caso de que se les encargara algún trabajo determinado. Especiales, aquellos a quienes, no obstante hallarse al servicio de otros centros culturales, les fuesen encomendados por el patronato estudios o investigaciones y mantuviesen, debido a eso, lazos con la Casa. Becados, aquellos a quienes ésta confiaba la elaboración de monografías o trabajos especiales. Véase la tabla 2.[15]

El campo de actividades cubierto por los miembros de la Casa de España, de acuerdo con las directrices de su patronato, fue muy amplio y variado. Abarcó principalmente las siguientes actividades: cursos, cursillos, conferencias y seminarios en instituciones culturales de la capital y de los estados; trabajos técnicos en departamentos oficiales y universitarios; e investigaciones destinadas a la publicación y edición de obras de diferentes clases—científicas, literarias, etc.—preparadas en el centro. Además de sostener tales labores, el patronato proporcionó ayuda para el establecimiento de laboratorios y para trabajos en ellos.

Casi todos los miembros de la Casa dieron cursos y conferencias sobre materias de su competencia en los planteles de enseñanza superior de la capital (Universidad Nacional, Instituto Politécnico y Escuela de Verano), y cursillos y conferencias en las universidades de los Estados (Morelia, Guadalajara, Puebla, Monterrey y San Luis Potosí); algunos de los miembros estuvieron adscritos permanentemente, como profesores regulares, a varias de estas últimas universidades (en la de Morelia hubo cuatro y uno en la de Guadalajara). Otros miembros trabajaron en laboratorios y en los servicios de instituciones públicas (tres en el Hospital General, dos en la Asociación para evitar la Ceguera, uno en el Instituto Politécnico, uno en el Instituto de Química de la Universidad, uno en el Instituto de Enfermedades Tropicales, y otro en el Departamento de Salubridad Pública). Bastantes de los comprendidos en los grupos anteriores dedicaron también parte de sus esfuerzos a la investigación; a ellos se deben estudios originales sobre algunos elementos químicos, sobre la mosca causante de la oncocercosis, sobre las membranas profundas del ojo y sobre la fauna de los lagos de Michoacán. La sola investigación fue el cometido de los becados; los pocos que tuvieron esta calidad nos dejaron trabajos referentes a la historiografía de la conquista de México, a la prensa insurgente y a la historia de la música mexicana. Muchos de los miembros humanistas prepararon obras de su propia creación, literarias en su mayor parte, y el patronato encomendó a algunos de éstos o de los dedicados a otras labores la publicación de libros clásicos. Por otra parte, sacrificando una cantidad importante de sus recursos, el patronato puso particular empeño en la creación de un Laboratorio de Fisiología, para que trabajaran en él los especialistas españoles en tal materia, y puso aún mayor interés en la erección de un edificio destinado a cobijar un Instituto de Física, cuya dirección confió a un notable físico hispano perteneciente a la Casa; ambos centros pasaron a formar parte de la Universidad Nacional, que los utilizó para la docencia en las respectivas disciplinas.[16]

Tabla 2: Clasificación de los miembros de la Casa de España

Honorarios	Residentes	Especiales	Becados
Ignacio Bolívar	José Carner, Pedro Carrasco, Roberto Castrovido, Alvaro de Albornoz, Juan de la Encina, Enrique Díez-Canedo, Juan José Domenchina, León Felipe, José Gaos, José Giral, Benjamín Jarnés, Gonzalo R. Labora, Manuel Márquez, José Medina Echevarría, Agustín Millares Carlo, José Moreno Villa, Francisco Pascual, Manuel Pedroso, Jaime Pi y Suñer, Luis Recasens Fiches, Aurelio Romero Lozano, Juan Roura Parella, Adolfo Salazar, Rafael Sánchez Ocaña, Juan Solares Encina, José Torre Blanco, Jesús Val y Gay, Joaquín Xirau	Urbano Barnés, Cándido Bolívar, Rosendo Carrasco, Isaac Costero, Fernando de Buen, Francisco Giral, Juan López Durá, Antonio Medinaveitia, Manuel Rivas Cherif, Juan Xirau, María Zambrano	Germán García, Ramón Iglesia, Otto Mayer Sierra, José María Miquel i Verges, Mariano Rodríguez Orgz, Leopoldo Zea

Producción bibliográfica de La Casa de España

Los recién llegados tuvieron una tarea inmediata ante sí: concluir los trabajos que la contienda civil les había impedido terminar. Las publicaciones de los primeros años son de una abundancia y calidad sorprendentes. Sus temas no son la Guerra Civil—ése es el tema de los periodistas y políticos—sus preocupaciones son las mismas que tuvieron en España.[17]

La Casa de España publicó 49 libros entre 1938 y 1942, año en que comienzan a aparecer ediciones con el sello de El Colegio de México. Los que corresponden a la Casa de España abarcan una amplia gama de asuntos; en la gráfica 1 se incluye la distribución temática de dichos libros, que pueden clasificarse en 13 categorías. Se advierte que la mayor parte de los textos son de carácter literario (16), seguidos por los de filosofía (10) y los de contenido médico (6), en cuarto lugar se encuentran los de historia (3). Corresponden dos títulos a bibliografía, sociología, paleografía, arte y música. Sobre derecho, educación, ciencia y teatro se publicó un impreso por cada tema.

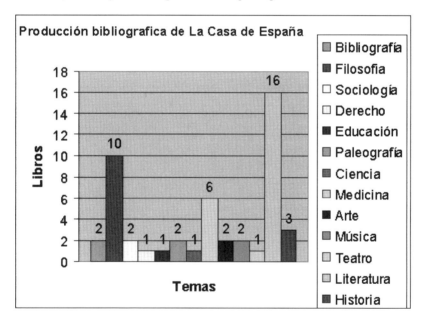

Gráfica 1.

La distribución cronológica de las publicaciones de la Casa de España se representa en la Gráfica 2. En ella se observa que la producción inicia en 1938 con un solo libro, se incrementa durante 1939 y alcanza su nivel más alto en 1940, declina en 1941 y durante 1942 aparece un libro con el sello de la Casa de España y comienzan a editarse las publicaciones de El Colegio de México.

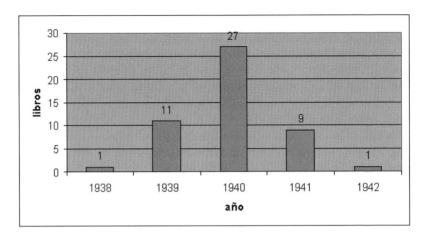

Gráfica 2.

La nómina de autores que publicaron en La Casa de España suma treinta y siete de treinta y una se publicó una sola obra, la tabla 3 incluye la producción de los seis restantes.

Tabla 3: Autores más editados por La Casa de España

Autor	No. de obras
José Gaos	5
Alfonso Reyes	2
José Medina Echavarría	2
Agustín Millares Carlo	3
Adolfo Salazar	2
León Felipe Camino	3
José Moreno Villa	2

Es de llamar la atención que a pesar de las condiciones económicas propias de La Casa, durante su corta vida hubiera podido editar un conjunto considerable de obras, lo que en buena medida se explica si se considera que varios de sus autores tuvieran avanzados los trabajos antes de venir a México. En el anexo 1, se ofrece el listado con la totalidad de los libros publicados por La Casa de España en México.

El Colegio de México

En palabras de José Miranda:

La Casa de España supo transformarse, mediante oportuna y sabia metamorfosis, en una institución de altos estudios: El Colegio de México (fundado a fines de 1940), en el que cuajó y fructificó aún más eficazmente la espléndida obra de su predecesora. La antorcha espiritual que encendió en México la Casa de España era traspasada, tras breve carrera—poco más de dos años— a un nuevo organismo, que, en ininterrumpido avance, seguiría haciendo flamear cada vez con mayor intensidad la antorcha representativa de la sagrada herencia.[18]

El Colegio está organizado en 7 centros de Estudios, el primero de ellos, fundado por Silvio Zavala se denominó Centro de Estudios Históricos (CEH, 1941); siguieron después: el Centro de Estudios Lingüísticos y Literarios (CELL, 1947); el Centro de Estudios Internacionales (CEI, 1960); el Centro de Estudios Económicos y Demográficos (CEED); Centro de Estudios Orientales (1964),[19] el Centro de Estudios Sociológicos (CES, 1973); y finalmente el Centro de Estudios Económicos (CEE) que se separó del CEED en 1981.

Cada uno de los Centros publica una revista especializada de reconocido prestigio que incluye trabajos de sus investigadores y de investigadores externos. Los títulos son: Revista de Filología Hispánica (inició en 1947), Historia Mexicana (1951), Foro Internacional (1960), Estudios de Asia y Africa (1966), Estudios Sociológicos (1983), Estudios Demográficos y Urbanos (1986), y Estudios Económicos (inició en 1986).

En 1961 se modificó el Acta Constitutiva de El Colegio para incorporar la fracción f al artículo 1° y se agregó a sus objetivos el impartir enseñanzas a nivel universitario, post-profesional o especiales, en las ramas de conocimientos humanísticos y de las ciencias sociales y políticas, creando los órganos apropiados para la realización de estos fines y otorgando los diplomas, títulos y grados correspondientes, de acuerdo con los planes y programas de estudios de la institución que se aprobaron. Actualmente se imparten 2 programas de licenciatura, 7 de maestría y 9 de doctorado en algunas de las ciencias sociales y las humanidades.[20]

Tomando como base el modelo de trabajo de El Colegio de México (COLMEX) el 1979, Luis González y González fundó El Colegio de Michoacán (COLMICH), ubicado en Zamora, Michoacán, con la idea de que realizara investigación sobre la región. A esta iniciativa se sumó la apertura de El Colegio de la Frontera Norte (COLEF, fundado en 1982, como Centro de Estudios Fronterizos del Norte de México), El Colegio de Sonora (COLSON, 1982), El Colegio de Jalisco (COLJAL, 1982), El Colegio Mexiquense (1986), El Colegio de Sinaloa (1992), El Colegio de la Frontera Sur (ECOSUR, 1994) y El Colegio de San Luis (COLSAN, 1997).

Los profesores investigadores de todos los Colegios colaboran en proyectos de investigación conjuntos y apoyan los programas de docencia. La Red de Colegios, como se la conoce, ha incidido de manera directa en las políticas nacionales y estatales del país a través de propuestas concretas para resolver problemas que afectan al país; contribuye también a la formación de recursos humanos para el sector público y el sector académico del país.

Investigación sobre migración

En cuanto a la investigación sobre Migración, del que se ocupa esta reunión de SALALM, "la labor del COLMEX fue, en muchos sentidos, pionera en cuanto al señalamiento del tema como fundamental en la comprensión de la realidad histórica y de la dinámica social del México contemporáneo".[21] De ahí que los estudios sobre la migración interna y la internacional se llevan a cabo en todos los Centros, con excepción del CELL. Su producción editorial incluye alrededor de 200 títulos, algunos de ellos resultado de proyectos de investigación con otras instituciones nacionales e internacionales.

Toda esta trayectoria ha favorecido y ha sido sustancialmente complementada con una política interna de fortalecimiento y desarrollo de sus propios recursos institucionales, tanto humanos como materiales, especializados para enfrentar el complejo y diverso campo de la migración internacional. En el caso del COLMEX, el tema ha favorecido la formación de recursos humanos especializados en el campo de la demografía, los estudios de población, las relaciones internacionales, la historia y la economía. Más recientemente, investigadores del CEDDUA y del CES tomaron la iniciativa de impulsar la creación de un Programa de Migración Internacional (PROMI), el cual se propone desarrollar actividades de difusión, información y extensión en el campo.[22]

En el año 2002 se creó el Grupo Guatemala-México sobre Migración y Desarrollo, en el que participan: el COLMEX, Catholic Relief Services (OCRS), Ford Foundation, Fundación Soros y la Facultad Latinoamericana de Ciencias Sociales; su objetivo es "elaborar una propuesta de lineamientos de política pública migratoria para ser presentados y discutidos en esferas gubernamentales y sectores sociales y políticos interesados".[23]

Los proyectos que actualmente se trabajan en el COLMEX son: (1) Liberalización comercial y migración internacional, (2) Encuesta sobre migración en la frontera Guatemala-México, (3) Las fronteras y su dimensión sociopolítica, (4) Migración y violencia en Guatemala, (5) La frontera sur de México: 1821–1980, (6) Grupo binacional México-Guatemala sobre migración, (7) Migración y mercados de trabajo y (8) Efectos de las reformas en la migración y la sustentabilidad de la agricultura mexicana.

Respecto al COLEF,

por su ubicación geográfica y por su misma definición, desde su fundación ha desarrollado con particular atención y con un criterio de prioridad dentro de su agenda temática, una serie de trabajos orientados a profundizar en el conocimiento de la migración internacional de mexicanos a Estados Unidos, así como también de las migraciones que se dirigen a o provienen de la región fronteriza del norte de México.[24]

La investigación sobre migración se lleva cabo, principalmente, en los Departamentos de Estudios de Población, de Estudios Sociales y de Estudios Culturales, de Estudios Económicos y del Medio Ambiente. Actualmente están en proceso 19 proyectos de investigación mismos que se incluyen en el anexo 2 de este trabajo.

En 1998, el COLEF, el COLMEX y la Sociedad Mexicana de Demografía (SOMEDE) acordaron organizar el Seminario Permanente sobre Migración Internacional,[25] con el propósito de constituir un foro de presentación y discusión continuo y sistemático de avances de investigación, tal que permita el intercambio y la socialización de los estudios en materia de migración internacional. A la fecha se han programado seis ciclos anuales, durante los cuales se realizaron 57 sesiones en las que se abordaron diversos aspectos del fenómeno migratorio internacional. En el 2004 se incorporó al conjunto de instituciones auspiciadoras la Organización Sin Fronteras. En las reuniones se presentan trabajos con distintos énfasis y carácter (avances teóricos, formulaciones metodológicas y hallazgos de investigación) con el propósito de propiciar intercambios, discusiones y reflexiones, lo que contribuye principalmente a alimentar el trabajo del cuerpo de investigadores del COLEF y del COLMEX especializados en el tema. Los informes de actividades del Seminario, correspondientes a los ciclos 1999 al 2004 contienen una detallada descripción de sus motivaciones y los objetivos alcanzados, así como del desarrollo de las sesiones, información sobre los participantes y del contenido de los temas específicos tratados.[26]

Tanto el COLMEX como el COLEF participan en distintas instancias nacionales, bilaterales y multilaterales que se relacionan con los procesos migratorios, como ejemplo de esto tenemos su participación en el Estudio binacional México-Estados Unidos sobre Migración y en el Comité del Sistema de Observación Permanente de las Migraciones (SOPEMI) de la Organización para la Cooperación y el Desarrollo Económico (OCDE).

Por su parte, el ECOSUR lleva a cabo investigación sobre el tema "Migración internacional en la frontera sur de México".

Sin duda alguna, la contribución que El Colegio de México ha hecho a la cultura y a las ciencias sociales en México es trascendente, se le reconoce como una institución de excelencia y seguirá siendo un ejemplo de que los refugiados no llegan a un país con las manos vacías.

ANEXO 1
Autores de la Casa de España

Arte, teatro y literatura

Bal y Gay, Jesús. *Romances y villancicos españoles del siglo XVI.* 1939.

Camino Galicia, León Felipe. *Español del éxodo y del llanto . . . doctrina, elegías y canciones.* 1939.

———. *El gran responsable: grito y salmo.* Colección Tezontle. 1940.

———. *El payaso de las bofetadas y El pescador de caña: poema trágico español.* 1938.

Díez-Canedo, Enrique. *El teatro y sus enemigos.* 1939.

Domenchina, Juan José. *Poesía escogida, 1915–1939.* 1940.

Garfias, Pedro. *Primavera en Eaton Hastings: poema bucólico con intermedios de llanto.* Colección Tezontle. 1941.

Giner de los Ríos, Francisco. *La rama viva.* Colección Tezontle. 1940.

Gutiérrez Abascal, Ricardo. *El mundo histórico y poético de Goya.* 1939.

Jarnés, Benjamín. *Cartas al Ebro.* 1940.

Millares Carlo, Agustín. *Antología latina: I Prosistas.* [1941].

Pellicer, Carlos. *Recinto y otras imágenes.* Colección Tezontle. 1940.

Reyes, Alfonso. *Capítulos de literatura española.* Primera serie. [1939].

Rodríguez Luna, Antonio, con textos de Luis Cardoza y Aragón. *Diez aguafuertes.* [1940].

Salazar, Adolfo. *Las grandes estructuras de la música.* 1940.

————. *Música y sociedad en el siglo XX.* 1939.

Sánchez de Ocaña, Rafael. *Reflejos en el agua.* 1940.

Los siete sobre Deva: sueño de una tarde de agosto. [1942].

Torrí, Julio. *De fusilamientos.* 1940.

Usigli, Rodolfo. *Itinerario del autor dramático.* [1940].

Villaurrutia, Xavier. *Textos y pretextos: literatura, drama, pintura.* 1940.

Bibliografía

Estrada, Genaro. *Bibliografía de Goya.* 1940.

Moore, Ernest Richard. *Bibliografía de novelistas de la revolución mexicana.* 1941.

Ciencia

Carrasco y Garrorena, Pedro. *Optica instrumental.* 1940.

Derecho

Recaséns Siches, Luis. *Vida humana, sociedad y derecho.* 1940.

Educación

Roura-Perella, Juan. *Educación y ciencia.* 1940.

Filosofía

Caso, Antonio. *Meyerson y la física moderna.* 1939.

Gaos, José. *Antología filosófica I: la filosofía griega.* 1941.

————. *Cátedra de filosofía. Curso de 1939.* 1940.

————. *La filosofía de Maimónides.* 1940.

————. *Introducción a la filosofía: cursillo de diez lecciones.* 1939.

Gaos, José, y Francisco Larroyo. *Dos ideas de la filosofía.* 1940.

García Bacca, Juan David. *Invitación a filosofar I: la forma del conocer filosófico.* 1940.

Menéndez y Samará, Adolfo. *Fanatismo y misticismo.* 1940.

Ramos, Samuel. *Hacia un nuevo humanismo*. 1940.

Zambrano, María. *Pensamiento y poesía en la vida española*. 1939.

Historia

Moreno Villa, José. *Cornucopia de México*. 1940.

————. *Locos, enanos, negros y niños palaciegos*. 1939.

Sierra, Justo. *Evolución política del pueblo mexicano*. 1940.

Paleografía

Millares Carlo, Agustín. *Gramática elemental de la lengua latina*. 1941.

————. *Nuevos estudios de paleografía española*. 1941.

Sociología

Medina Echavarría, José. *Cátedra de sociología*. 1939.

————. *Panorama de la sociología contemporánea*. 1940.

Temas médicos

Carrasco Formiguera, Rosendo. *Seis conferencias sobre endocrinología sexual*. 1941.

Giral Pereira, José. *Fermentos*. 1940.

Pascual del Roncal, Federico. *Manual de neuropsiquiatría infantil*. 1940.

Pi-Suñer Bayo, Jaime. *Las bases fisiológicas de la alimentación*. 1940.

Rivas Cherif, Manuel de. *La fotografía de las membranas profundas del ojo*. 1940.

Schwyzer, Julius. *La fabricación de los alcaloides*. 1941.

ANEXO 2
Proyectos de El Colegio de la Frontera Norte

1. Caracterización de emigrantes mexicanos en la ciudad de Chicago.
2. Caracterización de los flujos migratorios de población mexiquense a los Estados Unidos de América.
3. Correlates of HIV-Related practices among mexican migrants.
4. Educación y empleo de los migrantes guanajuatenses.
5. Efectos socioeconómicos del flujo migratorio internacional en localidades fronterizas sonorenses.
6. Encuesta de evaluación del Programa Paisano.
7. Encuesta de la Frontera Módulo Guanajuato.
8. Estudio de migrantes mexicanas en Chicago.
9. Estudio integral de migración en la región de San Quintín.
10. Los nexos que nos unen: Las comunidades mexicanas en el condado de San Diego y su relación con Tijuana (The ties that bind us: Mexican communities in San Diego county and other relationship to Tijuana).
11. Migración y cambio religioso: análisis de la relación entre nueva migración internacional y cambio religioso a partir de dos estudios de caso (Chinantla, Puebla y Alto Lucero Veracruz).

12. Migración, trabajo agrícola y etnicidad: la articulación de lo global, nacional y local en el Valle de San Quintín, Baja California.

13. Migraciones desde y hacia el Estado de Guanajuato (COESPO-GUANAJUATO I).

14. Movilidad laboral de carácter temporal en la frontera Norte de México con E. U.: evolución reciente y principales características.

15. Observatorio de flujos migratorios en la frontera Guatemala-México.

16. Observatorio de flujos migratorios en la frontera México-Estados Unidos.

17. Observatorio del proceso migratorio internacional hidalguense.

18. Operación y administración de un eventual programa de trabajadores temporales (PTT) en Estados Unidos.

19. Prevención de SIDA en comunidades de migrantes indígenas Oaxaqueños: Una propuesta de investigación acción con orientación cultural y enfoque de género.

NOTAS

1. Patricia W. Fagen. *Transterrados y ciudadanos: los republicanos españoles en México* (México, D.F.: Fondo de Cultura Económica, 1975), p. 11.

2. "La República española en el exilio", en *Nuestro México* 18 (1986): 3–6.

3. Fagen, *Transterrados y ciudadanos,* p. 24.

4. José Luis Abellán, "México y el exilio español", en *Los refugiados españoles y la cultura mexicana: actas de las primeras jornadas celebradas en la Residencia de Estudiantes en noviembre de 1994* (Madrid: Publicaciones de la Residencia de Estudiantes, 1998), pp. 13–14.

5. Emeterio Payá Valera, *Los niños españoles de Morelia: el exilio infantil en México* (México, D.F.: Edamex, 1985), p. [39].

6. *El Nacional,* junio 17, 1939.

7. Dolores Pla Brugat, "Els exiliats catalans: Un estudio de la emigración republicana" (Doctorado tesis, Universidad Nacional Autónoma de México, Facultad de Filosofía y Letras, 1998), p. 256.

8. *El Nacional,* junio 11, 1939.

9. Carlos Martínez, *Crónica de una emigración: la de los republicanos españoles en 1939* (México, D.F.: Libro Mex, 1959), pp. 21–22.

10. Rafael Segovia, "La difícil socialización del exilio", en *Los refugiados españoles y la cultura mexicana: actas de las primeras jornadas, celebradas en la Residencia de Estudiantes en noviembre de 1994* (Madrid: Amigos de la Residencia de Estudiantes, 1998).

11. Ibid., pp. 34–35.

12. Abellán, "México y el exilio español", pp. 15–16.

13. Daniel Cosío Villegas, "Un poco de historia", en *Historia mexicana* 25, no. 4 (abril–junio 1976): 506.

14. Clara Lida, José Antonio Matesanz, y Beatriz Morán, "Las instituciones mexicanas y los intelectuales españoles refugiados: La Casa de España en México y los colegios del exilio", *El pensamiento español contemporáneo y la idea de América* (Barcelona: Anthropos, 1989), p. 92.

15. José Miranda, "La Casa de España", en *Historia mexicana* 18, no. 1 (julio–septiembre 1968): 8.

16. Ibid., pp. 4–6.

17. Rafael Segovia, "La difícil socialización del exilio", p. 37.

18. Miranda, "La Casa de España", p. 8. Estos Centros llevan actualmente los nombres de Centro de Estudios Demográficos, Urbanos y Ambientales y Centro de Estudios de Asia y Africa respectivamente.

19. Estos Centros llevan actualmente los nombres de Centro de Estudios Demográficos, Urbanos y Ambientales y Centro de Estudios de Asia y Africa respectivamente.

20. Puede verse el desglose de carreras en la página web de la institución: http://www. colmex.mx.

21. El Colegio de la Frontera Norte, El Colegio de México y la Sociedad Mexicana de Demografía, Seminario Permanente sobre Migración Internacional, http://migracioninternacional.com/docum/seminari.html (consultado en el Internet marzo 3, 2006).

22. Ibid.

23. "Las migraciones y el desarrollo entre Guatemala y México: una propuesta de elementos de políticas y acciones" (Guatemala: Ediciones Amalia, 2003), p. 2.

24. El Colegio de la Frontera Norte, El Colegio de México y la Sociedad Mexicana de Demografía, Seminario Permanente sobre Migración Internacional, http://migracioninternacional.com/docum/seminari.html (consultado en el Internet marzo 13, 2006).

25. Mayores detalles sobre los antecedentes, objetivos y trabajos del Seminario, véase http://viejo.colmex.mx/ligas/semceddu.htm (consultado en el Internet marzo 3, 2006).

26. El Colegio de la Frontera Norte, El Colegio de México, http://200.23.245.225/Alwebaplicaciones/ (consultado en el Internet marzo 13, 2006).

11. La imagen como documento de la migración: colecciones en las bibliotecas mexicanas

Elsa Barberena
Carmen Block
Elda Mónica Guerrero

Existen varias maneras de acercarse al estudio de las migraciones a través de: la antropología, la economía, la sociología, la tradición y la cultura. Sobre la región latinoamericana y en particular sobre México, Pérez Gay nos dice que no se sabe con precisión cuál es el papel que tiene la migración mexicana en el marco de "la gran migración universal" y continúa exponiendo que la mexicana es una migración que nace en nuestro país, nuestras propias necesidades la generan y la cambian con los cambios que las mismas necesidades presentan. La migración de México puede verse como un accidente o una situación fortuita de combinaciones naturales que ninguna ley material o moral determina.[1]

De 1880 a 1930 la migración mexicana tuvo su origen principalmente debido a factores económicos.[2] De 1942 a 1948 se establece el Programa Nacional de Braceros que enviaría a Estados Unidos a cuatro millones de trabajadores para solucionar la ausencia de brazos en este país, cuando la mayoría de sus jóvenes se encontraban en la guerra. Los especialistas señalan que ésta fue una de las contribuciones más importantes para el crecimiento de la economía agrícola estadounidense. En esos años, además de llamarles "braceros", que según el Diccionario Larousse es, para México, una persona de una región pobre que emigra temporalmente a otra más prospera para trabajar como jornalero, también se les llamó "espaldas mojadas" para indicar el carácter ilegal de aquéllos que cruzaban a nado el Río Bravo para entrar sin documentos a intercambiar su trabajo por una forma de subsistencia.

El gran tema del siglo XXI es la migración, sin embargo en México no existe una política de Estado que se ocupe de este fenómeno y asocie los procesos migratorios con una perspectiva poblacional, demográfica y de mercados laborales.[3] El proceso de separación del emigrante no se limita a una simple cuestión entre el antes y el después de cruzar la frontera. El mecanismo de regulación social se ve obligado a clasificar a los emigrantes en legales e ilegales, admisibles y rechazables, tolerables e intolerables, ciudadanos y delincuentes, asimilables y peligrosos.

La cifra en apoyo a la larga historia de las relaciones entre México y Estados Unidos que da el último informe de la Oficina del Censo en Washington, es de 41.3 millones de hispanos, sin especificar su situación migratoria, lo cual puede incluir a los residentes ilegales. Otra cifra relevante apunta que siendo ésta la mayor minoría del país, es la responsable de la mitad del crecimiento de la población estadounidense que fue de 2.9 millones de habitantes en el año contado de julio de 2003 a agosto de 2004. Y una cifra más sin precedente, de la Oficina del Censo es que uno de cada siete habitantes de Estados Unidos es de origen hispánico.

En la actualidad estas amplias comunidades latinas en Estados Unidos cuentan ahora con mayor relevancia no sólo por su importancia como electores sino también como consumidores que gastan al año 55 mil millones de dólares en vestidos, alimentos y bebidas. Mostrando a la vez su característica principal que es la entrañable relación que mantienen con sus familias en México, de quienes son descendientes y a quienes enviaron en 2005, remesas por 20 millones de dólares.

Para nuestras bibliotecas los cambios culturales que refleja esta población es de importancia primordial, considerando que en Estados Unidos los latinos cuentan con 654 publicaciones nacionales, y los periódicos latinos venden un millón 700 mil ejemplares a la semana.[4] Y por otra parte, en México, la revista titulada *Conexión México,* única en su género, por lo menos en Ibero América, se dedica a documentar el fenómeno de la migración y sus efectos culturales, sociales y económicos en México y Estados Unidos. En sus programas los emigrantes pasan de ser los siempre protagonistas de nota roja o fuente de remesas, para informar cómo con su capacidad de trabajo y responsabilidad conquistan joyerías de la Quinta Avenida y restaurantes de primera en Nueva York y en Chicago; cómo con su trabajo pueden colaborar con la NASA en proyectos espaciales o dar clases de maya en Harvard. *Conexión México* se distribuye a través de Direct Tv en Estados Unidos.[5]

La fotografía como documento

En el caso que nos ocupa es el mundo de los emigrantes mexicanos que van a los Estados Unidos. La visualidad se vuelve una fuente poderosa de información y de conocimiento. Este recurso cognoscitivo incluye representaciones internas (imágenes mentales) y representaciones externas (cuadros, fotografías, películas).

La representación consiste en una construcción socio-cultural constituida por las relaciones de unos hombres con otros hombres. Se podría afirmar que el fotógrafo de emigrantes entra en estrecha relación con las personas que cruzan la frontera México-Estados Unidos para lograr una mayor comprensión del fenómeno, como lo afirma el fotógrafo mexicano Eniac Martínez o como sucede con la empatía que se da entre los Hermanos Mayo, emigrantes fotografiando emigrantes.

La representación actúa como una fuente de comunicación a un universo de usuarios de la información. Esta situación es común en las bibliotecas y archivos. En éstos se localizan bases de datos, catálogos, que además de ser herramientas colectivas de recuperación de información son también espacios colectivos de conocimiento y comunicación.

A continuación se mostrarán fotografías, disponibles en algunas bibliotecas mexicanas, de esta cultura de los emigrantes a través de la imagen de algunos fotógrafos mexicanos: Juan Rulfo, Eniac Martínez, Lola Álvarez Bravo, los Hermanos Mayo (Julio, Cándido, Pablo, Faustino y Paco).

La fotografía tiene uno o varios de estos valores: el estético, el documental y el de la calidad técnica. Esta selección de los fotógrafos mexicanos y sus fotografías ha contemplado estos tres factores.

Juan Rulfo

Nació en 1918 en Sayula, Jalisco, vivió en la Ciudad de Guadalajara y en la de México donde murió en 1986. No obstante que pasó su vida entre estas dos grandes ciudades le atraían profundamente los pueblos pequeños y el campo del México rural en general y el de Jalisco en particular. La reputación de Juan Rulfo en los círculos literarios ya estaba establecida cuando publicó su primera colección de fotografías en 1980. A pesar de su reconocimiento tardío como fotógrafo, Rulfo tomó sus primeras imágenes en los años 30 y llegó a ser un practicante serio de la fotografía en los años 40 y 50. Es decir sus años más productivos como escritor coincidieron con un período de interés intenso por la fotografía.[6] El hijo del escritor y fotógrafo, Juan Pablo Rulfo, opina que la mayoría de las fotografías de su padre que hasta ahora se han publicado o exhibido han sido mal interpretadas porque generalmente se acentúa un dramatismo que él no buscaba expresar. El primer libro donde aparecen las fotos lo más cercano al negativo original es *Juan Rulfo, Fotógrafo* de Andrew Dempsey.

Para Rulfo hijo, la interpretación artística sólo la puede hacer el creador. Pero ante su ausencia, la propuesta es que los negativos se traten como documentos.[7]

Otras opiniones incluyen la de Carlos Fuentes quien dice que en sus fotografías Juan Rulfo resucita al pueblo entero por la belleza de formas en donde convergen el arte literario y el arte plástico. Por otra parte Jorge Alberto Lozoya habla de cómo la característica artesanal de lo rulfiano es especialmente evidente en la fotografía. Para Eduardo Rivero, palabra e imagen, voz y acto de fotografiar se encuentran en íntima relación entre la experiencia vital y la fotografía. Erika Billeter afirma que Juan Rulfo no hace fotografías literarias. Sus fotos no cuentan nada. Sólo muestran a los hombres y su tierra.[8]

Eniac Martínez

"Eniac Martínez asumió un proyecto de fuertes características documentales pero dirigió la cámara hacia el tiempo de lo cotidiano, no se propuso hacer de la fotografía un instrumento de registro científico si es que las disciplinas sociales en verdad son ciencias. Por el contrario, privilegió la experiencia propiamente fotográfica. Aún así sus imágenes funcionan también como registro, y ésta es, muy probablemente, una de sus mayores virtudes".[9]

Eniac Martínez presenta sus fotografías que son parte de un proyecto llamado Mixtecos Norte/Sur en donde una de sus metas es lograr mayor comprensión hacia las personas que cruzan la frontera. Es la historia de indígenas mixtecos que emigran de las tierras cada vez más improductivas del estado de Oaxaca hacia el campo industrializado de Estados Unidos.

Lola Alvárez Bravo

Nació en Lagos de Moreno, Jalisco en 1907 su verdadero nombre es Lola Martínez de Anda. De formación autodidacta destacó en la fotografía artística, al dar libre curso a su imaginación visual y su sentido de la composición no pretendía modificar la realidad sino complementarla.

Desde joven enseñó su arte en la Academia de San Carlos y en otras escuelas, y trabajó para el Instituto de Investigaciones Estéticas de la Universidad Nacional Autónoma de México y para el Departamento de Fotografía del Instituto Nacional de Bellas Artes. En los años cincuenta dirigió la Galería de Arte Contemporáneo, donde presentó la primera exhibición de Frida Kahlo. Realizó un documental sobre los frescos de Diego Rivera en Chapingo. Representó a México en la exposición fotográfica *The Family of Man,* en el Museo de Arte Moderno de Nueva York. En 1964 expuso cien retratos en el Palacio de Bellas Artes, en la que fue su primera exposición individual.[10]

Los Hermanos Mayo (Julio, Cándido, Pablo, Faustino y Paco)

Desde su llegada a México con el exilio republicano español de 1939, los Hermanos Mayo se constituyeron como pilar de la historia documental y del fotorreportaje en el siglo XX.

Sin proponerse la denuncia sino la documentación, los Hermanos Mayo fotografiaron lo triste y lo terrible, pero también un panorama sonriente y entusiasta con imágenes que tienen su propio lenguaje.

El seudónimo Mayo, según la versión de Faustino, se dio como resultado de la publicación de unas fotografías de la represión de manifestantes el 1° de mayo en Madrid, a principio de los años 30.[11]

Mraz y Vélez Storey dicen que a pocas semanas de la intervención de Estados Unidos en la Segunda Guerra Mundial, las actividades productivas del país comenzaron a experimentar los efectos de una prosperidad inusitada, lo que se tradujo en una gran demanda de brazos para la agricultura y el mantenimiento de las vías férreas. La atmósfera ideológica creada por la guerra convenció a los principales líderes políticos de la necesidad de abrir las puertas a la libre importación de mano de obra mexicana.

A finales de mayo de 1942 la Casa Blanca elaboró un proyecto para la importación de braceros mexicanos y el 23 de julio de ese mismo año el Presidente de México, Manuel Ávila Camacho aprobó el Programa Nacional de Braceros.

Las imágenes en la serie denominada *Braceros* de los Hermanos Mayo dan una cara humana a los datos y a las estadísticas, mostrando a la gente que vivía en carne propia los hechos que los historiadores han podido sustraer y reconstruir de los documentos.

Las imágenes informan, además, sobre las estructuras y los patrones de la migración, así como sobre los eventos y detalles de la historia social de los braceros: aspirantes a braceros usando overoles representan la clase obrera urbana, los trabajadores agrícolas están vestidos con ropa de campesinos y las mujeres están vendiendo comida y bebida.[12]

Los Mayo tomaron 400 fotos de braceros, actualmente resguardadas en el Archivo General de la Nación de la Ciudad de México.

Nuestra conclusión es que mediante el análisis de las fotografías se busca comprender el fenómeno de los emigrantes mexicanos a través de la imagen. Es otra manera de enfrentarse al pasado además del apoyo que brindan las gráficas económicas y los datos políticos.

APENDICE 1
Fotografías presentadas

Hermanos Mayo

"Protesta de campesinos y aspirantes a braceros". Zócalo, México, D.F., 1945.
"Aspirantes a braceros y vendedora de aguas frescas". La Ciudadela, México, D.F., 1945.
"Cola de aspirantes a braceros dentro de la Ciudadela". México, D.F., 1945.
"Aspirantes a braceros de la clase obrera urbana afuera de la Secretaría del Trabajo y Previsión Social". Calle López, México, D.F., 1942.
"Bracero leyendo carta". Ciudad Juárez, Chihuahua, 1944.

Juan Rulfo

"Caminantes".
"Hombre en un pueblo".
"Patio de ferrocarril".
Sin título

Eniac Martínez

"Pisca de la fresa". Wattsonville, 1990.
"Casa del mayordomo". San Juan Mixtepec, 1989.
"La vieja reja en el bordo". Tijuana, 1991.

Lola Alvárez Bravo

"El sueño de los pobres".

Hermanos Mayo

"Los hermanos Mayo".
"Estación de ferrocarril". Buenavista, México, D.F., 1945.
"Cola de aspirantes a braceros y vendedora de agua". La Ciudadela, México, D.F., 1945.
"Indocumentados en un patio de tren". Ciudad Juárez, Chihuahua, 1950.
"Aspirantes a braceros de extracción campesina frente a la Ciudadela". México, D.F., 1945.
"Estación de ferrocarril". Buenavista, México, D.F., 1945.
"Aspirantes a braceros en el Estadio Nacional". México, D.F., 1942.
"Cola de aspirantes a braceros". La Ciudadela, México, D.F., 1945.
"Bracero dictando carta a un escribano público". Ciudad Juárez, Chihuahua, 1944.

APENDICE 2
Bibliotecas que resguardan libros con fotografías de emigrantes

Archivo General de la Nación
Biblioteca
Eduardo Molina y Albañiles s/n
Col. Penitenciaría Ampliación
15350 México, D.F.
Tel.5133 9900
http://www.agn.gob.mx/inicio.php?cu=in&comp=no

Biblioteca Nacional
UNAM. Instituto de Investigaciones Bibliográficas
Centro Cultural Universitario, CU
04510 México, D.F.
Tel.5622 6800
http://biblional.bibliog.unam.mx/bib/biblioteca.html

CONACULTA. Biblioteca de las Artes
Centro Nacional de las Artes
Río Churubusco 79 Col. Country Club
04220 México, D.F.
Tel.1253 9400 CONM EXT 1229 ADQ 1251
http://bibart.cnart.mx:4505/ALEPH/%20/file/instart.htm

CONACULTA. Centro de la Imagen
Plaza de la Ciudadela no. 2
Centro Histórico
México, D.F.
Tel.9172 4724
http://www.conaculta.gob.mx/cimagen/quienes.html

UNAM. Centro de Investigaciones sobre América del Norte
Biblioteca
Piso 9 y 10 Torre II de Humanidades
Circuito Interior, Ciudad Universitaria
04510 México, D.F.

Tel.5623 0308
http://www.cisan.unam.mx/biblio.html

UNAM. Instituto de Investigaciones Estéticas
Biblioteca "Justino Fernández"
Circuito Mario de la Cueva, Ciudad Universitaria
04510 México, D.F.
Tel.5622 7544
http://www.esteticas.unam.mx/

NOTAS

1. José María Pérez Gay, "El ocaso del futuro: el Limes romano y la gran migración", *La Jornada,* diciembre 19, 2005, p. 6.

2. *La emigración de San Luis Potosí a Estados Unidos. Pasado y presente,* 1a ed. (Monterrey, México: Senado de la República, 2001), p. 15.

3. Jorge Santibáñez, "De no tener política, a aceptar su importancia", *Demos: Carta demográfica sobre México* 16 (2003–2004): 9–10.

4. Pérez Gay, "El ocaso del futuro".

5. Elena Poniatowska, "La tv cultural debe dar servicio al público, dice Javier Aranda", *La Jornada,* febrero 19, 2006, p. 6a.

6. Douglas J. Weatherford, *Photographing Silence: Juan Rulfo's Mexico* (Jones y Boshard Galleries, enero 20, 2006–mayo 29, 2006).

7. Jorge Luis Espinosa, "Rulfo, la imagen sin sesgos dramáticos", *El Universal* (México), enero 31, 2006, cultura, p. 4.

8. Juan Rulfo, *Juan Rulfo: México fotógrafo,* textos por Carlos Fuentes, Margo Glantz, Jorge Alberto Lozoya, Eduardo Rivero, Víctor Jiménez, y Erika Billeter (Barcelona: Lunwerg Editores, 2001).

9. http://www.zonezero.com/exposiciones/fotografos/eniac/.

10. *Enciclopedia de México* (México, D.F.: Sabeca International Investment Corp., 2000), p. 370.

11. Cecilia Aguilar, "Los Hermanos Mayo, Pilar de la Historia Documental y del Fotorreportaje en el Siglo XX", *La Cultura.* Sala de Prensa. Noticias del Día (México: CONACULTA, 2002).

12. John Mraz y Jaime Vélez Storey, *Trasterrados: Braceros Vistos por los Hermanos Mayo* (México: Archivo General de la Nación; Universidad Autónoma Metropolitana, 2005).

BIBLIOGRAFÍA

Aguilar, Cecilia. "Los Hermanos Mayo, Pilar de la historia documental y del fotorreportaje en el Siglo XX". *La Cultura.* Sala de Prensa. Noticias del Día. México: CONACULTA, 2002.

Ceballos Ramírez, Manuel. *De historia e historiografía de la frontera norte.* México: Universidad Autónoma de Tamaulipas, Instituto de Investigaciones Históricas, y El Colegio de la Frontera Norte, 1996.

Cohen, Jeffrey H. *The Culture of Migration in Southern Mexico.* 1a ed. Austin: University of Texas, 2004.

Corona Vázquez, Rodolfo. "Cada vez más emigrantes". *Demos: Carta demográfica sobre México* 16 (2003–2004): 11–13.

Cuarto oscuro 12 (octubre/noviembre 1974): 17.

Debroise, Olivier. *Fuga mexicana. Un recorrido por la fotografía en México.* Barcelona: Gustavo Gili, 2005.

La emigración de San Luis Potosí a Estados Unidos. Pasado y presente. 1a ed. Monterrey, México: Senado de la República, 2001.

Enciclopedia de México. México, D.F.: Sabeca Internacional Investment Corp., 2000.

Espinosa, Jorge Luis. "Rulfo, la imagen sin sesgos dramáticos". *El Universal* (México), enero 31, 2006, cultura, p. 4.

Foto Hnos. Mayo: IVAM Centre Julio González. 8 julio/30 agosto 1992. Generalitat Valenciana.

Fuga mexicana. Un recorrido por la fotografía en México. 1a ed. México: Consejo Nacional para la Cultura y las Artes, 1994.

http://www.zonezero.com/exposiciones/fotografos/eniac/. Consultado en el Internet diciembre 27, 2005.

Mraz, John, y Jaime Vélez Storey. *Trasterrados: braceros vistos por los hermanos Mayo.* México: Archivo General de la Nación; Universidad Autónoma Metropolitana, 2005.

————. *Uprooted: braceros in the hermanos Mayo lens.* Houston, Tex.: Arte Publico, 1996.

Mummert, Gail, ed. *Fronteras fragmentadas.* Zamora, Michoacán: El Colegio de Michoacán, 1999.

Nuevas tendencias y nuevos desafíos de la migración internacional: Memorias del Seminario permanente sobre migración internacional. Vol. 1, 1a ed. México: El Colegio de la Frontera Norte, 2004.

Pérez Gay, José María. "El ocaso del futuro: el Limes romano y la gran migración". *La Jornada,* diciembre 19, 2005, p. 6.

Poniatowska, Elena. "La tv cultural debe dar servicio al público, dice Javier Aranda". *La Jornada,* febrero 19, 2006, p. 6a.

Rulfo, Juan. *Juan Rulfo: México, fotógrafo.* Textos por Carlos Fuentes, Margo Glantz, Jorge Alberto Lozoya, Eduardo Rivero, Víctor Jiménez, y Erika Billeter. Barcelona: Lunwerg Editores, 2001.

Santibáñez, Jorge. "De no tener política, a aceptar su importancia". *Demos: Carta demográfica sobre México* 16 (2003–2004): 9–10.

Weatherford, Douglas J. *Photographing Silence: Juan Rulfo's Mexico.* Jones y Boshard Galleries. enero 20, 2006–mayo 29, 2006.

Libraries, Librarians, and
Library Resources

12. Cine digital de acceso libre en el Internet: producciones españolas y latinoamericanas

Jesús Alonso-Regalado

El Cine en la era digital

La tecnología digital ha transformado la manera en que se produce y distribuye el cine. Desde el punto de vista de la producción, el abaratamiento de costos ha permitido que la creación audiovisual esté al alcance de cualquier persona. El auge del cine digital está supone una nueva era dentro del séptimo arte donde se abren nuevos cauces a la experimentación y a la renovación.

Con respecto a la distribución, desde la década de los 90 se generalizó la posibilidad de ver películas de reciente estreno a través de los servicios *pay per view* (pagar por ver) creados por canales de televisión. Esta tecnología permitía ver una película antes de su estreno en videocasete o en DVD. En la actualidad, existen en el Internet varios sitios que ofrecen películas pagando por el alquiler o por la descarga de una copia. Este año se ha dado un paso más allá, la película *Catarsis* del director Ángel Fernández Santos se estrenó simultáneamente el pasado 10 de marzo en salas cinematográficas y en el videoclub en línea Accine (http://www.accine.com), un servicio de alquiler de películas bajo demanda en el Internet.[1] Esto supone la primera experiencia en el ámbito hispánico hacia una nueva manera de tener acceso a las películas donde el espectador podrá decidir en cada momento qué plataforma prefiere usar.

El desarrollo de las nuevas tecnologías de la información ha permitido una mayor capacidad de procesamiento y almacenamiento. Al inicio del desarrollo del Internet, la información accesible se reducía a lo textual.

Actualmente podemos tener acceso además a imágenes estáticas, sonidos e imágenes en movimiento. En los últimos años la presencia en la red de estas últimas se ha generalizado: programas de televisión, anuncios publicitarios, tráilers, vídeoclips musicales, vídeos educacionales, vídeos caseros, noticias y películas. Los formatos de almacenamiento de recursos audiovisuales se han multiplicado en los últimos años como el estándar mpeg o los formatos creados por distintas empresas como Windows Media (.avi, .asf, .wmv), RealMedia (.rm), Flash (.swf) y QuickTime (.mov). Al mismo ritmo, salían al mercado una gran variedad de reproductores: Flash Player, QuickTime, Windows Media Player, Real Player, Google Media Player, etc.

En este contexto, me gustaría insertar esta presentación que pretende ofrecer un panorama general del cine digital accesible de manera gratuita a través del Internet y producido en España y Latinoamérica.

Búsqueda de imágenes en movimiento en el Internet

En primer lugar, analicemos brevemente las posibilidades de la búsqueda de imágenes en movimiento en el Internet. Los motores de búsqueda han incorporado recientemente este servicio. Entre los más conocidos se encuentran AlltheWeb, Alta Vista, Yahoo! y Google (el servicio Google Video fue inaugurado en el año 2005). Las posibilidades de estos buscadores son todavía muy limitadas. Yahoo! es actualmente uno de los que ofrece más opciones ya que pemite limitar las búsquedas por formato, tamaño y duración. AlltheWeb ofrece la posibilidad de activar un filtro de imágenes, limitar por tamaño y por tipo de descarga *(download* o *streaming).*

Alta Vista permite recuperar por formato y duración. Por último, Google no ofrece ninguna posibilidad de refinar la búsqueda. Se trata todavía de un proyecto experimental de su laboratorio.

La localización de películas digitales españolas y latinoamericanas en estos buscadores resulta una tarea difícil. La mayor parte de ellos permite recuperar distintos tipos de imágenes en movimiento como noticias, videoclips musicales, e incluso tráilers de películas pero apenas son eficaces a la hora de buscar producciones cinematográficas. Son capaces de localizarnos páginas web donde se incluyen listados o bases de datos que proporcionan el acceso a las películas pero raramente nos ofrece el acceso directo a la película en sí. Este terreno todavía pertenece en gran medida a lo que conocemos como Internet invisible. A esta situación hay que añadir que ninguno de estos buscadores permite buscar por país o lengua.

Por otro lado, existen proyectos de acceso a vídeos de dominio público en archivos abiertos como el Internet Archive que incluye imágenes en movimiento pero sólo sobre temática estadounidense.

En suma, el cine digital de acceso abierto en el ámbito iberoamericano es difícil de localizar, se encuentra muy disperso y todavía su presencia es reducida en Internet.

¿Dónde localizar cine digital en el Internet producido en España y América Latina?

Sitios Web especializados en cortometrajes

El cortometraje se ha convertido en nuestros días en el formato de duración más extendido para distribuir el cine de manera gratuita en la red. Las principales ventajas de combinar las potencialidades de la tecnología web y la digital son:

- La difusión de un formato que raramente se exhibe en salas comerciales.

- La promoción de nuevos creadores dado que el cortometraje disponible en Internet sirve como carta de presentación de nuevos directores que se quieren dar a conocer.

- La velocidad y calidad de descarga de imágenes permite la visualización de este tipo de producciones de breve formato con una calidad en general aceptable.

Una de las dificultades a la hora de localizar estos cortometrajes reside en la variada terminología que se utiliza para definir este formato: cortometrajes (o también denominados popularmente como cortos) en la red, online, en línea, en la web, cortometrajes comprimidos o para el Internet. La variedad de géneros es también extensa: animación, documentales, ficción, creaciones experimentales, videoarte, etc.

Algunos sitios webs especializados en cortometrajes dignos de mención son:

- Solocortos.com: Cortometraje On-line. http://www.solocortos.com. Éste presenta cortometrajes procedentes tanto de España como de América Latina. Su acceso requiere el registro como usuario. La organización de los mismos es por género o título. Este sitio web también ofrece un servicio de discusión donde los usuarios pueden enviar sus comentarios sobre los cortos.

- Hurluberlu Films: Short Films Online. http://www.hurluberlu.com. Hurluberlu Films se define como una plataforma internacional de acceso gratuito a cortometrajes. Según se indica en su página web, "El programa de Hurluberlu Films se basa en una selección internacional de películas que nos han llegado de directores de cine, casas de producción u otros distribuidores".[2] Actualmente incluye cortos de Argentina, Brasil y España. Todos ellos se acompañan de subtítulos en su lengua original.

Festivales de cortometrajes en Internet

Los festivales de cortos en la red han logrado que el acceso al cortometraje tenga una mayor visibilidad. Estos festivales se han consolidado en los últimos años como espacios donde la difusión de estas producciones breves esté al alcance de todo creador que desee mostrar su trabajo.

- Notodofilmfest.com. http://www.notodofilmfest.com. Se trata de uno de los mayores festivales internacionales de su género en la red. Cuenta con un buscador de los cortos participantes que permite localizarlos por autor, título, género y formato. Incluye también el acceso a los cortos de anteriores ediciones del festival. Recientemente se han presentado 1,400 cortos de un total de 25 países a la IV edición donde según los organizadores se han batido récords de descargas de cortos: más de 70,000.[3]

- Ingenio400.com. IV Centenario de El Quijote. http://www.ingenio400. com. Premio para cortos, videoarte y net-art inspirados en la novela *El Ingenioso Hidalgo Don Quijote de la Mancha.* Convocado por la Sociedad Estatal de Conmemoraciones Culturales con motivo del IV centenario de la publicación de su primera parte.

- Festival de Cortometrajes On-Line Minuto y Medio. http://www. minutoymedio.com. Este festival forma parte del portal Hispavista. Los cortos son en español y no pueden superar los 90 segundos. La última edición disponible en la red es la del año 2002.

- Fotogramas en Corto. http://www.fotogramasencorto.wanadoo.es/. Festival creado por la revista de cine Fotogramas. Permite el acceso a un archivo de todas sus ediciones desde su primera convocatoria en el 2004.

- Consurso de Cortometrajes Nontzefilm. http://www.nontzefilm.com/2006/ cast. El portal cultural Nontzeberri.com convoca este concurso con la ayuda del Festival de Cine Fantástico de Bilbao. Presenta vídeos tanto de España como de países latinoamericanos.[4]

- Certamen Gay-Lésbico de Cine Comprimido. http://www.fancinegay. com/2005/principal2005.htm. Este certamen, surgido en el año 2003, admite cortometrajes de ficción, documental y video creaciones procedentes de países del ámbito iberoamericano que traten sobre el deseo y/o sentimientos homosexuales. El sitio web sólo ofrece el acceso de los cortometrajes ganadores de cada edición.

Productoras

Algunas de las productoras que han prestado especial atención al mundo del cortometraje son:

- La Toma (http://www.latoma.cl)

- Producciones Colargol (http://www.produccionescolargol.com/)

- Tropofilms.com (http://www.tropofilms.com)

Escuelas de cinematografía

Las escuelas de cinematografía utilizan el corto como herramienta de trabajo en proyectos de prácticas en cursos y proyectos de final de carrera. En este sentido la Escuela Nacional de Experimentación y Realización Cinematográfica (ENERC; http://www.enerc.gov.ar/cortos/cortos_up_main.html) en Argentina ha creado una página web que incluye una sección de fragmentos de cortos en línea desde donde se pueden descargar trabajos realizados por alumnos y ex-alumnos de la escuela. Entre otros, se incluyen trabajos de cineastas contemporá-neos reconocidos internacionalmente como Tristán Bauer y Lucrecia Martel.

En un futuro próximo, una de las posibles tendencias será la promoción en la red de trabajos realizados por los alumnos a través de productoras vincula-das con las escuelas de cinematografía. De esta manera, se favorecería la incor-poración de los alumnos a la industria cinematográfica. Actualmente existen casos de productoras como Escándalo Films vinculada con la Escola Superior de Cinema i Audiovisuals de Catalunya (ESCAC) pero que no incluyen cortos de sus alumnos en la red.

Portales y videotecas digitales

La preservación y difusión del patrimonio cultural es el principal objetivo que comparten este tipo de proyectos que surgen con una voluntad de cober-tura nacional e incluso panhispánica en el caso de la biblioteca Virtual Miguel de Cervantes.

- Cinemateca Virtual de Chile. http://www.cinechileno.org/. Esta cin-emateca virtual está realizada por el Consejo Nacional de la Cultura y las Artes de Chile y la televisión virtual ArcoIris. Su misión es facili-tar el acceso al patrimonio audiovisual chileno a través del Internet. Actualmente incluye 130 producciones organizadas alfabéticamente, por fechas o por categorías de formato tales como cortometraje o largo-metraje y temática como historia y política.

- Nuestro.cl: El Sitio del Patrimonio Cultural Chileno. http://www.nuestro.cl. Portal desarrollado por la Corporación Patrimonio Cultural de Chile que se configura como el principal sitio en Internet para acceder a recursos digitales de calidad sobre el patrimonio cultural de Chile. A diferencia de la Cinemateca Virtual de Chile, la sección de vídeos de este portal se limita a presentar únicamente una selección de documen-tales no necesariamente incluidos en el primero.

- Memoria Digital de Canarias. http://bdigital.ulpgc.es/mdc. Proyecto creado en la Universidad de las Palmas con el objetivo de crear una colección de recursos digitales sobre las Islas Canarias. Actualmente incluye más de 100 vídeos, en su gran mayoría documentales.

- Videoteca de la Biblioteca Virtual Miguel de Cervantes. http://www.cervantesvirtual.com/bib_imagenes/. La Biblioteca Virtual Miguel de Cervantes se ha convertido con el paso de los años en uno de los más completos proyectos digitales de preservación y difusión del patrimo-nio cultural hispánico. Con respecto al material audiovisual (accesible por título y/o autor), presenta una valiosa videoteca sobre todo en lo referente a la literatura en forma de documentales, entrevistas a autores, recitales poéticos y filmaciones de representaciones teatrales. En cuanto a lo que se refiere a producción cinematográfica presenta una interesante colección de documentales con una amplia temática.

Dignos de mención son los documentales dedicados a escritores, a temas tan variados como el exilio republicano español de 1939 o el arzobispo salvadoreño Monseñor Romero así como colecciones como las que posee la División de Cine y Video de la Biblioteca Nacional de Venezuela.

Museos

Son cada vez más numerosos los museos que se deciden a ofrecer archivos audiovisuales de género fundamentalmente documental sobre cuestiones culturales e históricas. A modo ilustrativo, algunos ejemplos de museos que están explorando este tipo de proyectos son:

- Museo Chileno de Arte Precolombino. http://www.precolombino.cl/es/audiovisual/. A través de su archivo se puede acceder a documentales realizados por el área audiovisual del museo. Se trata de vídeos realizados desde perspectivas antropológicas, arqueológicas y culturales.

- Museo de la Palabra y la Imagen (El Salvador). http://www.museo.com.sv. Este museo incluye por ahora sólo un documental sobre la insurrección indígena en El Salvador en 1932. Otros proyectos se encuentran todavía en fase de producción. Actualmente, el acceso por el Internet de algunos de sus documentales está dirigido a la promoción de la venta de su catálogo audiovisual a través de su tienda en línea.

Asociaciones, redes comunitarias y ONGs

Un creciente número de asociaciones en países latinoamericanos se han preocupado por reflejar en imágenes la realidad social de diversos grupos populares, marginados y minorías. El género audiovisual al que recurren es un híbrido que se alimenta en gran medida de elementos del documental pero también del videoarte e incluso del mundo de la ficción. Su intención es mostrar una realidad muchas veces invisible donde estos sectores de la sociedad dejan de ser únicamente el objeto filmado para convertirse también en agentes y creadores de imágenes que reflejen sus propios problemas y formas de pensar. Desde este punto de vista, muchas de estas creaciones se les podría reconocer como video-testimonio.

Dos corrientes dentro de este género híbrido han cobrado especial atención:

- El vídeo popular llevado a cabo por grupos comunitarios donde "desde el mismo momento de su concepción exista plena participación de los miembros del grupo, de la comunidad en cuestión, con sus ideas, valoraciones, puntos de vista acerca del tema y su tratamiento en el material audiovisual".[5] Ejemplo de ello es la Red Nacional de Vídeo Popular en Chile http://www.alejandria.cl/videos/videos1.htm.

- El vídeo sobre temática indígena. En algunas ocasiones es realizado por las propias comunidades indígenas. Actualmente existen experiencias que promueven el uso del vídeo como vehículo de expresión de su identidad pero que no están disponibles en la red.[6] Por otro lado, existen proyectos realizados por ONGs como *Ser Indígena* (http://www.serindigena.cl) que utilizan el vídeo digital en Internet como medio para difundir las tradiciones y valores culturales de los pueblos indígenas actuales. Sus producciones han tenido siempre el apoyo de las mismas comunidades que han visto en el medio audiovisual una forma de proteger su legado cultural.

Videoblogs (vlogs)

El Videoblog o vlog es una variedad de blog cuyo contenido principal son vídeos. Normalmente, se acompañan de textos, imágenes y cualquier otro tipo de información que pueda ayudar a contextualizarlos. Los vídeos pueden ser comentados por aquellos que accedan al videoblog. De esta manera, estas bitácoras visuales se configuran como una valiosa herramienta para comunicarse con otros creadores y experimentar con la tecnología de vídeo digital en Internet. Actualmente, la mayor parte de los vlogs son diarios personales en los que sus creadores documentan su vida cotidiana y expresan sus ideas. El acceso a los vídeos incluidos en los videoblogs se ve dificultado por la imposibilidad de localizarlos en buscadores. En el ámbito del español existen recursos como Vlogespañol http://vlogespanol.com que proporciona un listado de vblogs en la red. En portugués, Videolog.com.br http://www.videolog.com.br/ es el primer proyecto de vlog en Brasil creado en el año 2004.

Conclusión

El cine digital de acceso abierto en Internet está abriendo nuevos espacios en el ámbito de la producción audiovisual iberoamericana, espacios abiertos a la creatividad, con nuevos contenidos, pluralidad de perspectivas, con propuestas originales y novedosas. El acceso gratuito a través del Internet supone una ventana abierta a la riqueza cultural de los países iberoamericanos. Ante las dificultades de exhibición comercial, la red permite dar visibilidad a imágenes que reflejan la complejidad y diversidad de nuestros países.

El uso potencial de estas creaciones audiovisuales en nuestras universidades es ilimitado ya que permite trasladar a las aulas el debate sobre problemáticas, sensibilidades y contenidos a los que no tendríamos fácil acceso de ninguna otra manera.

NOTAS

1. Accine (http://www.accine.com) incluye en su catálogo de alquiler bajo demanda en línea películas de Iberoamérica y Europa (fundamentalmente de temas de América Latina). Las producciones iberoamericanas provienen de los siguientes países: Argentina, Chile, Colombia, Cuba, Ecuador, España, México, Perú, Uruguay y Venezuela.

2. Información incluida en la página principal del sitio web de Hurluberlu Films, http://www.hurluberlu.com (consultado en el Internet marzo 10, 2006).

3. Agencia EFE, "El corto H5N1, de Fernández Miranda, gana el Notodofilmfest.com", Elmundo.es, http://www.elmundo.es/elmundo/2006/03/08/cultura/1141774155.html (consultado en el Internet marzo 8, 2006).

4. Para acceder al primer certamen de este concurso: http://www.nontzefilm.com/2005/cast/.

5. Elina Hernández Galárraga, "El video como medio de educación popular", http://tecnologiaedu.us.es/revistaslibros/carlos%20bravo/no7-5.htm (consultado en el Internet marzo 10, 2006).

6. Ejemplo de ello es el proyecto Vídeo nas Aldeias, http://www.videonasaldeias.org.br (consultado en el Internet marzo 10, 2006).

13. Proyectos de digitalización de materiales lusohispanos en la Biblioteca del Congreso para el siglo XXI

Georgette Magassy Dorn

El propósito de este trabajo es presentar algunos de los proyectos e iniciativas de la Biblioteca del Congreso de la digitalización de materiales sobre el mundo lusohispano. Títulos específicos de ciertos proyectos y de algunas tecnologías las menciono en inglés, puesto que traducir los mismos podría crear confusión.

Las bibliotecas en el siglo XXI están experimentando grandes cambios en lo que respecta a su adaptación a las nuevas tecnologías y a las nuevas necesidades y exigencias de sus usuarios. La Dra. Deanna Marcum, Associate Librarian of Library Services de la Biblioteca del Congreso, habló de desarrollos en torno a la biblioteca digital en una ponencia principal (keynote address) en una conferencia celebrada en la China.[1] No cabe duda, que la digitalización de materiales hace possible la diseminación de imágenes y publicaciones a través de Internet por todo el mundo para gran beneficio de todos los que tienen acceso a esa red. La posibilidad de comunicar en forma casi instantánea materiales digitalizados es la gran revolución tecnológica de nuestros tiempos. Los avances en estas tecnologías simplificaron las transacciones en el mundo de los negocios. Por su parte, en el ámbito de las ciencias, hace ya varios años que se han creado comunidades virtuales en especialidades como la química, la medicina y el medio ambiente.[2]

En 1998 la Biblioteca del Congreso implementó una "estrategia para digitalizar", por la cual se quiso examinar el estado actual de archivación y conservación de materiales digitalizados por las bibliotecas e instituciones en los Estados Unidos. Para lograr este resultado y por mandato específico del Congreso de los Estados Unidos, se organizó el National Digital Information Infrastructure and Preservation Program (NDIIPP). Colaboran con este programa a nivel nacional tanto entes gubernamentales como bibliotecas.[3]

Deanna Marcum, dictó varias conferencias en que explica los nuevos programas e iniciativas que tratan de los avances tecnológicos y el uso que pueden hacer las bibliotecas de los mismos. Entre ellas pronunció una ponencia de aperturea en la Joint Conference on Digital Libraries en la ciudad de Denver, Colorado, en la que describe la integración de iniciativas digitales como parte de la totalidad de los servicios brindados por bibliotecas.[4]

Ya durante 1990–1994, antes de anunciarse la "estrategia para digitalizar" y bajo la dirección del Director de la Biblioteca del Congreso, James Billington, se inició el proyecto titulado "American Memory", dirigido tanto a escolares de primaria y secundaria, como a investigadores a nivel universitario. El proyecto consistió en la digitalización de materiales en varios formatos, creando recursos electrónicos, para diseminar y preservar libros, imágenes, manuscritos, mapas y fotografías con el fin de documentar la historia y cultura de los Estados Unidos. Estos archivos virtuales, a los que se puede acceder a través del Internet, tuvieron gran éxito y fueron utilizados por escuelas y colegios por todo el país. Hasta ahora a través del proyecto American Memory se han digitalizado 7.5 millones de imágenes seleccionadas de las colecciones de la Biblioteca del Congreso.[5] Sin duda que estos recursos electrónicos promovieron el uso de materiales digitales.

Hay que hacer constancia que la Biblioteca del Congreso digitaliza y coloca en el Internet para uso público solamente materiales que no están protegidos por "Copyright Law", por la legislación que rige los derechos del autor (propiedad intelectual) y que ya forman parte del dominio público. Es decir, en 2006, todo lo posterior a 1921 se considera protegido por la ley de Copyright. Por lo tanto, no colocamos material en el Internet que sea posterior a esa fecha. Excepciones son las publicaciones del gobierno de los Estados Unidos considerados del dominio público. Por otra parte, sí están protegidos por Copyright las publicaciones de los gobiernos de algunos otros países.[6]

Como ya hemos visto antes, el Internet transformó radicalmente la presentación y diseminación de documentos. En 1994 la Biblioteca del Congreso comenzó un proyecto que se conoce bajo el nombre de la "National Digital Library", un proyecto que cuenta con el apoyo del Congreso de los Estados Unidos y de varias entidades filantrópicas privadas. Como se mencionó anteriormente, la Biblioteca ya había digitalizado unos 7.5 ítems dentro del programa de "American Memory". Algunos de estos proyectos son de interés para Latinoamérica, como por ejemplo el intitulado "Immigration and American Expansion". Este ilustra la expansion territorial de los Estados Unidos durante el período de 1821–1890 con la presentación de selecciones de manuscritos, fotografías, documentos cartográficos, y textos, creando un verdadero archivo virtual.

La Biblioteca del Congreso posee en sus fondos aproximadamente 135 millones de piezas (ítems). Libros y revistas suman unos 21 millones y el resto lo componen mapas, manuscritos, fotografías, grabados, películas, grabaciones, música, es decir, un verdadero tesoro que refleja los conocimientos y logros de la humanidad a través de los siglos. Más de la mitad de los libros que se encuentran en la Biblioteca del Congreso están en otros idiomas. Calculamos que las colecciones lusohispanas y caribeñas (en éstas incluimos las Islas Filipinas antes del 1898 y todas las regiones que formaban parte del imperio español o portugués) suman más de 12 millones de piezas, entre las que 2.5 millones son libros y revistas.

En lo que se refiere a la digitalización de materiales lusohispanos, hemos convertido a formato digital tanto piezas únicas y originales, como también valiosas bibliografías y guías para facilitar la tarea del investigador. La primera colección lusohispana que apareció en el servidor de la Biblioteca del Congreso es el "Handbook of Latin American Studies".[7] Esta bibliografía comentada, publicada anualmente, es una herramienta indispensable para los estudios de Latinoamérica en lo que se refiere a las humanidades y las ciencias sociales. Esta obra anual se prepara en la Hispanic Division de la Biblioteca del Congreso desde el año 1939 con la asistencia de unos 135 expertos y estudiosos de la América Latina y es editada por la University of Texas Press, desde 1978. Editoriales universitarias que imprimieron el "Handbook" antes de Texas fueron las de Harvard University (1935–1947) y la University of Florida (1948–1978).[8]

En 1993 el entonces presidente de la Fundación MAPFRE América, don Ignacio Hernando de Larramendi, con apoyo inicial de la Andrew W. Mellon Foundation, decidió encargar a la compañía española Digibis la conversión retrospectiva en forma digital de los primeros 50 tomos del "Handbook of Latin American Studies". Esta conversión electrónica de impresos producidos a través de más de 50 años, con tipos de imprenta muy diferentes y con textos en más de una docena de idiomas, fue un trabajo pionero y produjo una base de datos con la capacidad de OCR (optical character recognition). El CD-ROM de los 50 tomos digitalizados se presentó en una reunión de la Latin American Studies Association en octubre de 1995 en Washington, en la Hispanic Division, con la presencia de don Ignacio Larramendi, el Embajador de España y miembros del Congreso de Estados Unidos. La Fundación MAPFRE nos ayudó a producir un segundo CD-ROM-2 en 1997 que incluye los primeros 55 volúmenes del "Handbook".

Gracias a una donación de los herederos de Lewis Hanke, fallecido en 1993, la base de datos del "Handbook" en su totalidad (incluyendo la digitalización de los primeros 55 tomos) fue colocada en el servidor de la Biblioteca del Congreso, junto con los volúmenes "en preparación" (aún no publicados) en 1998. Fue Lewis Hanke quien al ser nombrado director de la Hispanic Foundation (ahora es la Hispanic Division), trajo consigo a la Biblioteca del Congreso el "Handbook" en 1939. A pesar de estar completamente automatizado desde 1994 y asequible gratis en el servidor de la Biblioteca, el "Handbook" sigue siendo editado también en forma de papel. El volúmen publicado este año es el número 61 dedicado a las ciencias sociales. Como a principios de la década de los 60 el número de publicaciones sobre Latinoamérica había aumentado considerablemente, el entonces director de la Hispanic Foundation, Howard F. Cline, decidió alternar los volúmenes anuales con humanidades y ciencias sociales, cada año por medio, en vez de incluir todas las materias en un tomo.[9] Esta medida nos permitió incluir más materiales en cada publicación anual.

La página web de la Hispanic Division ilustra brevemente los servicios brindados por este departmento. Puesto que se puede acceder tanto en inglés, como en español y portugués a este sitio de Web, www.loc.gov/rr/hispanic también puede servir de entrada a todas las colecciones digitalizadas y a los servicios brindados por la Biblioteca del Congreso.[10]

A continuación vamos a describir ciertas iniciativas de digitalización completadas en años recientes. Cada colección mencionada cuenta con su propio sitio Web y puede ser consultada a través de la página web de la Hispanic Division mencionada anteriormente.

El recurso electrónico "Puerto Rico at the Dawn of the Modern Age" ilustra aspectos de la historia en el siglo XIX y principios del XX de Puerto Rico, con imágenes, manuscritos, folletos, libros y documentación cartográfica. Entre otros materiales en este archivo virtual se reprodujeron documentos del Partido Autonomista Puertorriqueño y también el libro de Salvador Brau "Puerto Rico y su historia".

Otro fondo digitalizado es el titulado "Hispanic Music and Culture in the Northern Rio Grande: The Juan B. Rael Collection". Este archivo es la colección etnográfica del folclorista Juan Bautista Rael (1900–1993) que documenta la música, cultura y costumbres de los hispano-parlantes en el area rural del norte del estado de New Mexico y el sur del estado de Colorado.

"Hispanic Americans in Congress, 1822–1995", fue un libro preparado en la Hispanic Division y editado por el Government Printing Office, la imprenta oficial del gobierno estadounidense. El libro presenta un listado con biografías y fotografías de los miembros hispanos en el Congreso de los Estados Unidos comenzando con 1822 el año que el primer miembro hispano llega a la Cámara de Representantes. La publicación tuvo tanto éxito que para mayor diseminación lo convertimos a un formato digital. Seguimos añadiendo a esta base de datos cada dos años los nombres de los nuevos miembros elegidos a ambas cámaras. El sitio de Internet de este fondo digital se mantiene al día con los nuevos miembros hispanos pues tiene enlaces a los sitios Web de los actuales miembros del Congreso.

En 1997 preparamos en la Hispanic Division el proyecto "The World of 1898: The Spanish-American War", en vísperas del centenario de la Guerra entre Estados Unidos y y España. Este archivo digital documenta la historia de las áreas y regiones protagonistas durante el conflicto y la inmediata época posterior. El sitio Web presenta fotografías, imágenes, mapas, diarios y libros. Este recurso electrónico es el más asíduamente utilizado entre las que aparecen en la página web de la Hispanic Division, con un promedio de 100,000 visitantes virtuales cada mes.

"The Portuguese in the United States", consiste de una bibliografía sobre la inmigración portuguesa a los Estados Unidos y las comunidades portuguesas en este país. El archivo virtual presenta mapas, textos, imágenes, manuscritos y se incluyen enlaces a otras colecciones de la Biblioteca. Aquí se pueden ver imágenes de Salomon Nunes Carvalho, de la sinagoga de Touro de Rhode Island, fundada por judíos de orígen portugués, o escuchar música de John Philip Sousa digitalizada.

En el año 2000 el Director Billington firmó un acuerdo con la Biblioteca Nacional de España para preparar un archivo digital bilingüe inglés y español para explorar las relaciones entre los españoles y la población indígena de lo que hoy constituye los Estados Unidos y también relaciones de los españoles con otros europeos que llegaron al continente americano. El resultado es el proyecto "Parallel Histories: Spain, the United States and the American Frontier" que representa un archivo digital de libros, mapas, grabados, gráficos y manuscritos digitalizados por la Biblioteca del Congreso y la Biblioteca Nacional para documentar las "historias paralelas" de varios pueblos comenzando con el siglo XVI hasta los albores de siglo XIX. El primer tema dentro de este proyecto, ya completado, se titula "Estados Unidos y España: Exploraciones y Primeros Asentamientos".

Este proyecto con España ahora forma parte de una nueva iniciativa digital titulada "Global Gateway", que consiste en preparar archivos virtuales bilingües con varios países. Hasta ahora hay proyectos con Rusia, Brasil, Francia, Holanda y el ya mencionado con España. Ahora se está proponiendo una iniciatiava de las mismas características con la Biblioteca Nacional de Egipto.

El segundo archivo virtual lusohispano que llevamos a cabo es "The United States and Brazil: Expanding Frontiers, Comparing Cultures", con la Biblioteca Nacional del Brasil.

La inauguración formal fue en febrero del 2004. Este es un archivo digital bilingüe (inglés/portugués) que explora y documenta las relaciones entre el Brasil y Estados Unidos desde fines del siglo XVIII hasta principios del XX. Traza paralelos entre estos dos países de gran extensión y multíples culturas. El archivo electrónico presenta libros, fotografías, mapas, gráficos, manuscritos y otros documentos digitalizados en ambas bibliotecas, con ensayos y textos bilingües.

"The Hans P. Kraus Collection" es un archivo virtual de 162 manuscritos digitalizados relacionados con la historia de la América española durante la época colonial, de 1492 a 1819. Algunos de los manuscritos llevan firmas del emperador Carlos V y de su mujer, Isabel de Portugal.

"The Luso-Hispanic World in Maps: A Selective Guide to Manuscript Maps to 1900 in the Collections of the Library of Congress", es un archivo electrónico de una selección de mapas manuscritos que se encuentran en los fondos de la Biblioteca del Congreso.

Otro proyecto de digitalización que estamos completando es una colección que consiste de 800 libros ladinos, es decir, libros sobre temas relacionados con judíos de la península ibérica escritos en español-ladino, algunos usando el alfabeto hebreo y otros el latino.

Además de digitalizar piezas únicas o colecciones enteras, también hemos digitalizado exposiciones preparadas por la Biblioteca del Congreso. Debemos mencionar la digitalización de "1492: An Ongoing Voyage". La exposición que fue preparada para el Quinto Centenario de la gesta de Colón. En 2005 digitalizamos otra exposición titulada "The Culture and History of the Americas: the Jay Kislak Collection" con objetos precolombinos, pinturas y libros raros, que forman parte de una colección recientemente donada a la Biblioteca del Congreso por el coleccionista y filántropo Jay Kislak.[11]

Una de las iniciativas que estamos proponiendo es la digitalización del Archivo de Literatura Hispánica en Cinta Magnética. Este archivo cuenta con las grabaciones sonoras de unos 680 poetas y narradores lusohispanos caribeños e hispanoamericanos de Estados Unidos. Algunas de las grabaciones recientes fueron llevadas a cabo en video.

En 2005, el Dr. Billington anunció un nuevo proyecto titulado "The World Digital Library" con la cooperación de las bibliotecas nacionales de varios países en un marco más amplio de lo que es el programa de "Global Gateway". Se propone que la "World Digital Library" sería patrocinada por entidades filantrópicas privadas además de fondos públicos. En su conferencia ante la U.S. National Commission for UNESCO, Billington anunció que la biblioteca virtual que está proponiendo, presentará al público del globo entero materiales raros y únicos digitalizadoes en las grandes bibliotecas desde de todos los lugares del mundo.[12]

No hay duda que en los años venideros seguiremos seleccionando materiales de los fondos de la Biblioteca del Congreso y preparando recursos electrónicos para diseminar nuestros fondos más extensivamente y ponerlos a disposición del público de todos los países del mundo y con ello contribuir a un mejor conocimiento de los pueblos que lo habitan.

NOTAS

1. Deanna Marcum, "Digital Library Developments Today: An Overview" (discurso de apertura, Conference of Librarians of the United States and China, Shanghai, People's Republic of China, marzo 25, 2004).

2. James H. Billington, "Remarks to the Plenary Session", U.S. National Commission for UNESCO, Georgetown University, junio 6, 2005. Se puede consultar el texto entero en la siguiente dirección: www.loc.gov/about/welcome/speeches.

3. Para mas información, consultar www.digitalpreservation.gov/.

4. Deanna Marcum, "The Sum of the Parts; Turning Digital Library Initiatives into a Great Whole", Joint Conference on Digital Libraries, Denver, junio 8, 2005.

5. www.memory.loc.gov//ammem/.

6. Deanna Marcum, "The DODL, the NDIIPP and the Copyright Conundrum" (discurso de apertura, Fiesole 2004, European University Institute, Villa La Fonte, Florence, Italy, marzo 19, 2006).

7. Todas la colecciones lusohispanas y caribeñas digitalizadas por la Biblioteca del Congreso pueden ser consultadas en la página web de la Hispanic Division: www.loc.gov/rr/hispanic/.

8. Dan Hazen, "The Handbook of Latin American Studies at Volume Fifty: Area Studies Bibliography in a Context of Change", *Inter-American Review of Bibliography* 41, no. 2 (1991): 195–196. Guy Lamolinara, "The Hispanic Division: The Center for Latin American Scholarship", *Library of Congress Information Bulletin* (septiembre 10, 1990): 299–303.

9. Dolores Moyano Martin, "Editor's Note: 50th Volume of the Handbook of Latin American Studies", *Handbook of Latin American Studies,* vol. 50 (Austin: University of Texas Press, 1990), pp. xxi–xxviii es un ensayo excelente sobre la publicación.

10. José E. Serrano, "A Bridge from the Past to the Present", *Library of Congress Information Bulletin* 63, no. 12 (2004): 242.

11. Helen Dalrymple, "Treasures of the Americas; The Jay Kislak Collection Debuts at the Library", *Library of Congress Information Bulletin* 64, no. 4 (April 2005): 79–87.

12. "Library of Congress Efforts to Create a World Digital Library", Library of Congress Press Release, noviembre 22, 2005.

14. Crossing Over: Preparing Latin Americanists for Careers in Academic Librarianship

Sean Patrick Knowlton

Each year universities produce far more graduate degrees than available tenure-track faculty positions. Academic positions, however, exist in librarianship, which is facing a decline in qualified applicants. In this presentation I describe a collaborative program initiated by University Libraries and the Graduate Teacher Program at the University of Colorado at Boulder. This successful mentored fellowship program promotes academic librarianship as a viable career for current graduate students not enrolled in a library science program. To date, fellows have found librarianship to be an excellent career option in which they can use their advanced subject and/or language expertise outside of the traditional academic career track. This presentation also issues a call for similar programs at other institutions as a way of encouraging students with subject expertise and languages relating to Latin America and the Caribbean to consider academic librarianship as a career.

In 2001, Golde and Dore published a major research survey of doctoral students. Eighty-seven percent aspire to faculty positions, unaware that only 50 percent will ever become full-time tenure-track faculty (17). The same study reveals that many graduate students lack effective mentoring on other career options. The overproduction of Ph.D.'s forces many to seek employment outside of their area of expertise, accept low-paying non-tenure-track positions as adjunct instructors, or not complete their graduate education. Those who choose to end their graduate education at the master's level, a nonterminal degree in most fields, face more limited opportunities than those with a doctorate. Golde and Dore propose reducing the number of doctoral degrees awarded while encouraging new Ph.D.'s to consider careers outside of academia (11). Interestingly, they neglect to promote academic librarianship as a career option within academia for both master's and doctoral degree holders. As identified by Golde and Dore, the same interests that influence graduate students to pursue a faculty career are all present in academic librarianship: "love of teaching, enjoyment of research, and interest in doing service" (9).

Recent articles show that candidate pools for academic librarian positions commonly include only a few qualified applicants (Hardesty 2002; Hewitt, Moran, and Marsh 2003). Only 24 percent of new librarians possess a second master's degree in addition to a master's degree in library and information science; less than 2 percent of new librarians possess a doctorate (Millet and Posas 2005). Academic libraries especially seek librarians who possess foreign language knowledge, whether in speaking or reading (Kellsey 2003). For most subject specialist or bibliographer positions, including Latin Americanists, a second advanced degree is preferred, if not required.

In 2002, ACRL identified recruitment and education as core issues of concern for academic libraries and issued a call for all academic libraries to establish recruitment to the profession efforts at the local level (Hisle 2002). To date, most of these efforts have overwhelmingly focused on students already enrolled in library school. They also do not purposely target individuals who possess advanced degrees in other fields. The ARL Academy is a recent exception, although it focuses on the professional development of these individuals already enrolled in library school. Another approach involves the creation of library internships for current or recent doctoral students. Yale University Library, for example, offers a paid semester-long graduate internship that is limited to only those who have completed their Ph.D. coursework. The Council on Library and Information Resources Postdoctoral Fellowship takes a novel approach by placing humanities scholars at an academic research library for a period of one to two years in order to "establish a new kind of scholarly information professional." There is some concern in the literature that programs of this nature sidestep and devalue the accredited MLIS degree, while others embrace these initiatives as a necessary means of recruiting subject specialists (Berry 2003). Lastly, ALSTARS, a promising program at the University of South Florida School of Library and Information Science, uses an IMLS grant to provide library school scholarships for those who already possess advanced subject degrees or special language skills. Nevertheless, little has been done by the profession as a whole to identify and encourage graduate students to consider academic librarianship as a career before they even apply to a library and information science program. Graduate education is, after all, an exploratory period during which students define their specific career tracks.

The Provost's Fellowship at the University of Colorado at Boulder Libraries strives to take a long-term approach to recruitment to the profession. The libraries seek to identify future academic librarians early in their academic careers and provide them with a professional-level experience in the libraries. During a 150-hour mentored fellowship over the course of a semester, the fellows learn the skills required or valued in the profession and, most importantly, they see firsthand how they can apply their subject and language skills in a whole new way while still in the academy.

Formed in 2002 as a response to ACRL's call for local academic libraries to recruit to the profession, the aptly named Task Force on Recruitment to the Profession of Academic Librarianship at CU-Boulder began by giving presentations, creating exhibits, and advertising itself as a host site for MLIS student interns from other institutions. These efforts caught the attention of the director of the Graduate Teacher Program (GTP) on campus, whose mission is to assist graduate students in their professional development. The director, Laura Border, recognized academic librarianship as a great alternate career option for the many graduate students she mentors and quickly saw the potential for a collaborative effort with the libraries. As a participant in the national Preparing Future Faculty program, the GTP has significant know-how in developing, monitoring, and evaluating graduate student mentorship experiences. This expertise helped the task force move quickly to define the parameters of a library mentorship, develop requirements for both fellows and mentors, create application and evaluation documentation and, most importantly, identify funding sources on campus. Assisted by the GTP's considerable knowledge of campus funding politics, they are able to offer each fellow a $2,500 stipend, which is equivalent to a teaching or research assistantship.

The program's goals are straightforward: introduce academic librarianship as a career to graduate students; present the tenure process for librarians at CU-Boulder Libraries; and recruit fellows with subject and/or language expertise to the academic library profession by encouraging them to enroll in library school. Fellows perform a mentorship in the libraries under the guidance of a librarian-mentor who is dedicated to the professional development of the fellow. Two rounds of the fellowship have been completed during spring and fall 2005, with the third round set to begin in January 2007. The task force seeks graduate students who express a clear interest in pursuing academic librarianship as a career, have strong academic records, and are committed to personal and professional development. To date, the majority of applicants have been master's students. The task force has not selected a single doctoral student to participate in the program due to their lack of expressed interest in librarianship as a career. Most see the fellowship as an opportunity to improve their research skills as a future professor. The nine fellows who have participated in the program represent the Departments of Art History, Classics, Comparative Literature and Humanities, English, Germanic and Slavic Languages and Literatures, History, and Religion. Together, fellows have spoken and/or written the following languages: French, German, Greek, Latin, Russian, Sanskrit, Spanish, and Swedish.

During their mentorship, fellows become virtual members of the faculty; they attend faculty meetings, department meetings, and in-service presentations. They tour the off-site storage facility and meet with the libraries' tenure committee to understand the unique requirements for librarians as faculty. Together, at the beginning of the fellowship, fellow and mentor establish a mentorship plan to outline the experience. Each fellow's experiences vary widely. They provide general and discipline-specific reference, plan and teach library research seminars in a variety of fields, select and deselect materials, create collection development policies, catalog materials in a foreign language, and use their subject/language expertise to create online subject guides and compile bibliographies. Above all, fellows perform professional-level work and are not used as student assistants. Mentors engage their fellows in librarianship by providing them with the necessary theoretical background and practical application while sharing their passion for the profession. They assign and discuss library literature, discuss best practices, provide opportunities for exploration, and answer questions. Most importantly, mentors make special efforts to integrate the fellows' subject knowledge and/or language expertise into the experience.

Before the fellowship, fellows generally expressed that they did not fully understand the duties of academic librarians and were not aware of the faculty status of the librarians at their own institution. After the fellowship, fellows had a new perspective: "I didn't realize how many specialized jobs there were for librarians. . . . I didn't know they were so involved in so many different activities and that there were so many with their own specialties." As the fellows developed an awareness of the profession, they began to identify with why the librarians spoke so highly of their profession: "Many of the reasons [librarians] listed for loving their jobs are the criteria that I am looking for in my own career search as well." Another concisely wrote, "I've come to understand the role of librarians in educating users."

Although some applicants wrote in their applications that they were considering librarianship because they did not want to teach in their disciplines, they learned to expand their understanding of teaching to include research instruction and reference interactions. One fellow commented, "This and other micro-teaching experiences throughout my fellowship redefined my notion of pedagogical practices and helped me understand that teaching exists in many forms."

Multiple measures that emulate the standard annual evaluation mechanisms of librarians—teaching/librarianship, research, and service—are used to evaluate the fellows. While mentors write evaluative summaries of their fellows' accomplishments, the fellows themselves explore their future career goals in a Socratic portfolio. The Socratic portfolio emphasizes the preparation of graduate students for their academic careers and helps them become "quick starters," those incoming faculty who actually succeed and attain tenure. This experience helps graduate students understand the faculty evaluation process.

Golde and Dore found in their study that many graduate students lack effective mentoring on career options. Specifically designed to address this need, the fellowship inspired one fellow to write: "My mentor was open and willing to discuss my development and personal interests. . . . Sadly, I never felt the same depth of commitment and support and honesty toward my professional growth from my department faculty." Overwhelmingly, fellows reported that they were able to integrate their subject/language knowledge into their work in the libraries: "It gave me confidence that I could use my subject and language skills as a librarian and this was something that I was not sure about before the fellowship." Another wrote:

> My personal interest in the field has grown, and I have spoken with a number of CU-Boulder Libraries faculty about their perspectives and experiences as librarians. All the librarians I have spoken with have been so overwhelmingly positive and delighted with their jobs that I feel very motivated to pursue librarianship as a career.

Only two of the nine fellows are not pursuing academic librarianship as a career at this time. Of those who are, one is already enrolled in a distance program; three more have been accepted; one has recently applied, while the final two will apply as they near completion of their current graduate program. Of the two who are not pursuing a career in academic librarianship, one has begun a career in translation while the other is working in a public library.

These students now understand and appreciate academic librarianship as a career, are aware of the tenure model as it applies to librarians, and are aware of concrete ways to incorporate their subject and language expertise in a new career. It is my hope that the achievements of this program can serve as inspiration for the development of similar programs at other institutions. Although the minimal elements of such a program are financial support for the graduate students and dedicated librarian-mentors, what really allows this program to succeed is the collaboration between the library and the Graduate Teacher Program. Specifically, the expertise and experience of the graduate student teaching and professional development program on campus can provide an experienced framework for graduate students' professional development and greatly enhance the entire experience. The ultimate outcome of such collaboration can provide future colleagues in the academy who can work together for the betterment of both academic departments and academic libraries.

WORKS CITED

Association of College and Research Libraries. "ARL Academy: Careers in Academic and Research Libraries." http://www.arl.org/arlacademy/. Accessed March 11, 2006.

Berry, John N. 2003. "But Don't Call 'em Librarians." *Library Journal* 128, no. 18 (November): 34–36.

Council on Library and Information Resources. "Postdoctoral Fellowship in Scholarly Information Resources." http://www.clir.org/fellowships/postdoc/postdoc.html. Accessed March 11, 2006.

Golde, Chris M., and Timothy M. Dore. 2001. "At Cross Purposes: What the Experiences of Doctoral Students Reveal about Doctoral Education." Report prepared for the Pew Charitable Trusts, Philadelphia, Pa. http://www.phd-survey.org. Accessed March 11, 2006.

Hardesty, Larry L. 2002. "Future of Academic/Research Librarians: A Period of Transition—to What?" *Portal: Libraries and the Academy* 2, no. 1 (January): 79–97.

Hewitt, Joe A., Barbara B. Moran, and Mari E. Marsh. 2003. "Finding our Replacements: One Institution's Approach to Recruiting Academic Librarians." *Portal: Libraries and the Academy* 3, no. 2 (April): 179–189.

Hisle, W. Lee. 2002. "Top Issues Facing Academic Libraries: A Report of the Focus on the Future Task Force." *College and Research Libraries News* 63, no. 10 (November): 714–715, 730. http://www.ala.org/ala/acrl/acrlpubs/crlnews/ backissues2002/novmonth/ topissuesfacing.htm. Accessed March 11, 2006.

Kellsey, Charlene. 2003. "Crisis in Foreign Language Expertise in Research Libraries: How Do We Fill This Gap?" *College and Research Libraries News* 64, no. 6 (June): 391–397.

Millet, Michelle S., and Liza Posas. 2005. "Recruitment and Retention of New Academic Librarians in Their Own Words: Who They Are and What They Want." http:// www.trinity.edu/mmillet/professional/NewLibProject.htm. Accessed March 11, 2006.

University of South Florida. School of Library and Information Science. "USF School of Library and Information Science is Recruiting Applicants for ALSTARS: Academic Librarians for Tomorrow's Academic Researchers." http://www.cas.usf.edu/lis/alstars/grant.html. Accessed March 11, 2006.

Yale University Library. "Yale University Library Offers Graduate Internship Opportunity for 2005–06." http://www.library.yale.edu/lhr/jobs/intern/ gradinternship.html. Accessed March 11, 2006.

Library Resources:
The Canadian Experience

15. Latin American Collections in Two Montreal Universities: A Preliminary Survey

Juanita Jara de Súmar

Montreal is the largest city in the Province of Quebec, which is located on the eastern side of Canada. Quebec was discovered and colonized by the French in 1534 with the name of Nouvelle France. It kept the name until 1763, when the Treaty of Paris gave the colony to Britain and then it became the Province of Quebec. Although under British government, the right of Quebecers of French origin to use the French language was recognized by the Quebec Act in 1774. Later, as large waves of British immigrants arrived in the 1800s, more English was spoken. Yet French-speaking Quebecers kept the right to have all official documents in both English and French.

In 1871, about one-third of the inhabitants of the four original provinces that formed the Canadian Confederation in 1967 were French and most of the rest were of British origin. By 1996, a little over 23 percent declared French as their mother tongue, 59 percent declared English, and the rest of Canadians claimed other languages. French-speaking Canadians are concentrated in Quebec, New Brunswick, Ontario, and parts of Manitoba.[1]

In Quebec, increasing immigration and the decline in recent years of the birthrate among Quebecers raised serious concerns among the French-speaking population about the survival of the French language in an English-speaking continent. Therefore, when the Parti Québécois came into power in the province, they proposed a Charter of the French Language, which was adopted in August 1977 and is usually referred in English as Bill 101. The charter made the Quebec province officially unilingual in French. As a consequence, all arriving immigrants had the right to apply for free French language courses, and their children were required to attend public schools in French. But decrees cannot change reality. There were many unilingual Anglophones in Montreal in 1977, and there seem to be many multilingual Montrealers today. Also, although immigrant children must attend primary and secondary school in the French sector, they are still allowed to apply to colleges and universities in the English sector.

I have chosen to look at Latin American immigration to Quebec starting in 1974, with the arrival of a large number of immigrants from Chile. Table 1 shows immigration from selected Latin American countries to Quebec between 1974 and 1996, the latest year with complete immigration tables to which I have access.[2]

Table 1: Immigration from Latin America to Quebec 1974–1996— Selected Countries

	Argentina	Chile	Colombia	El Salvador	Guatemala	Mexico	Peru
1974	328	**619**	**339**	132	95	102	166
1975	190	**630**	**297**	82	77	93	124
1976	231	**520**	**293**	93	69	119	148
1977	290	358	199	59	43	128	132
1978	334	442	159	55	50	96	116
1979	154	350	135	63	23	89	98
1980	104	353	75	73	72	71	112
1981	125	248	137	147	51	65	150
1982	199	331	132	**504**	51	91	185
1983	109	315	100	**902**	117	93	122
1984	69	213	93	**739**	320	102	119
1985	45	164	61	**534**	443	66	131
1986	65	229	89	**714**	393	124	310
1987	108	378	95	**844**	319	170	344
1988	137	311	106	452	104	149	190
1989	154	306	109	410	162	205	296
1990	282	**528**	96	**1,110**	338	296	478
1991	343	**959**	177	**2,433**	963	399	665
1992	453	**518**	198	**1,296**	696	359	720
1993	324	287	99	**730**	394	259	638
1994	119	129	100	339	256	162	477
1995	102	73	118	166	211	140	401
1996	85	84	96	179	281	212	506
Total	4,350	8,345	3,303	12,056	5,528	3,590	6,628

Source: Citizenship and Immigration Canada, "Country of Last Permanent Residence by Province or Territory of Intended Destination and Gender" [table], *Citizenship and Immigration Statistics (1966–1996),* http://www.cic.gc.ca/english/pub/index-2.html#statistics.

This table shows that immigration from Chile predominated in the late 1970s, followed by Colombia. All through the 1980s and beginning of the 1990s, the largest groups of Latin American immigrants came mainly from El Salvador and Guatemala. And finally, there was a large increase in immigration from Peru after 1990. Argentina and Mexico, the other two countries with large immigration figures, show a more steady flow, with only a moderate increase in the 1990s.

From here on I have mainly anecdotal evidence. Early immigrants from Chile to Quebec in the 1970s seem to have been absorbed by the French sector as a result of Bill 101. I have noticed among those I know that their children speak fairly good Spanish, but they are not comfortable reading or writing in that language. Both parents and children favored francophone colleges and universities. The same pattern seems to have occurred with immigrants from El Salvador and Guatemala. On the other hand, immigrants from Mexico and Argentina, and some from Colombia, can be found in both the English and French sectors.

Recent immigrant children from most of the Latin American countries in the list, and from other parts of the world, seem to be trilingual, and many opt for English higher education, rather than French, in spite of having attended primary and secondary school in French. So far I have not found figures showing how many of the younger generation can properly read and write in Spanish. I know that some years ago there was great concern among the Latin American teachers of Spanish in Montreal about the level of knowledge of the Spanish language shown by the younger generation of Latin Americans living in Montreal. Unfortunately their plans to provide Spanish courses for native speakers never materialized. And it is obvious that there is a great degree of code-switching: regardless of the language Latin Americans are speaking, one can hear "foreign words" interspersed in their speech all the time. Yet Birgit Mertz-Baumgartner afffirms, "En comparación con la producción literaria de otras minorías culturales en Canadá, los autores latinoamericanos se destacan por su fidelidad al español, que sigue siendo la primera lengua de escritura." [3] This statement may not hold true for long regarding the younger generations.

The most recent *Facts and Figures* of Citizenship and Immigration Canada seems to confirm my perception of multilingualism in Quebec. Table 2, extracted from this website, shows that only 11.7 percent of immigrants coming to Quebec from all parts of the world in 1995 knew both English and French, but in 2004 this percentage had increased to 33.3 percent. Some of those immigrants can be seen at McGill University these days. The same chart also shows that the percentage of immigrants with no knowledge of English or French has gone down in the same period from 41.2 percent to 27 percent. [4]

Because of this "linguistic divide," there are universities for each of Canada's official languages in Montreal. McGill and Concordia offer instruction in English. Université de Montréal (UdeM) and Université de Québec à Montréal (UQUAM) teach in French. Immigrants and children of immigrants can choose among them. McGill and Université de Montréal are the oldest universities in the city, and they both have a Centre for Latin American Studies and a Department of Hispanic Studies. This is why I have chosen them as the starting point for this study.

Table 2: Canada—Permanent Residents by Province or Territory and Language Ability

	English	French	Both French and English	Neither	Language Ability Not Stated	Quebec Total
			Number			
1995	5,893	6,919	3,191	11,212	0	27,215
1996	6,783	8,171	3,422	11,421	0	29,797
1997	5,983	6,927	3,013	12,011	1	27,935
1998	4,691	7,143	3,544	11,243	0	26,621
1999	5,548	8,092	4,429	11,091	0	29,160
2000	6,009	8,733	5,968	11,791	0	32,501
2001	6,011	9,549	8,110	13,923	0	37,593
2002	5,948	9,170	9,286	13,181	0	37,585
2003	6,638	8,614	11,487	12,817	0	39,556
2004	7,838	9,732	14,743	11,926	0	44,239

	English	French	Both French and English	Neither	Language Ability Not Stated	Quebec Total
			Percentage Distribution			
1995	21.7	25.4	11.7	41.2	0.0	100.0
1996	22.8	27.4	11.5	38.3	0.0	100.0
1997	21.4	24.8	10.8	43.0	0.0	100.0
1998	17.6	26.8	13.3	42.2	0.0	100.0
1999	19.0	27.8	15.2	38.0	0.0	100.0
2000	18.5	26.9	18.4	36.3	0.0	100.0
2001	16.0	25.4	21.6	37.0	0.0	100.0
2002	15.8	24.4	24.7	35.1	0.0	100.0
2003	16.8	21.8	29.0	32.4	0.0	100.0
2004	17.7	22.0	33.3	27.0	0.0	100.0

Source: Citizenship and Immigration Canada, *Facts and Figures 2004: Immigration Overview—Permanent Residents,* http://www.cic.gc.ca/english/pub/facts2004/permanent/19a.html.

McGill University

McGill University received its charter in 1821. According to *McGill Facts 2005–2006,* there are currently 32,787 students.[5] Only 52.9 percent of them have English as their mother tongue, followed by French with 18.7 percent, and other languages with 28.4 percent. Except for the languages departments, all instruction is given in English, although francophone students are allowed to write exams, and sometimes papers, in French.

The Faculty of Arts with 7,268 students has a Hispanic studies department, which was created in 1939, with undergraduate and graduate programs. By 1974 the courses content had almost the same ratio Spain/Latin America that it has today. The current course calendar for this department lists thirty-two courses, fourteen of them on Spanish-American literature and culture. It also offers two Hispanic civilization courses for the arts students (150 students per course). It is interesting to note that although in the beginning there were professors from other Latin American countries, all the Latin American professors teaching in this department since 1974 came from Argentina, just by chance. Another interesting aspect is that there is currently an increase in the number of Latin American students enrolled at the graduate level. Of the 17 current graduate students, 9 come from Latin America.[6]

Other departments also offer Latin American courses, in addition to those of the Hispanic studies department. Anthropology offers a seminar on Contemporary Latin American Culture and Society; history has four courses; and political science has one course. Seminars in economics and in the International Development Studies program also touch on Latin America as one of the areas of study. All the departments mentioned above have at least one professor doing research on Latin America. To them one must add seven of the researchers in the Centre for Developing-Area Studies, whose projects are related to this geographic area.[7]

There is also an interdisciplinary Latin-American and Caribbean Studies Program with approximately 40 students. This interdisciplinary program was established in 1971. It offers research seminars and requires an independent research project.[8] Finally there is the McGill School of Environment, which offers a semester in Panama or Barbados.[9]

Université de Montréal

The Université de Montréal opened in 1878. It currently has more than 55,000 students. La Faculté des arts et des sciences has a Department of Literature and Modern Languages since 1989, and, within this department, a section of Hispanic studies. They offer a similar number of courses as McGill, but there are some courses that cover both Spain and Latin America. They also have several translation courses, as well as advanced studies of the Spanish language.[10] The history department offers five courses on Latin America, the anthropology department has two courses, political sciences three courses, and economics one course.

The Université de Montréal has a research group on Latin America, founded in 1980. Their main aim is to foster exchange and close relationships among those working on Latin American topics.[11]

Given the similarity in the courses offered due to the fact that each university is serving a different linguistic population, the questions to ask are the following: Is there any special effort being made to foster the development of a Latin American collection in the library of each university? Should the Latin American collections of both universities duplicate or complement each other? Is any coordination taking place?

It is too early in the research to be able to answer these questions. The methodology employed so far may need to be examined to assess if the results really reflect what I am trying to find. Maybe in a future report, some of the preliminary findings will be contradicted. Still, I wanted to bring this research to this event, and I will be grateful of any input I receive.

This paper offers more information about the McGill University Library, because of easier access to information from my university. Also, I worked using the respective OPACs. Because I am much more familiar with the McGill catalogue, I was able to refine my results better.

Before I start comparing the Latin American collections of the two universities, I would like to point out that there are two librarians of Latin American origin at McGill. Neither of the two was hired because of being Latin American or because they speak Spanish. Subject and language responsibilities came later. I started as a reference and instruction librarian, and because of my language and subject knowledge, I have been offering workshops in Spanish to the students in the Hispanic studies department since 2001. When the merger of the collections and reference departments of the Humanities and Social Sciences Library happened last year, it was only natural that I should become the liaison librarian for the Hispanic studies department. The second Latin American librarian works part-time and is the liaison librarian for Jewish studies. She was born in Mexico and had to do her librarianship degree all over again at the Université de Montréal.

At this point I only have data for the McGill University Library regarding the development and size of the collection. Comparable data for Université de Montréal will be gathered in the next phase.

McGill reports a collection of 3,568,651 volumes, including bound periodicals. At McGill, materials related to Latin America are bought by the fourteen various libraries, but mainly by the Humanities and Social Sciences Library (HSSL). All the numbers given here are for the Latin American holding in this library. I estimate that about 75 percent of subject headings related to Latin America represent materials in HSSL.[12] But there is no librarian whose main responsibility is selecting Latin American materials. Librarians responsible for history, political science, anthropology, economics, and Hispanic studies all request materials in their respective areas of responsibility, but do not keep separate figures by geographic area for their expenditure.

Information provided by the collections coordinator of HSSL shows an increased interest in the last four years that relates to monographs only, journals being bought on a central budget. The budget for Hispanic Literature and Culture (Spanish and Latin American) has been about Can$36,000 each year. Additionally, and for two consecutive years, 2001–2002 and 2002–2003, there was a special fund of Can\$25,000 for interdisciplinary studies in Latin America. My Latin American colleague, who was attached to the collections department during those years, was asked to be involved in the selection of materials for these special funds.

Besides these basic budgets, there were other acquisitions for films and special items, most of them in microform. Some of the notable acquisitions are the following: International Population Census, 1945–1967, Latin America and the Caribbean; North American Congress on Latin America (NACLA) Archive of Latin Americana (volumes on Chile, El Salvador, Guatemala, Mexico, Cuba, Colombia, and Nicaragua); Princeton University Latin American pamphlet collection, Colombia; CIA Research Reports for Latin America; Digital National Security Archive (sections on Cuba, El Salvador, and Nicaragua); U.S. State Department, Confidential Central files for Argentina internal and foreign affairs, 1945–1959; and Latin American pamphlets from the Yale University Library, 1600–1900 (covers Mexico, Peru, Central and South America).

The sections of the collection that are analyzed here are history and literature, where shelf counts by class number are easy to delimit. The shelf lists that I had access to make separate entries for each physical volume, not for distinct works, and they include duplicate copies, but exclude bound periodicals. Even if the numbers are not definitive, I think they give a good indication of the structure and volume of the collection in the two areas listed above.

Table 3 provides a breakdown of book volumes by country/region in LC class numbers F1201–F3799. It can be seen that in this area McGill has a small collection of 8,817 volumes. Individual Central American countries have been grouped with the general works on that region given that numbers are fairly small for each country. Non-Spanish-speaking countries are excluded, but Brazil has been included.

Mexico is the country better covered, with 22.6 percent of the collection and together with Central America represent almost 40 percent of the collection, followed by works on Latin America in general 16.8 percent, Brazil 7.74 percent, Peru 6.91 percent, Argentina 6.86 percent, and Cuba 5.55 percent. The next phase will have to determine the criteria that have been taken into account when selecting more materials for certain countries than others.

Table 4 offers the same kind of data as table 3, but this time for literature. In the PQ7081–8897 there are 12,012 volumes. This time Argentina is on top, by far, with 25.33 percent, followed by Mexico 17.34 percent, Latin America in general 9.04 percent, Central America 8.96 percent, Chile 8.60 percent, Cuba 6.84 percent, Uruguay 5.54 percent, Peru 5.44 percent, and Colombia 4.87 percent. Brazil is not included, because there are no courses being offered on Brazilian literature. I hope that for phase two of this study, comparable data will be available for the collection of Université de Montréal.

Table 3: Total Volume Count for Call Numbers F1201–F3799—
McGill University Library

Mexico	1,993
Latin America, General	1,481
Central America	1,054
Cuba	490
Puerto Rico	169
South America	443
Colombia	269
Venezuela	248
Brazil	683
Paraguay	78
Uruguay	58
Argentina	605
Chile	342
Bolivia	142
Peru	610
Ecuador	152
Total	8,817

Table 4: Total Volume Count for Call Numbers PQ7081–PQ8897—
McGill University Library

Latin America, General	1,087
Mexico	2,084
Cuba	822
Central America*	1,077
South America	17
Argentina	3,043
Bolivia	132
Chile	1,034
Colombia	586
Ecuador	332
Paraguay	82
Peru	654
Uruguay	666
Venezuela	396
Total	12,012

*Includes Puerto Rico

The first step to compare the Latin American collections of McGill and Université de Montréal for the first phase was to count the number of items that are retrieved by doing subject/keyword searches in the holding of the respective humanities and social sciences libraries, using the OPACs. The original intention was to do two separate counts, one for the name of the country and one for the adjective of the country. But there were some truncation problems with countries that have very short names. Comparing subject heading in French and English proved to be challenging with regard to adjectives (singular, plural, masculine, feminine). Therefore in the end the keywords used were the truncated names of the Latin American countries to get both the name and the adjective of each country. The results were then broken down by language: Spanish, English, French, and others.

This comparative study supposes that both libraries use centrally produced complete MARC cataloguing records and that they apply the same level of specificity in assigning subject headings to the items. Sampling will be needed to determine if this is true.

McGill Libraries have an Aleph catalogue (http://aleph.mcgill.ca/F) and its implementation provides great flexibility for cross-searching result sets, which yields very accurate results as long as the language code in the MARC records is correct. I found the Université de Montréal's catalogue (http://www-atrium.bib.umontreal.ca:8000/) not as helpful and some results seem to indicate that some records lacked language coding. Unfortunately this catalogue does not provide access to the MARC record.

First results indicate that the total number of hits for McGill is more than 65 percent higher than for Université de Montréal. This may, of course, indicate differences in subject heading policies, which will have to be analyzed later. As expected, McGill's results were stronger in English language materials (63 percent), but Université de Montréal's results were surprisingly low in French (14.66 percent). In fact many more results in English were obtained (44.13 percent). By comparison, McGill's French language collection gave expected low results (3.54 percent). Results from the Spanish language collections of both libraries were very similar though: 34.13 percent for McGill and 32.53 percent for Université de Montréal (see table 5).

Looking at individual searches, "Peru" in Spanish gives higher results than English or French at Université de Montréal, and they are also higher than McGill's results. At McGill, Argentina has more hits in Spanish. For all the other individual countries, English produces more results. I will also want to explore further the use of Spanish American/Hispano-Américaine, which is mainly found in literature.

I feel fairly confident that the results from the McGill catalogue in the *Other* column are correct. They represent titles mainly in Italian and German, but also Portuguese, Yiddish, and a few other languages. Results from the Université de Montréal, on the other hand, need to be looked at individually, as a quick glance at the titles indicated that they were either in Spanish or English. This task is left for phase two.

Table 5: Major Latin American Countries Represented in the
McGill and Université de Montréal Humanities and Social Sciences
Collections—By Geographic Subject Headings

		Total Hits	Spanish	English	French	Other*
Latin America	McGill	4,335	1,233	3,068	190	78
	UdeM	*3,242*	*797*	*1,634*	*501*	*310*
Spanish American	McGill	1,141	777	395	30	16
Hispano-Americaine	*UdeM*	*439*	*243*	*97*	*34*	*65*
Central America	McGill	1,120	84	1,005	38	11
	UdeM	*577*	*68*	*379*	*87*	*43*
South America	McGill	1,510	310	1,067	120	54
	UdeM	*979*	*160*	*526*	*177*	*116*
Mexico	McGill	4,990	1,547	3,371	122	67
	UdeM	*3,624*	*1,233*	*1,651*	*503*	*237*
Argentina	McGill	1,480	837	583	33	40
	UdeM	*917*	*449*	*289*	*105*	*74*
Cuba	McGill	1,255	403	816	41	19
	UdeM	*705*	*277*	*260*	*105*	*63*
Peru	McGill	1,231	401	742	46	76
	UdeM	*1,140*	*509*	*396*	*149*	*86*
Chile	McGill	939	372	524	37	26
	UdeM	*658*	*205*	*259*	*115*	*79*
Colombia	McGill	698	343	353	12	5
	UdeM	*510*	*182*	*209*	*82*	*37*
Venezuela	McGill	560	287	261	11	7
	UdeM	*333*	*152*	*116*	*40*	*25*
Uruguay	McGill	1,231	401	742	46	76
	UdeM	*265*	*81*	*93*	*66*	*25*
Total	McGill	20,490	6,995	12,927	726	475
	UdeM	*13,389*	*4,356*	*5,909*	*1,964*	*1,160*

*Languages are identified in the McGill OPAC, and presumably in the UdeM too, fol-
lowing the coding in the MARC cataloguing record. The totals do not add up because there
are some bilingual and multilingual records. The *Other* column for McGill University
represents materials in other languages, mainly Italian and German. For Université de
Montréal, *Other* represents the balance of cataloguing records not coded for any of the
three languages, although a quick glance at the titles did not reveal other languages than
the three analyzed here. We assume that there must be some incomplete MARC records
which lack language code.

Because individual literary works do not have subject headings, I decided
next to analyze the collections by looking at a sample of major Latin American
authors, searching them as authors of the works *(by)* and as subjects in critical
works about them *(about)*. The selection of names was done somewhat arbi-
trarily based on the Hispanic studies course descriptions and the strength of the

McGill collection as shown by the shelf list. All the Nobel prizes were included, as well as authors representing the major countries. A selection of women writers was also included to reflect current interest found in the curriculum.

Two separate tables have been produced, one for each university library (see tables 6 and 7). Totals have been added for general reference about the importance of the authors, but cannot be taken as absolute values, given that cataloguing practice makes the same work appear in *by* and *about* when some original works and critical studies appear in the same volume, and may be different in the two universities. Again, language results follow the coding in the MARC records. Some works in the McGill catalogue are found to be coded for several languages when they contain one poem or short essay in another language. This produces multiple hits in the language counts. Lastly, the *Other* column for Université de Montréal reflects the balance of the total, which may simply reflect lack of coding, as there were no visible titles in other languages.

Works *by* more recent authors (Fuentes, Paz, Poniatowska, Vargas Llosa, etc.) in the Spanish language are equally represented in both collections, but there are more works *about* those same authors at McGill. There is no surprise in finding that earlier authors such as Borges, Mistral, and Darío are better represented (both *by* and *about*) at McGill. The number of translations of primary literary works to the respective official language of the university is comparable: 26.53 percent of the results of works by an author was in English at McGill and 23.98 percent was in French at Université de Montréal. Both libraries have a small percentage of translations in the other official language, 2.27 percent in French at McGill and 3.84 percent in English at Université de Montréal (see table 8). Works in other languages are very few at McGill and, as already mentioned, the Université de Montréal's number needs reviewing.

Results for searches *about* the authors show a different picture. First, McGill is comparatively stronger in terms of size. Second, Université de Montréal has a stronger collection in English than in French. Publication patterns will need to be analyzed to determine the level of coverage in the French language.

Much work needs to be done yet. The second phase will aim at obtaining comparable data from Université de Montréal and expanding the analysis of total number of volumes to other relevant call numbers, particularly in the social sciences. Regarding the literature section, some research needs to be done to determine the top authors represented in the collection at Université de Montréal. Duplicates need to be removed and distortions introduced by the multiple language coding in the MARC record for minor language presence need to be eliminated. The authors who are currently studied at the undergraduate level at both universities need to be found and how much overlap needs to be determined. Maybe even looking at the interlibrary loan requests will determine how well each library is meeting the research needs of the users.

Table 6: Representative Latin American Literary Authors in the
McGill Library Collection

		Total Hits	Spanish	English	French	Other
Sor Juana Inés	by	37	33	10	0	0
	about	78	59	19	1	0
Carlos Fuentes	by	80	53	28	0	0
	about	39	27	12	0	0
Octavio Paz	by	111	80	41	5	(m)
	about	59	39	19	1	1
Elena Poniatowska	by	33	27	8	0	0
	about	8	3	5	0	0
José Martí	by	51	45	8	0	0
	about	95	81	13	0	0
Alejo Carpentier	by	50	39	11	0	0
	about	69	44	17	6	3
Rubén Darío	by	79	76	5	0	0
	about	113	100	14	1	1
Miguel A. Asturias	by	52	39	12	1	0
	about	40	34	4	3	0
Jorge L. Borges	by	180	126	47	9	7
	about	261	161	82	15	11
Julio Cortázar	by	89	71	21	0	0
	about	86	60	25	3	0
Victoria Ocampo	by	31	26	5	0	0
	about	13	9	4	0	0
Cristina Peri Rossi	by	19	16	3	0	0
	about	6	3	3	0	0
Gabriela Mistral	by	41	32	8	3	0
	about	47	38	8	2	0
Pablo Neruda	by	131	102	54	5	1
	about	117	89	31	1	3
Isabel Allende	by	30	14	16	0	0
	about	23	8	17	0	0
Gabriel García M.	by	75	52	23	0	0
	about	133	86	44	2	5
Jorge Icaza	by	12	11	1	0	0
	about	3	2	1	0	0
José M. Arguedas	by	32	28	4	0	0
	about	36	32	4	0	0
César Vallejo	by	53	46	9	2	1
	about	75	67	7	3	1
Mario Vargas Llosa	by	88	61	24	4	0
	about	67	38	27	4	2
Total by		1,274	977	338	29	9
Total about		1,368	980	356	42	27
Total		2,642	1,957	694	71	36

Table 7: Representative Latin American Literary Authors in the Université de Montréal Library Collection

		Total Hits	Spanish	English	French	Other
Sor Juana Inés	by	24	19	2	3	0
	about	*40*	*32*	*4*	*3*	*1*
Carlos Fuentes	by	80	51	2	24	3
	about	*32*	*19*	*8*	*4*	*1*
Octavio Paz	by	111	63	8	31	9
	about	*27*	*15*	*4*	*7*	*1*
Elena Poniatowska	by	32	29	1	1	1
	about	*2*	*1*	*1*	*0*	*0*
José Martí	by	29	23	2	3	1
	about	*43*	*33*	*3*	*3*	*4*
Alejo Carpentier	by	50	30	3	13	4
	about	*36*	*19*	*9*	*7*	*1*
Rubén Darío	by	26	24	0	2	0
	about	*43*	*37*	*5*	*1*	*0*
Miguel A. Asturias	by	47	25	1	17	4
	about	*23*	*16*	*0*	*6*	*1*
Jorge L. Borges	by	91	45	5	30	11
	about	*119*	*48*	*27*	*33*	*11*
Julio Cortázar	by	71	50	1	15	5
	about	*46*	*28*	*12*	*5*	*1*
Victoria Ocampo	by	4	1	1	2	0
	about	*3*	*1*	*0*	*2*	*0*
Cristina Peri Rossi	by	13	12	0	1	0
	about	*1*	*0*	*1*	*0*	*0*
Gabriela Mistral	by	12	9	1	2	0
	about	*15*	*12*	*2*	*1*	*0*
Pablo Neruda	by	78	49	2	17	10
	about	*35*	*16*	*7*	*7*	*5*
Isabel Allende	by	21	13	0	7	1
	about	*5*	*3*	*2*	*0*	*0*
Gabriel García M.	by	64	40	3	19	2
	about	*61*	*28*	*24*	*4*	*5*
Jorge Icaza	by	7	7	0	0	0
	about	*0*	*0*	*0*	*0*	*0*
José M. Arguedas	by	26	23	1	2	0
	about	*25*	*23*	*1*	*1*	*0*
César Vallejo	by	29	29	0	0	0
	about	*45*	*37*	*3*	*3*	*2*
Mario Vargas Llosa	by	73	42	1	24	6
	about	*39*	*22*	*10*	*5*	*2*
Total by		888	584	34	213	57
Total about		*640*	*390*	*123*	*92*	*35*
Total		1,528	974	157	305	92

Table 8: Representative Latin American Literary Authors—Language Percentage Distribution*

		Total Hits	Spanish	English	French	Other
By authors	McGill	1,274	76.68	26.53	2.27	0.70
	UdeM	888	65.76	3.84	23.98	6.40
About authors	*McGill*	*1,368*	*71.63*	*26.02*	*3.07*	*1.97*
	UdeM	*640*	*60.93*	*19.21*	*14.37*	*546.00*

*Total is greater than 100% for McGill because bilingual and multilingual works produced hits under each of the languages.

The first phase seems to confirm that there is an overlap in the Spanish language material, which is expected and considered normal, particularly in literature. For the second phase, it will be necessary to analyze the methodology to determine if it is really going to give accurate data for comparison. Then it will be possible to determine how well both collections complement each other.

NOTES

1. Office of the Commissioner of Official Languages, "Language Policy," rev. by Barbara J. Burnaby, in *Canadian Encyclopedia* (Toronto: McClelland and Stewart, 2002).

2. Citizenship and Immigration Canada, "Country of Last Permanent Residence by Province or Territory of Intended Destination and Gender" [table], *Citizenship and Immigration Statistics (1966–1996)*, http://www.cic.gc.ca/english/pub/index-2.html#statistics (accessed February 8, 2006).

3. Birgit Mertz-Baumgartner, "Imágenes del Exilio y de la Migración en la Literatura Latinoamericana en Canadá," in *Coloquio Internacional Migración y Literatura en el Mundo Hispánico,* ed. Irene Andrés-Suárez (Madrid: Editorial Verbum, 2002).

4. Citizenship and Immigration Canada, "Permanent Residents by Province or Territory and Language Ability" [table], *Facts and Figures 2004: Immigration Overview—Permanent Residents,* http://www.cic.gc.ca/english/pub/facts2004/index.html (accessed February 8, 2006).

5. McGill University, *McGill Facts 2005–2006,* http://www.mcgill.ca/facts2005-06/ (accessed February 8, 2006).

6. Department of Hispanic Studies, McGill University, http://www.arts.mcgill.ca/hispanic/ (accessed February 11, 2006).

7. Centre for Developing-Area Studies, McGill University, http://www.mcgill.ca/cdas/ (accessed February 11, 2006).

8. Latin-American and Caribbean Studies, McGill University, http://www.mcgill.ca/lacs/ (accessed February 11, 2006).

9. McGill School of Environment, McGill University, Field Study Semesters, http://www.mcgill.ca/mse/programs/fieldstudies/ (accessed February 14, 2006).

10. Faculté des arts et des sciences, Université de Montréal, Secteur de lettres et sciences humaines, Département De Littératures Et Langues Modernes, http://www.littlm.umontreal.ca/ (accessed February 11, 2006).

11. Groupe de recherche sur l'Amérique latine (GRAL), Université de Montreal, http://www.recherche.umontreal.ca/pub/unite_affichage.asp?unite_rech_c=117 (accessed February 11, 2006).

12. Elaine Yarosky, 2006.

BIBLIOGRAPHY OF TABLES

Citizenship and Immigration Canada. "Country of Last Permanent Residence by Province or Territory of Intended Destination and Gender" [table]. *Citizenship and Immigration Statistics (1966–1996)*. In *Research and Statistics,* http://www.cic.gc.ca/english/pub/index-2.html#statistics. Accessed February 8, 2006.

———. "Permanent Residents by Province or Territory and Language Ability" [table]. *Facts and Figures 2004: Immigration Overview—Permanent Residents.* http://www.cic.gc.ca/english/pub/facts2004/index.html. Accessed February 8, 2006.

McGill University. *McGill Facts 2005–2006.* http://www.mcgill.ca/facts2005-06/. Accessed February 27, 2006.

McGill University. Centre for Developing-Area Studies. Centre for Developing-Area Studies. http://www.mcgill.ca/cdas/. Accessed February 11, 2006.

McGill University. Department of Hispanic Studies. Department of Hispanic Studies at McGill University. 2005. http://www.arts.mcgill.ca/hispanic/. Accessed February 11, 2006.

McGill University. Latin-American and Caribbean Studies. Latin-American and Caribbean Studies. http://www.mcgill.ca/lacs/. Accessed February 11, 2006.

McGill University. McGill School of Environment. Field Study Semesters. http://www.mcgill.ca/mse/programs/fieldstudies/. Accessed February 14, 2006.

Mertz-Baumgartner, Birgit. "Imágenes del Exilio y de la Migración en la Literatura Latinoamericana en Canadá." In *Coloquio Internacional Migración y Literatura en el Mundo Hispánico. Université de Neuchatel,* edited by Irene Andrés-Suárez. Madrid: Editorial Verbum, 2002. Pp. 280–293.

Office of the Commissioner of Official Languages. "Language Policy." Revised by Barbara J. Burnaby. In *Canadian Encyclopedia.* Toronto: McClelland and Stewart, 2002. Pp. 1293–1295.

Université de Montréal. Faculté des arts et des sciences. Secteur de lettres et sciences humaines. Département de Littératures et Langues Modernes. 2005. http://www.littlm.umontreal.ca/. Accessed February 11, 2006.

Université de Montréal. Groupe de recherche sur l'Amérique latine (GRAL). Groupe De Recherche Sur L'amérique Latine (GRAL). 2003. http://www.recherche.umontreal.ca/pub/unite_affichage.asp?unite_rech_c=117. Accessed February 14, 2006.

16. Spanish in Saskatchewan: Newcomers Influencing the Development of Curricula and Library Collections in Latin American and Iberian Studies at the University of Saskatchewan

Donna Canevari de Paredes

Saskatchewan: The Province and Its Peoples

The Province of Saskatchewan celebrated its centennial in 2005. Unlike eastern North America, and also much of Central and South America, immigration to and settlement of the Canadian Prairies happened almost entirely in the late-nineteenth and twentieth centuries. Canada acquired from the Hudson's Bay Company the western interior of what was then known as British North America in 1870. The land was an immense tract, which the new government of Canada initially intended to govern as a colony. Political events such as the Red River Resistance in 1870 and the North-West Rebellion in 1885 (both of which concerned native and Métis discontent and desire for national self-determination), however, helped to persuade the federal government to change its plans and bring this vast parcel of land into the confederation of eastern provinces that from 1867 was known as Canada. Manitoba became a province in 1870 and British Columbia in 1871, while what became Saskatchewan (and Alberta) in the twentieth century was first known as the North-West Territories.[1]

One can divide the population of what was formed from the North-West Territories into the twentieth-century Province of Saskatchewan into two groups: indigenous peoples and newcomers.

There is evidence that indigenous peoples, also known as native, aboriginal or First Nations peoples, have lived in the geographic area since 10,000 B.C., initially as nomadic tribes and hunter-gatherers. With the settlement of British North America, the First Nations entered into treaties, first with the British Crown and after 1867 with the newly formed government of Canada, and began settling on reserves.[2] Presently, the Federation of Saskatchewan Indian Nations represents seventy-four First Nations in Saskatchewan.[3]

The first Europeans in the area were explorers who came in the late-seventeenth century in search of fur trade routes. Newcomers as settlers, however, have immigrated to Saskatchewan only since the nineteenth century.

Indeed, within the first ten years of the province's incorporation, the population nearly doubled thanks to homesteaders attracted by inexpensive land. Those first settlers mainly originated from the British Isles, but were followed by other European immigrants of German, Irish, Russian, Ukrainian, and other European origins, as well as those Europeans from various countries who migrated for religious reasons, such as the Doukhobors, Jews, and Mennonites. In addition there were Chinese immigrants, many of whom were initially hired as workers for the Canadian Pacific Railway in the 1880s and came to Saskatchewan via British Columbia. Also people of African origin began to homestead in Saskatchewan after emigrating from the United States in the post–Civil War era.[4]

Latin American and Spanish Migrations to Saskatchewan

Emigration from Spanish-speaking countries to Saskatchewan, however, is a much newer history—and one that began in earnest only in the latter half of the twentieth century. Liberalization of Canada's Immigration Act in the 1960s resulted in a greater influx of newcomers from non-European sources.[5] Although there was a very minor number of residents from Spain and other Spanish-speaking countries earlier, Spanish speakers did not become noticeably present within Saskatchewan until the 1970s, following a major migration from Chile. This was a result of the 1973 overthrow of the Allende regime, coupled with Canada's response to that political event and its liberal immigration policy.[6] From 1973 to 1976, large numbers of Chileans came as political refugees to many parts of Canada, including Saskatchewan, as part of the Special Chilean Movement initiated by the Canadian government.[7] In the 1980s there was also a major influx of Central American refugees to the country and to the province, many from El Salvador and Nicaragua, following the civil wars in those countries. Although there continues to be a small number of Spanish speakers from Spain, the vast majority of the individuals who make up the province's Hispanic community are Latin American. Most reside in one of the two major urban centers: Regina, site of the province's government; or Saskatoon, site of the province's largest city.[8] It is also important to note that the Spanish-speaking community within Saskatchewan should actually be referred to in the plural, as the origins of the members of the collective Hispanic population are from many countries and there is much cultural and social life segmented by country of origin, principal among which are Chile, Colombia, Guatemala, Mexico, Nicaragua, and El Salvador.[9]

Spanish-Speaking Communities of Saskatchewan and Their Influence on Language and Culture

The Latin American immigrations of the past thirty years have had a significant impact on the culture of the province and, consequently, on the initiatives, academic programs, and library collections of the University of Saskatchewan.

In addition to such recent phenomena as popular "Latin Nights" at local night-clubs, which massively attract Hispanic and non-Hispanic individuals from undergraduate to retirement age, there are a number of organizations that have evolved as a result of the presence of Spanish-speaking Saskatchewanians. In the city of Saskatoon, where the University of Saskatchewan is located, an association called the Círculo Hispánico was founded in 1972, partly as a result of the large university-related contingent among the founders. The mandate of the Círculo Hispánico originally included the desire that it be an adjunct body to the university's Spanish program and a means by which students and other nonnative speakers could practice Spanish; and also a means through which the various Hispanic cultures represented by the migrations to the area could be promoted within the Saskatchewan cultural mosaic.[10] Many of the individuals who have assumed directorship roles in the club since its founding, including the current president, have been University of Saskatchewan faculty. Consequently, over the span of its existence, it has not been unusual for meetings and special events of the Círculo Hispánico to be held on campus. The close connection between the Círculo Hispánico and the university has facilitated communication and links among the following: the university Hispanic community (faculty, staff, and students); non-Hispanics in the university community involved in Spanish language and Latin American initiatives, programs, and research; and the wider provincial Hispanic population.

An offshoot of the Círculo Hispánico is the Escuela Hispánica, which was founded in 1980 with the input of many native Spanish speakers from the University of Saskatchewan. The Escuela Hispánica maintains both a Saturday school for the children of Spanish-speaking immigrants and an evening school for adult learners of the language. A look at some of the early educational materials written for use by the Escuela Hispánica, along with the roster of its founding teachers and in combination with the mandate of its parent organization, make it clear that the university connection was strong from the start.[11] The Círculo Hispánico is one of many Latin American/Spanish-oriented associations formed in the province from the 1970s to the present, but it remains the one most closely tied with the University of Saskatchewan.

Various other Hispanic-themed clubs exist in the province, and new ones continue to be formed, for the pleasure of learning and conversing in Spanish and appreciating related cultures, dances, and sports. These are enjoyed by Hispanic and non-Hispanic residents of Saskatchewan. Some examples are the Regina and Saskatoon Chilean Associations; the folk music group Mamma Llajta; the Salvador Allende Folklore Group; and the dance troupe Raíces Chilenas. Additionally, there are such groups as the Arauco and Barrabases, which are adult men's soccer clubs that compete within the province's soccer leagues and have been instrumental in promoting the growth and enjoyment of that sport within Saskatchewan.[12]

Perhaps because of a need for winter beach holidays in destinations such as Cuba and Mexico, the study of Spanish for recreation and tourism has been extremely popular in Saskatchewan for more than thirty years. In addition to the Escuela Hispánica, there are many opportunities for non-Spanish speakers in Saskatchewan to learn the language. The University of Saskatchewan began teaching noncredit Spanish language courses through its Extension Division in 1973; those courses continue through the university's Language Centre.[13] The Saskatchewan Organization for Heritage Languages lists, in addition to the Escuela Hispánica, various Spanish schools within the province that provide classes to preschool through adult Spanish language learners. These language, cultural, and sport clubs have been influential in the creation of associations that attest to the large immigration to and multiculturalism of the province. The Saskatchewan Intercultural Association and the Multicultural Council of Saskatchewan are umbrella associations concerned with the preservation of heritage cultures and languages. Coordination by the Saskatchewan Intercultural Association has, for example, facilitated the participation of Hispanic communities of the province in a number of initiatives, notably, the two annual multicultural festivals of the province: "Folkfest" in Saskatoon and "Mosaic" in Regina.

Teaching of the Spanish language has also been facilitated and coordinated initially through the Saskatoon Multilingual School—in which during the 1980s both the Escuela Hispánica and the Saskatoon Chilean Association participated—and currently, provincially through the Saskatchewan Organization for Heritage Languages.[14] The Saskatchewan Organization for Heritage Languages, a direct result of the Saskatoon Multilingual School, further helped to bring Spanish language education into the realms of the Saskatchewan Department of Learning, from which a Spanish language secondary school curriculum was developed and is now currently in place; and the University of Saskatchewan, which, in addition to the Spanish and Latin American studies programs to be discussed immediately following, established the Heritage Language Teachers Certificate Program within the College of Education.[15]

University of Saskatchewan and Latin American and Iberian Studies

The University of Saskatchewan has been impacted in various ways by the Spanish-speaking populations. By 1991 the first cohort from the university's College of Education two-year evening program to prepare heritage language teachers received their diplomas. The mainstream degree programs, notably those within the Colleges of Arts and Science and Graduate Studies, have also been altered by the presence of Hispanic newcomers.

Although various sectors of the university had long been involved in internationalization, and the institution had a list of exchange partners and projects in all parts of the world, the push to "globalize" came in 1993 with the establishment of a new administrative unit known as U of S International.

In 2000 the university's main academic governance body, University Council, passed an Internationalization Mission Statement and initiated an International Activities Committee.[16] In 2003 the University Council endorsed a major policy and planning document titled "Globalism and the University of Saskatchewan: The Foundational Document for International Activities at the University of Saskatchewan."[17]

Specific to Latin American studies, the foundational document and the university's course calendar and website point out a variety of Latin American–centered initiatives that have been in progress at the U of S for up to the last quarter-century. Principal among those are the degree programs offered through the College of Arts and Science: Spanish language, linguistics, literature, and civilization; Latin American area studies; Spanish and Latin American–themed graduate research offered through programs in the College of Graduate Studies; and Latin American–based research projects and exchange programs.

Spanish Language and Literature Studies

The teaching of Spanish language and literature began in 1964, simply with the commencement of the first Spanish language courses within the French department, which was then renamed the Department of French and Spanish. A baccalaureate program in Spanish was initiated with the 1969–1970 academic year. In 1989 Spanish came under the administration of the newly created Department of Modern Languages, while French became an independent department. But in 1998 the Department of Modern Languages was amalgamated with both the Department of French and the College of Arts and Science's interdisciplinary program in linguistics to form the current Department of Languages and Linguistics, where Spanish language and also Iberian and Latin American literature and cultural studies are currently administered.[18] Through the College of Arts and Science, the Department of Languages and Linguistics offers the B.A. degree in Spanish; Spanish/Linguistics; Spanish/Comparative Literature; and Spanish Area Studies. Through the College of Graduate Studies, the M.A. in Spanish is offered on a special case basis.[19]

International Studies Program—Latin American Studies Stream

Although International Studies, as an undergraduate self-directed interdisciplinary program, has been available at the U of S for thirty years, it was not until academic year 1999–2000 that Latin American Studies, as a formally recognized area of study within International Studies, was specifically named in the university's course calendar.

The International Studies program is one of several undergraduate interdisciplinary programs of the College of Arts and Science. It is run by an administrative committee composed of faculty from each of the College of Arts and Science departments that are official partners in the program.[20] International Studies at the University of Saskatchewan provides students with a broad introduction to the concepts of international studies and a strong emphasis in one of four areas, one of which is Latin American Studies. The degree offered is the B.A.

The distinctive factor of the Latin American Studies program is the Guatemala Term Abroad. This term is a joint program with the University of Guelph (Ontario) and offers students the opportunity to complete up to twenty-one University of Saskatchewan credit units while resident in Guatemala. This is a unique opportunity not duplicated, with the exception of Guelph, at other universities in Canada. In combination with the required and recommended courses, the Guatemala Term Abroad, held biennially, contributes to a strong Latin American Studies program.[21]

Additional Undergraduate Spanish and Latin American Area Studies Initiatives

In addition to the Latin American Studies program with its Guatemala Term Abroad, there are a number of other "taught abroad" and "study abroad" student opportunities focusing on Latin America that have become part of the university's academic programs in recent years. Examples include a one-term international health course taught in Nicaragua and offered by the College of Medicine's Department of Community Health and Epidemiology, and another International Studies course taught on site is titled "Cuba: Social Revolution and Change." The College of Arts and Science also has a variety of study programs in Mexico available under the terms of a formal exchange agreement with a consortium of campuses at Instituto Tecnológico y de Estudios Superiores de Monterrey (ITESM).[22]

Graduate Studies, Research, Projects, and Exchanges

On the graduate and faculty research levels, there is work being done on Latin American topics through a variety of disciplines. Further, research in Latin American topics at the University of Saskatchewan is expanding and the area has become a priority in internationalization initiatives. Notable examples include current-funded graduate and faculty research on agricultural development and rural healthcare in Peru, and peasant society and environmental issues in Guatemala. Current faculty and student reciprocal programs in such areas as veterinary medicine, nursing, and indigenous studies exist with various Latin American entities, and the university maintains exchange programs with several partner institutions.[23]

Graduate thesis research has been done on such topics as the position of Canada in the OAS, women writers of the Spanish Caribbean, and the current political situation in Venezuela, but also on a number of other Latin American–related areas of study. A search of the University of Saskatchewan theses collection for graduate research that resulted in master's and doctoral theses on Latin American topics reveals work predominantly in agriculture, geography,

geology, history, linguistics, and political studies, and with the majority of the
resultant degrees awarded within the last fifteen years.[24]

The University of Saskatchewan Library and the Development of the Collections in Support of Latin American and Iberian Studies

Latin American area studies, as noted, can and does encompass a great
many disciplines—many more areas than those noted either as core departments for the International Studies program or as necessary to support the
Spanish program within the Department of Languages and Linguistics. Many
audiences are being served by the University of Saskatchewan library and the
collections have been developed to cover a number of needs from a variety
of viewpoints.

The collections' parameters of the library endeavor to reflect the teaching, research interests, priorities, and initiatives of the university as a whole.
Library support for Latin American studies within agriculture, economics,
history, indigenous studies, law, political studies, sciences, and women's and
gender studies (among other aspects of Latin American studies), as well as for
language, literary, and cultural studies, is accomplished through the library's
subject-specific allocations in support of those programs; the library's general
"discretionary" operating funds; and through endowments, trusts, and other
special funds.[25]

Active development of the collection of Spanish language material and
of the literature of Spain and the Spanish-speaking countries of the Americas
began only in 1976. This was after the first major migration of Latin Americans
to the province and after the approval of a B.A. program in Spanish language
and literature. The collection began to be actively developed because of the recognition by then associate librarian Mary M. Brady, a former Fulbright scholar
in Argentina and the president of SALALM in 1976–1977, of the importance
of Spanish and Latin American area studies material to the university and its
library within the context of research libraries in North America.

In language and literature, the guideline is to endeavor to at least represen-
tatively (of fiscal necessity in moderation) collect the major literature of Spain
and of all Spanish-speaking countries in the Americas.[26] The Latin American
areas studies collection, in its widest sense (beyond even the interdisciplinary
confines of the International Studies program), is more difficult to qualify or
quantify. Beyond the materials classed within Latin American studies specific
ranges, Latin American studies material can be found throughout the library's
collections of physical holdings and electronically accessible information
resources. This young collection continues to be developed, based on the
needs of various university programs (notably the Guatemala Term Abroad)
by subject librarians responsible for various disciplines and has been enhanced
through electronic resources and document delivery. Retrospective development of the traditional print collections is essential for this young collection

and, in addition to regular retrospective development through purchase, the collection has recently been enhanced by a major gift-in-kind of approximately 2,500 titles on Latin American history, anthropology, ethnography, literature, and art.[27] The small traditional print serials collection has been greatly strengthened in Latin American studies by consortial and individual purchases of electronic resources, including access to serial publications from and about Latin America in all disciplines, and also by electronic access to standard databases and reference material.

Because the university has recently completed an external assessment process titled Systematic Program Review for each of its degree programs, the library, as part of that process, assessed its collections for the support of appropriate Latin American studies materials within the library collection assessments that were done in response to the review of each program. These collection assessments provided an opportunity for subject librarians to review the collections vs. the programs they are meant to support, to assess strengths and weaknesses, and to prioritize needs.[28] The collection is still very young, but during the last thirty years, in response to the multiple challenges posed by the Hispanic community and their influence on curricula and research and coupled with the internationalization mandate given to the university, the library has entered the realm of the North American standard for academic library collections in Latin American area studies.[29]

Influences: How We Arrived Here

Newcomers have influenced the programs and collections of the University of Saskatchewan to make them more Spanish language and Latin American studies inclusive. The presence of Spanish-speaking newcomers in the province was, of course, not the sole influence on the university's programs and collections, but was certainly an important contributing factor. The time was right, for a number of reasons including the Latin American migrations to the province, for a shift from parochialism to globalism in the priorities of the university. When the University of Saskatchewan was founded in 1907, the original faculty complement was drawn primarily from the universities of eastern Canada, Great Britain and other parts of Europe, and from the United States; the student body, at the same time, was almost exclusively from western Canada and mostly from Saskatchewan. It was a university very much reflecting the origins, traditions, and worlds of its faculty and student body.[30]

The influx of immigrants from the Spanish-speaking countries of the Americas brought new ideas to the province in general and to the university in particular. Most of the adult immigrants came into the workforce and/or the educational stream of the province immediately. For those who arrived as professionals, including the academics, making their presence known within their cultural community and within the university was normal and natural. Other

Hispanic immigrants arriving with the desire or need for further education entered the university and became part of the formation or strengthened the various cultural groups that were in the process of formation. The last several years have seen an influx of the children of the Spanish-speaking immigrants of the 1970s and 1980s entering the University of Saskatchewan; some of these children were born in the country of their parents, others were born in Canada. Almost all of them have some proficiency in Spanish and, it appears from their undergraduate and graduate library research, many have a passion to study and research the literature, history, politics, and cultures of their origins.

As a result of many influences, including a visible Hispanic community presence, the University of Saskatchewan has become more international and a more complete "universe of knowledge." The university's Internationalization Mission Statement begins thus: "Universities are by necessity rooted in a particular place and society. Yet, they must constantly seek to forge links across cultures, to broaden knowledge, and to meet varied responsibilities to society." The Spanish-speaking newcomers of the last thirty years have, indeed, left their mark on and enhanced the province and the University of Saskatchewan.

NOTES

1. Bill Waiser, *Saskatchewan: A New History* (Calgary: Fifth House, 2005), pp. 3–4.

2. Norman Ward, "Saskatchewan," *The Canadian Encyclopedia* (Historica Foundation of Canada, 2006), http://www.thecanadianencyclopedia.com/.

3. Federation of Saskatchewan Indian Nations, http://www.fsin.com/ (accessed February 24, 2006).

4. Waiser's *Saskatchewan* contains information on immigration and settlement of many European groups, see index, pp. 550–551.

5. Bernard D. Thraves, "Urban Ethnic Diversity," *The Encyclopedia of Saskatchewan* (Regina: Canadian Plains Research Center, 2005), p. 976.

6. Miguel Sanchez, "Chilean Community," *The Encyclopedia of Saskatchewan,* p. 169.

7. Wilson Ruiz, "Latin Americans," *The Canadian Encyclopedia,* http://www.thecanadianencyclopedia.com/.

8. *Total Immigrant Population by Place of Birth: Saskatchewan, Regina and Saskatoon (2001 Census—20% Sample Data)* (Regina: Bureau of Statistics, 2002).

9. Rodolfo Pino, "Hispanic Community," *The Encyclopedia of Saskatchewan,* pp. 443–444. See also *Total Immigrant Population by Place of Birth,* above.

10. Information based on conversations with founding members of the Círculo Hispánico.

11. Information based on conversations with past and current members of the directorship of the Círculo Hispánico and the Escuela Hispánica and on available curricular material from the first five years of the Escuela Hispánica.

12. Sanchez, "Chilean Community," p. 169.

13. University of Saskatchewan Language Centre. See http://www.extension.usask.ca/ExtensionDivision/resources/CSLI/index.html (accessed February 24, 2006).

14. Rodolfo Pino, "Saskatchewan Intercultural Association," *The Encyclopedia of Saskatchewan,* p. 811.

15. See College of Education, within University of Saskatchewan website. Information on the Certificate in Methods of Teaching Heritage Languages is directly at http://www.usask.ca/education/program/heritage.htm (accessed February 24, 2006).

16. See http://www.usask.ca/university_council/international/ for the terms of reference of the International Activities Committee and for the Internationalization Mission Statement.

17. "Globalism and the University of Saskatchewan: The Foundational Document for International Activities at the University of Saskatchewan" (September 2003). See this document at http://www.usask.ca/vpacademic/integrated-planning/plandocs/foundational_docs.php (accessed February 24, 2006).

18. University of Saskatchewan Archives, http://www.usask.ca/archives/. See fonds 2038 and 2050.

19. Within the University of Saskatchewan website, see information on the Spanish programs at http://www.arts.usask.ca/languages/spanish/index.php (accessed February 24, 2006).

20. Those departments are archaeology, economics, geography, history, political studies, religious studies and anthropology, sociology, native studies, and women's and gender studies. In addition, the following units also contribute courses: the Department of Community Health and Epidemiology of College of Medicine; the College of Law; and the Centre for the Study of Cooperatives.

21. Within the University of Saskatchewan website, see information on the Latin American Studies program directly at http://www.arts.usask.ca/intnl/ (accessed February 24, 2006).

22. See information on the "Taught Abroad" programs in the University of Saskatchewan Calendar at http://www.students.usask.ca/academic/studyabroad/taught/options/ (accessed February 24, 2006). See information on the Spanish language in Mexico programs at http://www.arts.usask.ca/languages/exchange.php (accessed February 24, 2006).

23. See the University of Saskatchewan International site at http://www.usask.ca/usi/ (accessed February 24, 2006) for a listing of current partners and projects and to access the International Opportunities Handbook.

24. See the University of Saskatchewan library at http://library.usask.ca/. Information specific to the theses collection is at http://library.usask.ca/spcoll/major.html (accessed February 24, 2006).

25. For a brief description of the library system, collections, and budget, see "Basic Library Facts," http://library.usask.ca/info/basicfacts.html (accessed February 24, 2006); and for a list of subject areas in which collection development is currently being directly supported, see "Current Selection and Ordering of Library Materials," http://library.usask.ca/info/librarianliaisons.html (accessed February 24, 2006).

26. See Spanish library collection profile within Donna Canevari de Paredes and MaryLynn Gagné, "Systematic Program Review—Languages and Linguistics Programs: University of Saskatchewan Library Response" (2004).

27. Dr. Beate Salz's gift-in-kind, 2004–2006, approximately 2,500 items.

28. See especially the report for the International Studies program: Donna Canevari de Paredes, "Systematic Program Review—International Studies Program: University of Saskatchewan Library Response" (2003).

29. Also see the library's Latin American and Iberian Studies subject page at http://library.usask.ca/subjects.php?subject=span (accessed February 24, 2006).

30. Michael Hayden, *Seeking a Balance: The University of Saskatchewan 1907–1982* (Vancouver: University of British Columbia Press, 1983), see references to faculty and student complements in index, specifically under "Faculty," p. 373, and under "Students," p. 378.

BIBLIOGRAPHY

Anderson, Grace M. "Spanish." Revised by Antonio Cazorla-Sanchez. In *The Canadian Encyclopedia*. Historica Foundation of Canada, 2006. http://www.thecanadianencyclopedia.com.

Federation of Saskatchewan Indian Nations. http://www.fsin.com/. Accessed February 24, 2006.

"Globalism and the University of Saskatchewan: The Foundational Document for International Activities at the University of Saskatchewan." September 2003.

Pino, Rodolfo. "Hispanic Community." In *The Encyclopedia of Saskatchewan*. Regina: Canadian Plains Research Center, 2005.

———. "Saskatchewan Intercultural Association." In *The Encyclopedia of Saskatchewan*. Regina: Canadian Plains Research Center, 2005.

Ruiz, Wilson. "Latin Americans." In *The Canadian Encyclopedia*. Historica Foundation of Canada, 2006. http://www.thecanadianencyclopedia.com. Accessed February 24, 2006.

Sanchez, Miguel. "Chilean Community." In *The Encyclopedia of Saskatchewan*. Regina: Canadian Plains Research Center, 2005.

Saskatchewan Organization for Heritage Languages. http://www.heritagelanguages.sk.ca/. Accessed February 24, 2006.

Thraves, Bernard D. "Urban Ethnic Diversity." In *The Encyclopedia of Saskatchewan*. Regina: Canadian Plains Research Center, 2005.

Total Immigrant Population by Place of Birth: Saskatchewan, Regina and Saskatoon (2001 Census—20% Sample Data). Regina: Bureau of Statistics, 2002.

University of Saskatchewan. http://www.usask.ca/. Accessed February 24, 2006.

University of Saskatchewan Archives. http://www.usask.ca/archives/. Accessed February 24, 2006.

University of Saskatchewan Language Centre. http://www.extension.usask.ca/ExtensionDivision/resources/CSLI/index.html. Accessed February 24, 2006.

University of Saskatchewan Library. http://library.usask.ca/. Accessed February 24, 2006.

Waiser, Bill. *Saskatchewan: A New History*. Calgary: Fifth House, 2005.

Ward, Norman. "Saskatchewan." In *The Canadian Encyclopedia*. Historica Foundation of Canada, 2006. http://www.thecanadianencyclopedia.com. Accessed February 24, 2006.

17. Immigration and Globalization: Meeting the Needs of an Emergent Clientele

Nicole Michaud-Oystryk

Manitoba and Immigration from Latin America

The Province of Manitoba is located in the center of Canada. It has a population of nearly 1.2 million with almost 75 percent of the population residing in the capital city of Winnipeg. Manitoba has a long history of immigration, a rich cultural diversity, and a strong humanitarian tradition.

Closely conforming to the Canadian trend, Latin American immigration to Manitoba started in the mid-1970s with the Chileans and Argentineans who were seeking refuge from political strife in their native country. In fact, Winnipeg was the gateway for these immigrants who were entering Canada. The 1980s saw the arrival of large groups of Salvadorans and smaller groups of Nicaraguans and Guatemalans, the vast majority of these classified as refugees and sponsored either by the government or private agencies. It appears that Mexicans immigrated at a slow, even pace. Temporary workers and exchange students make up a good proportion of the Mexican immigrant population. The most recent wave of immigration to the province is that of Argentine Jews who are sponsored by a community organization. Over one hundred families have settled in Winnipeg since the mid-1990s and the number continues to soar. These immigrants are well-educated individuals who fill high-demand professional positions.

The census of Canada provides statistics relating to mother tongue and ethnic origin. In the 1981 census, a total of 70,160 respondents across Canada declared Spanish as their mother tongue; 1,855 of these resided in Manitoba.[1] Ten years later, over twice as many respondents (186,255) claimed Spanish as their mother tongue; 4,650 of these were from Manitoba.[2] The 2001 census reported another significant increase with 245,500 responding Canada-wide that Spanish was their mother tongue; in Manitoba there were 5,210.[3]

According to the census, the number of Latin Americans in Manitoba, which includes those of Caribbean origins, reached 3,695 in 1981[4] and rose only slightly to 4,650 in 1991.[5] In the 2001 census, the number of respondents who gave their ethnic origin as Latin, Central, or South America was 244,430 for the whole of Canada and 7,020 for Manitoba, almost double the number of the 1981 census. The largest communities in order of size were Mexican, Chilean, Salvadoran, Paraguayan, Nicaraguan, and Brazilian. Since 2000, the number of immigrants from the region has been steadily rising.[6] The vast majority of immigrants from Latin America settle in Winnipeg. Today, it is home to small but vibrant, thriving Spanish communities. Three local radio programs are broadcasted in Spanish and two newspapers are published. Several restaurants and markets specializing in Latin American food are flourishing. A Spanish Toastmasters Club, a dance studio, and a Spanish club enhance the cultural vitality. A Spanish church serves the community and a Roman Catholic church offers a Sunday mass in Spanish. During the summer the largest Latin American groups participate in Folklorama, a spectacular multicultural event held annually in Winnipeg.

In addition to English and French, Manitoba's public education system offers a variety of languages of study. Spanish language instruction has been offered in schools since the 1970s but has been growing in popularity since the early 1990s. Currently, approximately thirty schools offer basic Spanish, primarily at the senior 1–4 levels; in 2004–2005 approximately 1,300 students were enrolled. In September 2006, a Spanish-English bilingual program will be launched in the largest school division.[7]

The immigration of Latin Americans to Manitoba has contributed to the multicultural mosaic and the economic development of the province. However, it is difficult to quantify the impact or to state categorically to what degree immigration has influenced the development of university programs and initiatives, and consequently library collections and services. As much as immigration has brought a distinct international outlook, globalization is also playing an important role in the development of linkages and partnerships with Latin America. Formal accords have strengthened economic ties and offered unique educational, social, and cultural opportunities.

The University of Manitoba

The University of Manitoba, founded in 1877, was the first university in western Canada and it remains one of the largest universities in the country. In 2005–2006, student enrollment reached an all-time high of over 28,000. The foreign student enrollment (9.4 percent) was also unprecedented.

The Student Population

This year's statistics on the distribution of students by citizenship show that of the 2,661 foreign students, only a fraction or an estimated 70 originate from Latin America. The greatest number comes from Mexico (34), Brazil (14), and Colombia (7). The total number of students from Latin America has been climbing since the early 1990s.[8]

The number of students enrolled in the Spanish section of the Department of French, Spanish, and Italian provides another measure of the growing importance of Spanish at the university. Enrollment has risen steadily over the past few years, reaching 416 this year, an increase of 99 students over the previous year. The faculty whom I consulted remarked that the second-generation immigrants from Latin America do not form a uniform group. The Spanish language is common to them but they do not mix or identify as a "Latin American" group.[9]

The Programs

The Department of French, Spanish, and Italian has the university's greatest concentration of courses related to Latin American culture and society. It offers a minor, a major, and an advanced major degree in Spanish language and literature. Spanish-American culture and civilization, nineteenth century, twentieth century, and contemporary literature, and Latin American cinema are the primary areas of focus. The Spanish section employs four professors and four instructors.

While a growing number of the general student population is interested in taking Spanish as an option, a significant number of second-generation Latin American students is also. For the most part, many speak Spanish but do not read or write it. In view of this situation, a new course "Spanish for Native Speakers" was introduced. Students who are fluent in Spanish are encouraged to take this course to develop their reading and writing skills. As well, the department accommodates native Spanish students in translation courses by encouraging them to translate from English to Spanish to help them improve their English language skills.[10]

New initiatives in the department illustrate the vitality of the Spanish language program. *Los Títeres de Don Quijote* is an English-Spanish puppet show produced in 2005 to commemorate the four-hundredth anniversary of Don Quixote. It is available on the department's website as is the telenovela *Amanda, una Historia en Español,* a short video with exercises intended for English-speaking students of Spanish.[11]

Other programs related to Latin America are relatively limited. Language and literature courses may be combined with courses in anthropology, economics, geography, and history in an interdisciplinary program leading to a minor in Latin American Studies. In summer 2006, a travel/study course titled "Women in Nicaragua" will be offered for the first time. This is a twelve-credit course, which features one month of study on the Caribbean coast of Nicaragua.

International Research Projects

The University of Manitoba is an active participant in the Program for North American Mobility in Higher Education. Established in 1995, this program was created to "encourage co-operation in higher education and training among the three countries (Canada, Mexico and the United States) with a focus on student mobility."[12] The University of Manitoba is currently involved in six of these trilateral projects in areas as diverse as disability studies, food safety, conflict resolution, multiculturalism, and technology.

The University of Manitoba also participates in projects funded by the Canadian International Development Agency. Two current projects, one on environmental health risk assessment and management, the other on nursing practice, are being delivered in Cuba, and a third project on soil resource information is based in Costa Rica.[13]

Beyond these major projects, 113 faculty members reported linkages with Latin America in the latest inventory of expertise and involvement in the international community. The faculties with the highest number are medicine (14), agricultural and food sciences (14), arts (12), and social work (10). There are linkages with all of the Latin American countries with the exception of Haiti.[14]

International Centre for Students

The number of international students has steadily increased over the past several years due in large part to new immigration policies. The nonpermanent resident policy has opened up opportunities to foreign students by allowing them to use their study permits at any institution in the country, by enabling them to work off-campus, and by granting them postgraduate one- to two-year work permits. As well, the provincial nominee program offers a special immigration stream for university graduates.

The International Centre for Students offers a gamut of valuable services including a pre- and post-arrival program, on-call student advisors, financial advice, a housing registry, and help with study permits and visa extensions. The center sees a lot of students who are interested in immigrating.

The International Centre for Students also manages the student exchange programs and acts as an advisor to departments who administer their own exchanges. The university benefits from two major agreements between Canada, the United States, and Mexico. One, the North American Mobility in Higher Education agreement, provides students with work experience in a wide range of academic and professional disciplines throughout North America. The other, the Consortium for North American Higher Education Collaboration (CONAHEC), promotes student exchanges and provides funding for conferences and think tanks.

In terms of bilateral accords, the University of Manitoba has formalized student exchange agreements with two institutions in Brazil: Pontificia Universidade Católica do Paraná, and Universidade Federal da Paraiba; and several in Mexico: nine universities of the Instituto Tecnológico y de Estudios Superiores de Monterrey, the Universidade de Guadalajara, Universidad Latina de America, and the seven universities in the state of Jalisco. It should be noted that the demand from Latin American students exceeds the demand from the Canadian students in large part due to the language barrier. While the Latin

American students are generally fluent in English, the Canadian students often lack the language skills necessary to pursue a program of study in Spanish or, in the case of Brazil, in Portuguese. However, this is an area where participation from second- and third-generation Latin American immigrants is increasing. They view these exchanges as opportunities to return to their roots and often to connect with family.[15]

In addition to these exchange programs, there are department-based programs. For example, the Faculty of Architecture has a tripartite agreement with the University of Waterloo and Mexico. Students from Mexico enroll in six-week studio courses at the University of Manitoba. Also the faculty is in the process of formalizing an exchange program between the University of Manitoba and the University of Valparaiso, Chile. The launch of this program, which will involve faculty and students, is scheduled for September 2006. As well, the Faculty of Management has a well-developed exchange program with universities worldwide. Its exchange program with Mexico sees 10 students from that country enrolling annually at the University of Manitoba and 3 going from Manitoba to Mexico. Another program involves Brazil and the exchange of 2 to 5 students per year.

How Are Library Collections and Services Responding to This New Environment?

Libraries Collections

The University of Manitoba Libraries consist of twenty libraries and satellites, with collections totaling approximately 2.2 million volumes and a staff of around 215 employees, including 60 librarians. The Elizabeth Dafoe Library, which serves the humanities and social sciences, is the main repository of materials related to Latin American studies.

Although there was minimal collecting of materials related to Latin America in earlier years, the collection flourished in the 1970s corresponding to the establishment of a Latin American studies program at the university. The growing interest in Latin America provided the impetus for the library to build a stronger collection. In the past decade, new funds have been allocated to fill gaps in the collection and to set up approval plan profiles. Today the approval plan generates works on the history of Mexico, general historical works in the area of Latin and South America, and critical works in Latin American literature. For a few years, a literary author-based plan was also in place but it was discontinued in favor of firm ordering. In recent years, monograph budgets have been quite stable and in fact have profited from the favorable exchange rate of the Canadian dollar. The acquisition of gift collections has also enriched the collection, most often providing retrospective materials. Today, there are approximately 20,000 monographs in the collection related to Latin America. This is a modest collection but all signs point to the continued sustainability and growth of the collection in the future.

In terms of serials, the collection holds over 100 titles in various areas of study and research on Latin America. The library has current subscriptions to about half of these titles and provides access to some thirty electronic journals, many of which are new titles received as part of aggregated packages. The library maintains subscriptions to two Spanish-American newspapers, *Uno más uno* and *La Nación*.

The collection supports the growing Spanish language program and advanced undergraduate study in Latin American literature. Primary works are purchased almost solely in the original language, with the majority of secondary works being in English. In time, an emerging interest in comparative literature and literature in translation will shift collecting patterns. Also with a growing number of students having some degree of fluency in Spanish, the library will be more receptive to purchasing secondary works in that language.

In the social sciences, the history collection is the strongest. It covers colonial and contemporary Latin America with a particular emphasis on Mexico, Central America, and Cuba. The collection deals with Latin America in the context of globalization, international politics, and the world economy. It emphasizes ethnic and multicultural studies and supports courses that examine aspects of Latin American immigration, culture, and society. The majority of the materials selected are in English. However, basic texts, major reference sources, and specific Spanish language works requested by faculty are acquired.

The collections support interdisciplinary graduate studies in selective areas of scholarship and the basic research needs of faculty specializing in Latin American anthropology, history, and literature. The libraries' membership in the Center for Research Libraries provides access to the center's rich collection of international newspapers and Latin American area studies materials.

Other libraries are selective in their collection of material related to Latin America, and they focus on very specific material that support their areas of teaching and research. For instance, the Albert D. Cohen Management Library collects Spanish-English business dictionaries; guides and monographs related to international business in the Caribbean, Latin America, and South America; and books on corporations in Latin America. The Architecture/Fine Arts Library subscribes to a few journals and orders books in support of faculty research and design projects in Brazil, Chile, and Mexico. The education library supports two courses on Teaching Heritage, Aboriginal and International Languages. As the Spanish programs grow in schools, the education library will no doubt intensify its collection of related curriculum and support materials.

Library Services

A few library services are of particular value to the growing Spanish-speaking student population and to students pursuing Latin American studies.

One is the Multi-Lingual Library Service. Posted on the website is a list of staff who are fluent in languages other than English and who have volunteered to serve as contacts for international students who wish to talk in their native language about library services and collections.

In collaboration with the International Centre for Students, the library offers orientation sessions for international students at the beginning of a term to familiarize them with the library and to create a comfortable and inviting environment for them. The library has also provided staff training on cultural diversity awareness.

The management library has produced a bibliographic guide entitled "Doing Business in the Caribbean, Latin America, and South America." It is anticipated that it will soon be posted on that library's website.

Most importantly, however, librarians have become aware that they more frequently encounter students who are able to read Spanish and do not recoil when materials written in Spanish are recommended to them. This is an interesting development that should grow as more students with Spanish language skills attend the university.

Challenges for the Future

The province's and the university's relationship with Latin America holds a lot of promise for the future. Social, cultural, and economic factors, as well as global trends, contribute to this positive outlook.

In order to meet the expectations and to take advantage of the opportunities offered by a stronger partnership with Latin America and its immigrants to the province, the university will have to focus its attention on several levels:

- It will have to secure ongoing funding for the development of new research programs and for the expansion of the student exchange programs.

- It will have to overcome the language barrier. Faculty and students will have to improve their Spanish language skills in order to facilitate linkages and increase collaborative projects. The development of Portuguese language skills would also be desirable given the current partnerships with Brazil. (Currently, Portuguese is not taught at the University of Manitoba.)

- It will have to strengthen its ties with the community. It must be prepared to respond to the needs and expectations of second- and third-generation immigrants.

As the role of the university increases in relation to Latin American interests, the university libraries will have to support any new initiatives through the development of collections and services, and perhaps take the lead in some areas of endeavor.[16]

NOTES

1. Statistics Canada, *Population: Mother Tongue,* 1981 Census of Canada, catalogue no. 92–902 (Ottawa: Industry, Science and Technology Canada, 1982), pp. 1–5, 1–6.

2. Statistics Canada, *Mother Tongue,* 1991 Census of Canada, catalogue no. 93–313 (Ottawa: Industry, Science and Technology Canada, 1992), pp. 14, 34.

3. Statistics Canada, "Detailed Mother Tongue, Sex and Age Groups, for Canada, Provinces, Territories, Census Metropolitan Areas and Census Agglomerations 1996 and 2001 Censuses: 20% Sample Data" [table], *Language Composition of Canada: Topic-Based Tabulations, 2001 Census,* Statistics Canada catalogue no. 97F0007XCB2001001, released December 10, 2002, http://www12.statcan.ca/english/census01/products/standard/themes/index.cfm (accessed February 24, 2006).

4. Statistics Canada, *Population: Ethnic Origin,* 1981 Census of Canada, catalogue no. 92–911 (Ottawa: Supply and Services Canada, 1984), pp. 1–13, 1–14.

5. Statistics Canada, *Mother Tongue,* pp. 22–25.

6. Statistics Canada, "Ethnic Origin, Sex and Single and Multiple Responses for Population for Canada, Provinces, Territories, Census Metropolitan Areas and Census Agglomerations, 2001 Census: 20% Sample Data" [table], *Ethnocultural Portrait of Canada: Topic-Based Tabulations, 2001 Census,* Statistics Canada catalogue no. 97F0010XCB.2001001, released January 21, 2003, http://www.statcan.ca/english/census01/products/standard/themes/index.cfm (accessed February 24, 2006).

7. Tony Tavares, Manitoba Department of Education, electronic message to author, February 24, 2006.

8. University of Manitoba, Office of Institutional Analysis, *Institutional Statistics Book* (Winnipeg, 1979/80–2005/06), http://www.umanitoba.ca/admin/institutional_analysis/isbook/index.htm (accessed March 22, 2006).

9. Enrique Fernandez, Professor, Department of French, Spanish, and Italian, University of Manitoba, conversation with author, February 2006.

10. Fernandez, conversation with author.

11. University of Manitoba, Department of French, Spanish, and Italian, *Los Títeres de Don Quijote,* http://www.umanitoba.ca/fsi/spanish/titeres.htm; and *Amanda, una Historia en Español,* http://www.umanitoba.ca/fsi/spanish/amanda.htm (accessed March 22, 2006).

12. Canada, Human Resources and Skills Development, "Program for North American Mobility in Higher Education," http://www.rhdcc.gc.ca/asp/gateway.asp?hr=/en/hip/lld/lssd/iam/north_american/purpose.shtml&hs=iyp (accessed February 23, 2006).

13. University of Manitoba, Office of International Relations, "Current and Recently Completed International Projects in Latin America Involving University of Manitoba Faculty Members" (Office of International Relations, University of Manitoba, Winnipeg, 2006), computer printout.

14. University of Manitoba, Office of International Relations, "University of Manitoba Faculty Expertise Concerning Latin America," comp. C. Zywina (Office of International Relations, University of Manitoba, Winnipeg, 2006), computer printout.

15. Robyn Tully, Communications Coordinator, and Rhonda Friesen, Exchange Coordinator, International Centre for Students, University of Manitoba, conversations with author, March 2006.

16. In addition to acknowledging the contributions of the individuals cited above, the author wishes to thank the following colleagues at the University of Manitoba who shared information and perspectives with her: Dennis Felbel, Donald K. Gordon, Mary Lochhead, María Inez Martinez, Nada Subotincic, and John Wiens.

BIBLIOGRAPHY

Bellan, Matt. "Argentine Jewish Immigration to Winnipeg Still Soaring: Population Has More Than Doubled in Past 12 Months." *Jewish Post and News.* http://www.jewishpostandnews.com/argentinejews.html. Accessed February 23, 2006.

Burnet, Jean R. *"Coming Canadians": An Introduction to a History of Canada's Peoples.* Toronto: McClelland and Stewart and Multiculturalism Directorate, 1988.

Canada. Department of Citizenship and Immigration. *Facts and Figures: Immigration Overview. Permanent and Temporary Residents.* Ottawa: Citizenship and Immigration Canada, 2005.

Canada. Department of Employment and Immigration. Public Affairs. Immigration Policy Branch. *Immigration to Manitoba: A Statistical Overview.* Ottawa-Hull, Ontario, 1989.

Canada. Department of Human Resources and Skills Development. "Program for North American Mobility in Higher Education." http://www.rhdcc.gc.ca/asp/gateway.asp?hr=/en/hip/lld/lssd/iam/north_american/purpose.shtml&hs=iyp. Accessed February 23, 2006.

Frideres, James S. "Changing Dimensions of Ethnicity in Canada." In *Deconstructing a Nation: Immigration, Multiculturalism and Racism in '90s Canada,* edited by Vic Satzewich. Halifax: Fernwood Publishing; Saskatoon: Social Research Unit, Department of Sociology, 1992. Pp. 47–67.

Manitoba. Department of Culture, Heritage, and Citizenship. Immigration and Settlement Services Branch. Citizenship Division. *Manitoba Immigration Information Bulletin 1987–1990.* Winnipeg, n.d.

Manitoba. Department of Employment Services and Economic Security. Immigration and Settlement Branch. *Manitoba Immigration Information Bulletin. Annual Report 1982, January 1 to December 31.* Winnipeg, n.d.

———. *Manitoba Immigration Information Bulletin. Annual Report 1983, Preliminary January 1 to December 31.* Winnipeg, n.d.

———. *Manitoba Immigration Information Bulletin. Annual Report 1987.* Winnipeg, n.d.

Manitoba. Department of Labour and Immigration. Immigration and Multiculturalism Division. *Manitoba Immigration Facts 2002 Statistics Report.* Winnipeg, 2003. http://www.gov.mb.ca/labour/immigrate/infocentre/pdf/statsum2002.pdf. Accessed March 5, 2006.

———. *Manitoba Immigration Facts 2003 Statistical Report.* Winnipeg, 2004. http://www.gov.mb.ca/labour/immigrate/infocentre/pdf/mif_booklet.pdf. Accessed March 5, 2006.

———. *Manitoba Immigration Facts 2004 Statistical Report.* Winnipeg, 2005. http://www.gov.mb.ca/labour/immigrate/infocentre/pdf/mif_web.pdf. Accessed March 5, 2006.

———. *Manitoba Immigration Statistics Summary 2000 Report.* Winnipeg, 2001. http://www.gov.mb.ca/labour/immigrate/infocentre/pdf/statsum2000.pdf. Accessed March 5, 2006.

Manitoba. Department of Labour and Immigration. Immigration and Multiculturalism Division. *Manitoba Immigration Statistics Summary 2001 Report.* Winnipeg, 2002. http://www.gov.mb.ca/labour/immigrate/infocentre/pdf/statsum2001.pdf. Accessed March 5, 2006.

Simmons, Alan B. "Latin American Migration to Canada: New Linkages in the Hemispheric Migration and Refugee Flow System." *International Journal* 48 (spring 1993): 282–309.

Statistics Canada. *Canada's Ethnocultural Portrait: The Changing Mosaic.* 2001 Census: Analysis Series. Catalogue no. 96F0030XIE2001008. Ottawa: Statistics Canada, 2003. http://www12.statcan.ca/english/census01/products/ analytic/companion/etoimm/contents.cfm. Accessed February 24, 2006.

———. "Detailed Mother Tongue, Sex and Age Groups, for Canada, Provinces, Territories, Census Metropolitan Areas and Census Agglomerations 1996 and 2001 Censuses: 20% Sample Data" [table]. *Language Composition of Canada: Topic-Based Tabulations, 2001 Census.* Statistics Canada catalogue no. 97F0007XCB2001001. Released December 10, 2002. http://www12.statcan.ca/ english/census01/products/standard/themes/index.cfm. Accessed February 24, 2006.

———. *Ethnic Origin.* 1991 Census of Canada. Catalogue no. 93–315. Ottawa: Industry, Science and Technology Canada, 1993.

———. "Ethnic Origin, Sex and Single and Multiple Responses for Population for Canada, Provinces, Territories, Census Metropolitan Areas and Census Agglomerations, 2001 Census: 20% Sample Data" [table]. *Ethnocultural Portrait of Canada: Topic-Based Tabulations, 2001 Census.* Statistics Canada catalogue no. 97F0010XCB.2001001. Released January 21, 2003. http:// www.statcan.ca/english/census01/products/standard/themes/index.cfm. Accessed February 24, 2006.

———. *Mother Tongue.* 1991 Census of Canada. Catalogue no. 93–313. Ottawa: Supply and Services Canada, 1992.

———. *Population: Ethnic Origin.* 1981 Census of Canada. Catalogue no. 92–911. Ottawa: Supply and Services Canada, 1984.

———. *Population: Mother Tongue.* 1981 Census of Canada. Catalogue no. 92–902. Ottawa: Supply and Services Canada, 1982.

Tomic, Patricia, and Ricardo Trumper. "Canada and the Streaming of Immigrants: A Personal Account of the Chilean Case." In *Deconstructing a Nation: Immigration, Multiculturalism and Racism in '90s Canada,* edited by Vic Satzewich. Halifax: Fernwood Publishing; Saskatoon: Social Research Unit, Department of Sociology, 1992. Pp. 163–181.

Ujimoto, K. Victor. "Multiculturalism and the Global Information Society." In *Deconstructing a Nation: Immigration, Multiculturalism and Racism in '90s Canada,* edited by Vic Satzewich. Halifax: Fernwood Publishing; Saskatoon: Social Research Unit, Department of Sociology, 1992. Pp. 351–357.

University of Manitoba. Department of French, Spanish, and Italian. *Los Títeres de Don Quijote,* http://www.umanitoba.ca/fsi/spanish/titeres.htm; and *Amanda, una Historia en Español,* http://www.umanitoba.ca/fsi/spanish/amanda.htm. Accessed March 22, 2006.

University of Manitoba. Office of Institutional Analysis. *Institutional Statistics Book.* Winnipeg, 1979/80–2005/06. http://www.umanitoba.ca/admin/institutional_ analysis/isbook/index.htm. Accessed March 2006.

University of Manitoba. Office of International Relations. "Current and Recently Completed International Projects in Latin America Involving University of Manitoba Faculty Members." Office of International Relations, University of Manitoba, Winnipeg, 2006. Computer printout.

———. "University of Manitoba Faculty Expertise Concerning Latin America." Compiled by C. Zywina. Office of International Relations, University of Manitoba, Winnipeg, 2006. Computer printout.

Women Writers across
Latin American Borders

18. How the Three Julias Won Their Fame/ *Como las tres Julias ganaron su fama*

Nelly S. González

If one word in Spanish could be used to summarize the essence of Julia Alvarez, it might be *polivalente*. In English, one might refer to her as versatile. For rhetorical purposes, I refer to three Julias in the title of my talk. The first Julia is the Latina writer of the immigrant experience in the United States. The second Julia is the writer of feminist literature. And, the third Julia is the writer of Latin American historical and political fiction. However, Julia Alvarez really defies categorization or perhaps demands a multiplicity of categories. In truth, there are not just three Julias. There are five, there are seven, and perhaps there are ten Julias. Consider that in a literary career that has spanned three decades, Julia has written and published in two languages; she has written essays, poems, short stories, and novels; and she has even written a cookbook and a children's book.

The keys to understanding Julia Alvarez as a literary phenomenon are the following:

a. the Dominican upper-middle class and its reverence of literature as an ornament of prestige

b. the Dominican immigrant experience in the United States

c. the post–World War II political history of the Dominican Republic

d. the rise of ethnic writing in the United States following the Civil Rights movement

e. Julia's overnight success took twenty-five years of dedication to her craft

Family Background—Upper-Middle-Class Roots

Julia Alvarez came from a large, upper-middle-class family. Her paternal grandfather had twenty-five legitimate children and as she states, "who knows how many illegitimate children could be added." This kind of statement is itself a cliché. (Legitimate were the children born from a couple in matrimony, and illegitimate were the rest of the children born out of wedlock.) Julia was fond of her grandfather from her maternal side of the family. She describes him as a tall, slim, good-looking grandpa who liked to talk to her and often asked what she was going to be when she grew up. On a certain occasion, Julia's reply was that she was going to be a "poet." This was music to the grandfather's ears and he smiled proudly with this answer. As one can see, the choice of "poet" as an aspiration was not an act of bohemian rebellion, but rather well within the mainstream of her social class, which looked at poetry as a sign of refinement and prestige.

Born on March 27, 1951, in New York City, Julia promptly moved with her family back to the Dominican Republic and lived the first ten years of her life surrounded by a troupe of maids, since her family was relatively affluent. Although she confesses that she hated books, school, and anything that had to do with work, she became adroit at reciting poetry, which she often did to entertain guests.[1]

Well Educated

It is important to note that Julia benefited from a first-class education. During her years in the Dominican Republic, she attended the elite American School. When she moved to the United States, her parents sent her to the Abbott Academy, a private boarding school for girls. She was educated at Connecticut College and Middlebury College. She received a Master of Fine Arts degree from Syracuse University. For nearly twenty-five years she taught creative writing at the college, prep school, and high school levels. In sum, she spent many years being exposed to the literary world and working to perfect her craft. When she published her first novel in 1991 to great acclaim, her "overnight" success was really anything but that.

The Trujillo Dictatorship and the Struggle for Democracy

During the dictatorship of Trujillo (twenty-five years long), many Dominicans were involved in the struggle for democracy and suffered persecution. Among these Dominicans was Julia's father. Once he was discovered as one of the opposition trying to overthrow the government of the dictator, there was no other choice but to escape, and it is then that the entire family left home to look for another place to call home again. It is in this situation that the family moved to New York with the help of a friend, who was an American doctor (Julia's father was also a doctor).

This move meant that Julia had to leave everything behind: her room, her home, her friends, her school, her way of living, her language, and many other things. She had to begin a new life in a different country with different surroundings, another house, another school, and a new language to learn in order to be able to communicate and function in her "new home." This move "redefines this critical period through multiple perspectives that enrich and complement a certain understanding of past [the change] provides [her] with voices and experiences that have helped to develop her writing career."[2]

Julia Alvarez states that she began writing essays, poetry, and in her words "how could the wild, multitudinous, daily things in anybody's head be inventoried in a form? . . . But that is the pretext of essays: we have something to declare."[3]

The Immigrant Experience

Her immigrant status and her desire to succeed in life are clearly stated in her own words: "I was abruptly uprooted from everything that I had known and loved. I lost almost everything: a homeland, a language, family connections, a way of understanding warmth."[4]

Adjusting to her new homeland was an experience of considerable difficulty. It meant that Julia had to adjust not only to her neighborhood in a large city (New York) but to a completely different set of rules, customs, language, environment, school, teachers, and classmates. All that had to be done as fast as she could. So she had to swim fast, if she wanted to survive. And as she states: "I landed not in the US, but in English?"[5] And proudly she adds that in her future "English became her homeland." Perhaps this interview conveys her feelings:

> Suddenly everything changed overnight-the way the air
> smelled, the way the light felt, the way the people responded,
> the language in which people responded, the food that was
> given to us in school, the structure of the family, which was
> no longer extended and varied but suddenly a nuclear
> family, which put a lot of pressure on all of us.[6]

Budding Literary Career

As she became comfortable with her newly acquired language, she began writing to express herself. Sometimes it was in the form of poetry or essays, and she started to send them for publication. Julia acknowledges that a number of these essays have been published in magazines and anthologies and for that she was helped by numerous editors and muses. She also thanks Roberto Véguez, who helped her with her Spanish. And most of all she thanks the *Virgencita de la Altagracia* who put them all in her *camino, ¡alta y última gracias!*[7] Julia's critics recognize that Julia was ten years old when she and her family fled to the United States, and it is understandable that she writes in English due to the fact that she was educated in this country. She even acknowledges that she had help with her Spanish.

Julia's first published literary works were books of poetry. Her first was *Homecoming* (1984). This book contains her poems "33," in which she takes stock of her life at age thirty-three (no husband, no children, no secure employment), and the poem "Housekeeping," in which domestic chores are presented as serious crafts worth mastering.

Latina Writer of the Immigrant Experience in the United States

Julia's most well-known works in the genre of literature of the immigrant experience are the breakthrough novel *How the Garcia Girls Lost Their Accents*

(1991), which was named a "Best Books of 1991" by *Library Journal,* and the sequel *!Yo!* (1997), which was acclaimed for its narrative inventiveness.

U.S. Latino literature is a new field and is also known as Hispanic American literature. It is the subject heading used by the Library of Congress classification system. It has been enriched by "writers who were formed and educated in their native countries and later emigrated or were forced to flee to the United States, and the other category includes writers who were born and raised in the United States, and who for the most part write in English."[8]

As a "Latina writer," Julia Alvarez was promptly established among the literary criticism and interpretation and hailed as one of the representatives of the development of Latina writers.

Her works are examined through "somatic dialogs addressing reason and emotions traditionally subordinated to reason because of their connection to women."[9]

The Feminist Writer

The feminist movement's impact on literature can be traced in the writing of several female writers in contemporary literature by women of minority groups. Some refer to them as women of color. Among them, Julia Alvarez is considered as a "female postcolonial—a hybrid region of literary production that dovetails the psychoanalytic strain of feminism [offering] a model which not only continues to flow out the hybrid exclusions of social interaction but also re-writes that understanding through an openly gendered lens."[10]

Literary critics examining the criticism and interpretation of the feminist movement include a concept of "Betweenness," which developed meaning the crossing of "borders by transnational feminist practice that is embodied in the creative and theoretical writing of a diverse group which comes together in the way that they each integrate the use of a generic literary form, like the historical romance or the melodrama, that is often associated, negatively, with being feminine, with the articulation of feminist agenda."[11] Nichols's focus for her thesis on Alvarez's *Time of the Butterflies* builds upon this foundation by describing how a feminist intervention into the genres of *testimonio* and romance can be reappropriated and redeployed in service of a Latina feminist project of storytelling. Something like "tracing roots and posting new possibilities, of writing 'old new fashioned love stories of writing Latina feminism through fiction.'"[12]

Diaspora

But Julia Alvarez holds one more merit and that is to employ and articulate the notion of "DiaspoAmerica" in her narrative, as other writers like herself from Cuba and Puerto Rico have done in their Caribbean texts. Campos Brito states that by representing America as a crossroad of diasporas, as a transnational imaginary, these texts not only expand the territorial boundaries of Hispanic Caribbean nations and the U.S. itself, but also undermine conventional assumptions of who is Dominican, Cuban, Puerto Rican, or American. . . . More importantly, through this process they move from a politics of identity to a politics of representation . . . and that is what Julia does, the construction of transnational and hybrid identities in her work.[13]

The Writer of Latin American Historical and Political Literature

After firmly establishing her reputation as a writer, based on her literature of the Latina immigrant experience and her feminist literature, Julia was ready for the broader challenge of writing historical and political fiction. Given her life experiences, it would come as no surprise that she would take on the almost mythical Trujillo dictatorship as her subject matter. Julia's most ambitious novel is *In the Time of the Butterflies* (1994), which is based on the true story of three sisters, known as the "butterflies," who defied the Trujillo dictatorship and paid for it with their lives. This novel won strong critical acclaim. It was an American Library Association Notable Book and a finalist for the National Book Critics Circle Award.

Good Timing—Fame and Awards

Julia Alvarez, together with Isabel Allende, is probably the most well-known Latina writer currently at work in the United States. There are thirty-nine doctoral dissertations written about her, her feminism, her Latina status, and her place in American literature, and studies comparing her to writers like Toni Morrison, Cristina Garcia, Le Ly Hayslip, Jamaica Kincaid, and many more too long to list. If one looks up Julia's name in Google, 1,350,000 hits could be searched that include her name in them. She also has her own "official webpage" with excellent and orderly presentation and information that provides a sense of credibility and true information, which emanates from Julia herself. She includes what she wrote, the awards and prizes that she won, her feelings, etc. A nice feature that I find interesting and up-to-date is "News" section. For example:

NEWS

"Charm," appears in the January 2006 issue of *O, The Oprah Magazine.* It is also part of a really wonderful collection of essays, *Why I'm Still Married: Women Write Their Hearts Out on Love, Loss, Sex, and Who Does the Dishes,* edited by Jean Trounstine and Karen Propp. The collection is in bookstores now, just in time for Valentine's Day! I'm currently reading it myself: one essay every night. Enlightening!

My new children's book, *A Gift of Gracias: the Legend of Altagracia,* was published last October, 2005, in English and Spanish, *Un regalo de Gracias:*

la leyenda de la Altagracia. I am making a pilgrimage to Higüey on la Virgencita's feast day, January 21st, 2006, to present her with a copy, *promesa cumplida!*

My new novel, *Saving the World,* will be published this coming April 2006. I will be on the road with a book tour that takes me to 15 cities. Stay tuned. I will post the details on my APPEARANCES page as soon as I have them.

APPEARANCES

I will be the guest of "La Plaza, Conversations with Ilan Stavans" on WGBH, Tuesday, January 10th at 7:30pm. This is the Boston premiere. There is also a video/audio podcast available online: wgbh.org/conversations.

I will be going on a 15-city book tour, beginning in April. Please check back on this page for details about appearances near you.

Stops will include Manchester, VT; South Hadley, MA; Boston; New York City and Brooklyn; D.C.; Miami; Chicago; Milwaukee; Minneapolis; Portland, OR; Seattle, WA; San Francisco, CA; Los Angeles; Tempe, AZ; Denver; and Dallas.

Then, they'll ship me home in a little baggie marked "Author Leftovers." I do hope I will see some of you at these stops. It's what makes touring worth it, getting to meet my readers.[14]

Julia Alvarez has been recognized as a poet and narrator who has received many awards, prizes, and grants, which is needless to list when I could give you her official webpage where they are all listed: http://www.juliaalvarez.com/about/vita.php. Cocco de Filippis states that it has been said that the literary creativity, in general, is the product of the author's obsessions. But, in the case of Julia Alvarez, her literature is the result of her desire to find a resolution to her conflict of being a Latina writer, which involves the concept of being a woman, Latina, and writer.[15]

How Julia Gets Her Inspiration

Julia Alvarez in her own words states how she gets involved in her writing when she tells how she wrote the poem titled "Reading the Coffee Cup":

> Then, one morning, I thought, why don't I try this out. I had such a vivid memory from childhood of old Chucha reading the future from the stains left in coffee cups, a tradition in the Dominican Republic. Soon I was deep inside the poem. I could smell the beans. I could see that old woman so clearly, her lined face, her wise eyes, old Chucha who had been dead for a decade, who had read my coffee cup and predicted a future I couldn't remember.

"Reading the Coffee Cup" by Julia Alvarez

Old Chucha used to read
the coffee cups.
After they were drained,
she'd turn the cups over
on their saucers
and let the future form.

As I waited I'd feel the sun
warm on my brown skin,
I'd watch the hummingbirds plunge
their beaks in the bougainvillea.
In the sky, a plane glinted north.
I lifted my hand to wave.

My cup always took longest.
Finally, she'd turn it over,
eyes narrowed
so that her wrinkled face
grew even more wrinkled.
Her future was almost over.

But mine was just beginning.
¡Ten years old!
Chucha's eyebrows lifted.
She saw towers! Strangers!
She heard an odd Spanish
issuing from my lips!

Weeks later, I landed
in the United States of America,
skyscrapers so tall
it hurt my neck to look up,
and coffee so weak
it left no stain on the cup.

And Chucha faded
into one more old face
who died while I was gone,
her art of reading the cup
turned into a superstition
in an underdeveloped nation.

Or so I was taught
in the towers by the strangers,
English coming from my lips
as if I had been born to it;
assimilated into the mainstream,
I learned to swim.

But still, in some café
in Boston or New York City,
I finish my coffee
and Styrofoam or mug
I turn the cup over
and let the dregs dry.

Then holding it in my hands
I gaze down into Chucha's face;
I smell the brilliant sun
baking the bougainvillea,
the hummingbirds buzzing
above the honking of traffic.

I go back for refills
until all I had lost returns
so palpably I can taste it!
A new art like her old art -
reading the past
in a coffee cup.[16]

Julia Alvarez's creative and enthusiastic prose is proof of her fame. Having written on various topics covering fiction, poetry, and nonfiction, she has something about something "to declare."

NOTES

1. Silvio Serias, *Julia Alvarez: A Critical Companion* (Westport, Conn.: Greenwood Press, 2002), p. 1.

2. Amarilis Ortiz, "La narrativa como rescate de la historia privada: Poder, resistencia y transición en la sociedad dominicana de 1960 a 1965" (Ph.D. diss., Vanderbilt University, 2004).

3. Julia Alvarez, *Something to Declare* (New York: Plume, 1999), p. xiv.

4. Heather Rosario-Sievert, "Conversation with Julia Alvarez," *Latin American Literature and Arts* (spring 1997): 32.

5. Melita Marie Garza, "Sharing Secrets," *Chicago Tribune,* November 21, 1994, pp. 1, 5.

6. Darren Kash Broome, "Strategies of Resistance in Alvarez's 'In the Time of the Butterflies'" (Ph.D. diss., University of Alabama, 2002), p. 7.

7. Alvarez, *Something to Declare,* p. x.

8. Broome, "Strategies of Resistance," p. 7.

9. Judy Rivera-van Schagen, "Conformity and Resistance: Somatic Dialogics and the Construction of the Female Self in the Works of Ana Castillo, Rosario Castellanos, Rosa María Britton, and Julia Alvarez" (Ph.D. diss., Indiana University of Pennsylvania, 2002).

10. David Thomas Mitchell, "Conjured Communities: The Multiperspectival Novels of Amy Tan, Toni Morrison, Julia Alvarez, Louise Erdrich and Cristina García" (Ph.D. diss., University of Michigan, 1993).

11. Susan E. Nichols, "Between Feminine and Feminist: Contemporary United States Latina Writers Negotiate Genre and Politics (Emma Perez, Julia Alvarez, Sandra Benitez, Alicia Gaspar de Alba)" (Ph.D. diss., University of California, Los Angeles, 2002).

12. Nichols, "Between Feminine and Feminist."

13. Rosa Cecila Campos Brito, "Hacia una diaspo-America: Imaginarios transnacionales en textos contemporaneous."

14. http://www.juliaalvarez.com/.

15. Daisy Cocco de Filippis, *Desde la diáspora/A Diaspora Position* (New York: Ediciones Alcance, 2003), p. 107.

16. http://www.juliaalvarez.com/napa/ (accessed March 1, 2006).

BIBLIOGRAPHY

Works by Julia Alvarez

"Alvarez Describes Home." In *Writer's Choice: Composition and Grammar Text for Eight Graders.*

"An American Childhood in the Dominican Republic." *The American Scholar* (winter 1987).

Before We Were Free. New York: A. Knopf, 2002.

"Black Behind the Ears." *Essence Magazine* (February 1993).

A Cafecito Story. With an afterword by Bill Eichner and woodcuts by Belkis Ramírez. White River Junction, Vt.: Chelsea Green, 2001.

A Cafecito Story/El cuento del cafecito. Translated by Daisy Cocco de Filippis. White River Junction, Vt.: Chelsea Green, 2002.

El cuento del cafecito. Mexico: Debolsillo, 2004.

Finding Miracles. New York: Knopf, 2004.

"Flight Plans." *The Washington Post Magazine,* August 13, 1995.

"Hold the Mayonnaise." *Hers* Column, *New York Times Magazine,* January 12, 1992. Reprinted in *The McGraw Hill Reader* (New York: McGraw Hill, 1994); and in *Aims and Options: A Thematic Approach to Writing* (Boston: Houghton Mifflin, 1994).

Homecoming: New and Collected Poems. New York: Plume, 1996.

Homecoming: Poems. New York: Grove Press, 1984.

How the García Girls Lost Their Accents. Chapel Hill: Algonquin Books, 1991.

How Tia Lola Come to Stay. New York: Knopf, 2001.

In the Name of Salome. Chapel Hill: Algonquin Books, 2000.

"An Unlikely Beginning for a Writer." In *Máscaras.* Berkeley, Calif.: Third Woman, 1997. Pp. 189–199.

19. Adaptación y traslación de la historia puertorriqueña en *La casa de la laguna* de Rosario Ferré

Nashieli Marcano

Mediante la crónica y la memoria, *La casa de la laguna* de Rosario Ferré, establece una conexión entre las nociones de "género" y "raza" en el contexto de la historiografía de la mujer afro-puertorriqueña, las cuales han sido—por lo general—estudiados por separado. Es imprescindible fusionar ambos elementos pues es en este contrapunto de género y raza en donde podemos hacer un acercamiento a la mujer afro-puertorriqueña en esta novela. Trataremos el efecto de los códigos lingüísticos empleados por la autora al momento de publicar su trabajo, más las imágenes de la mujer negra creadas para su historicidad.

Ferré: ¿Dónde se ubica su historiografía?

La escritura puertorriqueña producida en los EE.UU. ha estado bajo el escrutinio de varios críticos puertorriqueños. Algunos, como Juan López Bauzá, aseguran que la literatura producida en el continente debe ser excluida del espacio literario de la isla, ya que, "la literatura puertorriqueña escrita en inglés en los Estados Unidos es una ramificación autónoma de la isleña, no la mitad ausente de ésta" (1999, 2). Es decir, que esta escritura se desvincula de la obra literaria puertorriqueña. Para López Bauzá, en Puerto Rico no existe mercado en el que sobreviva la literatura puertorriqueña en inglés, y quienes comparten su opinión, afirman que la nacionalidad boricua está muy ligada a la lengua española.

Por otro lado, los ensayistas Arcadio Díaz Quiñones y Jorge Duany debaten este pensamiento, ya que definen la literatura puertorriqueña de los EE.UU. como una relación íntima entre la isla y el continente, como una relación que más bien disuelve la frontera atlántica. Díaz Quiñónes articula que, gracias al movimiento de la diáspora, la literatura puertorriqueña se posiciona en un espacio más abierto e inclusivo. La literatura de Rosario Ferré, precisamente desmarca los límites fronterizos entre ambos países. Y como bien lo explica Duany: "Puerto Rico is a nation on the move" and the "political, geographic, and linguistic categories long taken as the essence of national identity . . . no longer capture the permeable and elastic boundaries of the Puerto Rican nation" (37). Ferré rompe el nexo entre la geografía, el idioma y la identidad nacional.

Para el boricua no es nada nuevo el publicar obras en otros idiomas. El considerado "Padre de la Patria" puertorriqueña, Ramón Emeterio Betances, publicó casi todas sus obras en francés, y la gran poeta Julia de Burgos, escribió sus últimas obras en inglés durante su exilio en Nueva York. Dada la situación política, social y cultural del país bajo el dominio colonial, historizarse en otros códigos lingüísticos deviene un acto natural y para algunos, algo necesario en el proceso de redefinirse.

El desterritorializar la literatura boricua no significa para Ferré hibridizar su escritura, puesto que esto implicaría el inscribir el ingrediente norteamericano en su obra; simplemente se reafirma como escritora bilingüe. Su elección de escribir sus primeras novelas largas *The House on the Lagoon* y *Eccentric Neighborhoods* originalmente en inglés, según la propia Ferré, ha sido para facilitar la difusión de sus novelas. De hecho, *Eccentric Neighborhoods,* fue la más vendida en Puerto Rico en 1998. La capacidad de Ferré de posicionarse en otro espacio para su escritura y de sus novelas de ser tan bien recibidas en la isla por los lectores, desata una polémica entre los críticos, contradiciendo el punto anterior de Bauzá; ya que se comprueba que la problemática de la historicidad del puertorriqueño trasciende los límites geográficos y lingüísticos. Como nos indica el crítico Juhász-Mininberg,

> Los variados circuitos de desplazamiento entre Puerto Rico y los Estados Unidos, entre el "aquí" y el "allá", de la experiencia puertorriqueña no sólo han relativizado el marco de referencia territorial que se asocia a la formulación tradicional del concepto de nación, sino que también ha multiplicado los registros lingüísticos en que se reclama y afirma el concepto de identidad nacional puertorriqueña. (2003, 142)

Ferré comienza escribiendo un cuento de 200 páginas titulado "La casa de la laguna", el cual le sirve como germen literario para más tarde escribir la novela *The House in the Lagoon*. Inmediatamente luego de publicar *The House on the Lagoon,* Ferré escribe la versión española la cual titula, *La casa de la laguna.* La traslación del texto original se da a dos niveles: a nivel de publicación (de cuento en español, a novela en inglés, a novela en español) y a nivel de contenido, pues la trama involucra el descubrimiento del manuscrito de Isabel. El hecho de referirnos a un manuscrito el cual tiene existencia material sólo en plano de ficción, nos encontramos entonces con la traslación al inglés de un texto fantasma. Valga la cita de Guillermo Irizarry, quien ha estudiado más de cerca traducciones de diversos autores caribeños:

> It is clear that as we attempt to value the canonicity of these writings we experience an affect of deterritorialization, as we have a displaced original and a phantasmagoric primary cultural-referential space. These narrations make reference to an original locus of culture, encoded in Spanish, while existing in and interpolating another (encoded in English).

En otras palabras, que la reproducción que hace la protagonista Isabel de la historia, de la cultura, y de la identidad de su familia, se traslada al inglés y va construyendo la "otredad" del sujeto mismo de la narración. Petra, sacerdotisa negra, y trabajadora doméstica en la casa Mendizabal, es quien protege el manuscrito, para luego ser publicado, sufre un desdoblamiento, y el lector de *The House in the Lagoon,* tiene también un encontronazo con su realidad, a través de un código lingüístico diferente.

La novela trata de Isabel Monfort, mujer blanca y burguesa, quien produce un manuscrito, precisamente titulado "La casa de la laguna", en el cual se revela la historia de su familia y la de su esposo Quintín Mendizábal. Quintín, hombre con vanas aspiraciones a ser historiador, descubre y lee el manuscrito, más comienza a corregirlo, ya que para él, el texto no le parece fiel a la historia de ambas familias. Con el manuscrito, Isabel socava la autoridad de la sociedad patriarcal, revelando las lagunas dentro de la historia oficial de la familia y la vez de la isla, ya pronunciadas anteriormente por el discurso masculino.

La trama de *The House in the Lagoon* tiene una fuerte inscripción histórico-social y étnica, ya que está acompañada de momentos y procesos claves de la isla, haciendo hincapié en 1898, año de la invasión militar norteamericana. Durante esta época, se historizaba la raza y la clase, mas se omite el género, dándose en especial, la ausencia de la negra; algo que a la novela de Ferré no se le escapa pues se abre un espacio narrativo en contexto femenino.

La visibilidad de la mujer negra a lo largo del manuscrito

En los primeros capítulos vemos como la clase y la raza a comienzos del siglo XX se inscriben en las discusiones sobre el otorgamiento de la ciudadanía norteamericana a los puertorriqueños. En este imaginario construido, la negra queda invisible en la historicidad del país. La otra estrategia empleada para mantener este imaginario del puertorriqueño blanco fue la antigua práctica de las iglesias españolas de mantener un "libro de limpieza de sangre", para evitar los matrimonios mixtos en la isla. Cuando la discriminación racial en los EE.UU. se une al ya existente discrimen racial en PR, se binariza aun más la raza. Se comienza entonces a imitar este racismo importado y se le da continuidad a la imagen del *jíbaro* para definir al puertorriqueño. La mulata implícitamente es historizada en los libros de limpieza de sangre.

Cuando Isabel nos adelanta a las décadas de los veinte, treinta y cuarenta, el lector se percata de que el problema de la representación de la negritud aun continúa. Estamos hablando de una negritud que existe, pero que se esconde y se viste de blanco. Isabel, mujer blanca y bien acomodada, nos describe a una mulata que se duele de su mulatez y que siente que debe pasar como blanca para establecerse social y económicamente. Isabel la historiza haciendo eco a la obra Vejigantes de Arriví. El manuscrito de Isabel nos da a conocer papel en la sociedad dentro del ámbito de los trabajos manuales (trabajo doméstico, cocinera, costurera). A diferencia del trabajo doméstico, el cual recibe un estatus social bajo al éste asociarse históricamente con la esclavitud, el de la costurera disfrutaba de mejor de un prestigio social. Este "ascenso" en la sociedad, bien se pudo haber dado por dos razones: (1) el trabajo de modista se hacia por medio de una "invitación a trabajar" a la casa de la "dueña" y (2) por el mero hecho de la costurera absorber conocimientos sobre las modas impuestas a las clases altas, participando de forma oblicua de este mundo. Esmeralda personifica a la mulata de esta época.

En la década de los setenta, el discurso de la afro-puertorriqueñidad entra en auge, y los autores redefinen y "mulatizan" la historia con personajes femeninos. Estos son autores que han sido influenciados por los sucesos históricos a nivel internacional: independencias africanas, la Revolución Cubana, el movimiento feminista, etc., que impactan la literatura de forma especial pues se van fundiendo las literaturas feministas y negroides. Podemos hacer una reflexión de esta escritura leyendo el manuscrito de Isabel. La mujer negra va adquiriendo mas presencia en la historia y en la historicidad del puertorriqueño.

Vemos a la mulata Coral iluminando intelectualmente a su novio Manuel (hijo de Isabel), instruyéndolo en los escritos de Mao, Carlos Marx y Albizu, y haciendolo miembro del partido independentista. Coral, quien reporta para el diario *The Clarion,* historiza al Puerto Rico de su época. Vemos como las nociones de género, raza, nacionalismo y clase se van intersectando y reforzándose mutuamente.

Ya leyendo los últimos capítulos, en donde el contexto progresa a la década de los ochenta, vemos que Petra, la sirvienta en la casa de los Mendizábal, ha estado activamente involucrada en la escritura del manuscrito de Isabel. Por un lado tenemos a Isabel, urgiéndole historizar acontecimientos que han pasado por desapercibido y que han sido versionados por el discurso masculino, mientras que por otro tenemos la presencia y la influencia de Petra para insertarse en el discurso negroide. Como consecuencia se inscribe a África como la otra **Madre Patria** dentro del árbol genealógico puertorriqueño en el manuscrito. Isabel y Petra, antes percibidas como objetos en su historicidad, reversan esta objetificación, asumiendo sus propios discursos.

La intervención de Petra fue imperante en este proceso, ya que ella se reivindica ella preservar el manuscrito de Isabel, logrando que este saliera a la luz pública mas tarde. Petra sacrifica mucho su identidad al proteger el manuscrito de Isabel, pues en este proceso ella debe reemplazar la palabra oral por la escrita. Ella transigió a que sus experiencias y su historia se escribieran y se publicaran en el lenguaje del colonizador, pero con la tranquilidad de ser ésta una escritura femenina.

La mulata textualizada en la casa

La casa de la laguna es—a primera instancia—una representación de la sociedad patriarcal puertorriqueña. La casa, de principio a fin sufre la mutación, ya que pasa por varias etapas de construcción y demolición a través de la dinastía Mendizábal. La casa viene a ser un borrador en donde se desplazan los cuerpos. Con cada construcción, destrucción y reconstrucción se busca hacer borrón y cuenta nueva, contar la historia de otra manera, adaptarse a los continuos cambios de contextos sociales y políticos. La presencia de Petra no permite que la casa sea una estructura fija, y que dentro de esta reescritura se quede fuera la negritud del puertorriqueño.

Buenaventura, el dueño de la casa, y Petra, la sirvienta, hacen de la casa un lugar para arraigarse, para estar en contacto con sus antepasados; Buenaventura como patriarca y Petra como matriarca de la familia. Vemos como el árbol genealógico de ambos individuos—que según la historia oficial, han ido corriendo paralelamente sin intersecar—se entrelazan. Para llegar a Petra, quien vive en el sótano de la casa, debe pasar uno por un túnel oscuro y húmedo. Es como entrar en el cordón umbilical . . . al llegar al pozo, todo el que entra en el se puede dar un baño purificador.

La mulata textualizada en la comida

Existe un determinismo ambiental al inscribir a la negra en lo puertorriqueño. Este determinismo se da a través de la comida y la naturaleza misma. Elementos como el agua y el fuego corporealizan a la negra en el manuscrito de Isabel. Ya sea por la dieta que ella consume o por los olores o sabores que emanan de su cuerpo en la novela de Ferré, la comida crea una imagen erotizada, y en casos, animalizada de ella. El consumir la carne del cangrejo, por ejemplo, ha sido una forma de acceder a la negra, como un rito de pasaje. Es una forma de asimilación a la hora de copular con ella.

Los sentidos del gusto y el olfato se ponen en función al detectar la presencia de la mulata, describiendo como un objeto apetecible y a la vez sexual. "En los casinos y otros centros sociales, la gente bien empezó a susurrar que de las mulatas emanaba un extraño olor a café con leche que las hacia muy atractivas" (36). Todos los hombres de la familia Mendizábal mantuvieron relaciones con negras. En el caso de Ignacio, este "no quería perder el sabor a buñuelos de crema de mocha que le quedaba en la boca después de que Esmeralda Márquez lo besara. . . . Lo único que le apetecía era recordar el olor a arroz con canela que le había humeado a Esmeralda Márquez del fondo de los sobacos cuando había bailado con ella la conga en el Jack's Place la noche anterior" (242).

Buenaventura inclusive, admite lo siguiente mientras comía sentado en la playa: "Cuando me muera, quiero que me entierren cerca de este lugar. Quiero subir al cielo en alas de un bacalaito frito y descansar la cabeza sobre una alcapurria gigante" (227). Este momento sobre indulgencia, Buenaventura fantasea con llegar a la gloria rodeado de una negritud feminizada. La mujer negra se corporealiza con productos de consumo. Al ser la comida, tan central en la organización social como la sexualidad en la novela, la mulata es aceptada como un cuerpo "comestible". El bacalaito frito y la alcapurria gigante son productos que pasan por el proceso de freír, lo que nos trae al siguiente elemento que textualiza a la mujer negra: el fuego.

La mulata textualizada en el fuego y en el agua y la tierra

El manuscrito de Isabel nos describe a la mulata a través de los elementos fuego y agua. En gran parte de su texto, estas dos fuerzas se yuxtaponen, creando una oposición fundamental que toman dominio de la trama. Ambos elementos pueden lograr perder su esencia al unirse, pero es precisamente en este momento que la imagen de la mulata se erotiza con doble carácter. Leamos una cita del manuscrito en donde el fuego y el agua se yuxtaponen:

> Coral sintió que se transformaba en un arrecife de fuego; su cuerpo era la ensenada en donde atracaría la proa de Manuel.
>
> --Así debe ser la muerte, mi amor—le susurro Coral cuando se encontraron.
>
> --Te equivocas—le contesto Manuel—Así será nuestra vida juntos. (365)

En esta segunda cita el fuego se introduce como relámpago acompañando la lluvia:

> El fogonazo eléctrico bajo corriendo por el tronco y entro de un salto a la casa por la ventana; la cuna de Altagracia estaba cerca, y se salvo de milagro. Pero el dios del fuego se alojo de todas formas en su cuerpo. Solo que, en lugar de en el corazón, se le metió en donde no debía: en la chochita.

Este determinismo es generacional y vemos que corre por la línea materna. Mientras que a la hija de Altagracia, Carmelina, la tachan de "dragón" a su nieta la acusan de tener al dios del fuego metido entre sus piernas. Sus caderas son descritas como "dos calderos bailando sobre la estufa" (328). Vemos nuevamente la yuxtaposición del fuego y agua, pues en estos recipientes se utilizan para hacer sopas.

Atravesando los manglares para llegar a la casa de los Mendizabal, llega Petra, sacerdotisa negra y soberana del arrabal Las Minas. Los ancestros de Petra eran guerreros de la tribu africana Ndongo Kumnundu, y quien—aun llevando la función de sirvienta—es quien manipula el espacio femenino y desmonta los mitos patriarcales que regían en la casa. El manglar evoca ese sendero que cruza el cimarrón, un sendero que nos remonta a sus antepasados y nos lleva a la África ancestral. Chamoiseau lo pone de ésta manera: "The mangrove is, in fact, a sensitive figure in our collective consciousness; it is, in our nature, a cradle, a source of life, of birth and rebirth" (390).

La tierra del manglar, al estar en contacto con el agua, es una tierra ablandada por la constante presencia de este liquido. Este ablandamiento es simbólico al cuerpo de la mujer negra quedando rendida por la importunación del deseo del hombre.

El agua es un elemento esencial en la novela. En el sótano de la casa de los Mendizábal, con piso de tierra, se encuentra un pozo, que para Petra representa la separación del mundo de los vivos del de los muertos. Buenaventura, aunque deseaba morir y subir al cielo con alas de alcapurria, fallece en el pozo en brazos, no de su esposa, sino de Petra: "Cuando vio a Petra ayudando a cargar el cuerpo y sosteniendo todavía la mano de Buenaventura, le dio un empujón y la saco a gritos del cuarto. . . . Quería asegurarse de que su alma llegara al otro mundo sana y salva, siguiendo la ruta subterránea del agua hasta su origen" (1998, 278). Aquí vemos una yuxtaposición entre el agua y la tierra.

A través del agua se procrea el mulato en la familia Mendizábal. En las afueras de la casa, entre el manglar y la laguna, se encuentra la playa Lucumí. Es en esta playa dónde copulan los personajes masculinos de la dinastía Mendizábal con los personajes femeninos negros. Se presentan aquí las dicotomías (hombre-mujer, blanco-negro, Dios-Elegguá, etc.) en plena confrontación.

En el caso de la afro-puertorriqueña, las constantes del agua, fuego y tierra son parte de su composición. El agua evoca la naturaleza femenina y su fertilidad. Por este médium, ella logra transmutarse en organismos. El mar convierte a la mulata en autora de la fecundación y albergue de vida. De la misma manera, el fuego le da el aspecto de un ente eterno. El termino proviene del latín *focus* que quiere decir "hoguera" u hogar. Vemos entonces que ambos elementos son puntos de ida y partida, de procreación y muerte, la conexión entre tiempos diferentes.

En el desenlace del manuscrito, la casa, rodeada de agua, se consume en llamas, dándole continuidad a un rito de fertilidad que prepara el terreno para la re-versionar lo puertorriqueño. En un estudio realizado por Ana Rivera Lassen, titulado "La mujer puertorriqueña negra", es uno de los pocos en donde se discute el tema del racismo y de su efecto en la mujer negra. Aunque Ferré trabaja el cuerpo de la mujer negra desde la perspectiva de una mujer burguesa, blanca, ella logra un nivel de complejidad en donde se revelan las relaciones de poder que lidian con el género, la raza y la clase. La problemática de la identidad nacional encarna en la figura femenina negra, pero no una relegada a una mera imagen, sino que existe como sujeto, no como objeto.

Conclusión

La estructura binaria de Ferré, con las dicotomías de hombre/mujer, blanco/negro, clase proletaria/clase burguesa, Dios/Elegguá, historia/ficción, nos lleva a ese proceso de ruptura. Mientras que en el imaginario puertorriqueño (incluyendo la literatura) se glorifica a la mujer negra por su función en el ámbito laboral doméstico, por su rol de madre nodriza y por su exuberante sexualidad, la novela debate los mitos creados e insertan a la mulata como personaje desmitificador de la realidad puertorriqueña. Ambas protagonistas, Isabel y Petra, señalan que ha significado la raza tanto para la mujer blanca, como a la mujer negra, mas como ésta ha estructurado la vida ambas.

BIBLIOGRAFÍA

Chamoiseau, Patrick. 1998. *Le discours antillais.* Paris: Seuil.

Díaz Quiñones, Arcadio. 2000. *El arte de bregar: Ensayos.* San Juan: Ediciones Callejón.

Duany, Jorge. 2002. *The Puerto Rican Nation on the Move: Identities on the Island and on the United States.* Chapel Hill: University of North Carolina Press.

Ferré, Rosario. 1997. *La casa de la laguna.* New York: Vintage.

Juhász-Mininberg, Emeshe. 2003. "Construyendo la puertorriqueñidad: ciudadanía, cultura y nación". En *Políticas de identidades y diferencias sociales en tiempos de globalización,* editado por Daniel Mato. Caracas: FACES-UCV. Pp. 117–146.

López Bauzá, Juan. "Rosario Ferré; el debate del idioma, los escritores de ayer y hoy". *Paliques,* February 19, 1999.

20. Diálogo a través de las fronteras: reformulaciones femeninas del pasado

Ylonka Nacidit-Perdomo

Una introducción necesaria

Los estudios bibliográficos y bibliotecológicos no pueden echar a un lado la necesidad de conocer la geografía y la territorialidad de la creación femenina. Todo discurso del saber siempre trae consigo dicotomías, fragmentaciones, y un desafío de oponer el pasado al presente.

Esta ponencia aborda el tema de las escritoras dominicanas del siglo XIX, de aquellas que tuvieron que adoptar otra patria, de otras que murieron en tierras lejanas, víctimas del destierro, del exilio involuntario, huyendo de la persecución política, o que temporalmente migraron como una forma de salvar sus vidas ante el acoso del tirano de turno.

Reconstruir la autoría femenina de *fin-de-siglo,* hacer el hallazgo de textos dispersos de la época decimonónica en el archipiélago de las islas caribeñas, es una manera de romper con la exclusión, a la cual ha sido empujada la mujer en el discurso dominante patriarcal, aún en el sistema de recolección de datos sobre una temática que como la migración se tiene aún cierta resistencia en torno a la investigación desde una perspectiva de género.

Todo empieza con mi relación con la Universidad de Concordia en Montreal, se inicia en 1994, época en la cual la doctora Catharina Vanderplaats de Vallejo me contacta por un puro y simple azar del destino. Entonces, lejos estaba yo de saber que sería parte de una *historia,* que tendría delante de mí la oportunidad de reconstruir la vida de Virginia Elena Ortea (1866–1903), una escritora dominicana casi desconocida, de la cual en 1989 yo había escrito un breve ensayo para leer a mis estudiantes en la Biblioteca Nacional titulado "Virginia Elena Ortea: sus juegos de alusión en *Risas y Lágrimas*", partiendo de un libro que extrañamente cayó en mis manos editado en 1978 por Alfa y Omega, libro detrás del cual anduviera la Dra. Vanderplaats, y que para suerte suya yo poseía.

Desde entonces se inició mi proceso de *movilidad,* de *desplazamientos,* de viajes al interior y al exterior. El *leitmotiv* consistía en localizar los manuscritos inéditos de Virginia Elena Ortea, sus textos publicados en el extranjero, en los países a los cuales emigró, y en medio de todo esto: rescatar todo texto (poema, ensayo, artículos periodísticos, etc.) de autoras dominicanas del siglo XIX, édito e inédito, olvidado en algún archivo familiar, o en un baúl centenario como fue el caso con algunos de los de Virginia Elena Ortea.

La meta a alcanzar sería en conexión y en contacto con las bibliotecas de Vanier y Webster de Concordia University, para hacer llegar a la Dra. Vanderplaats de Vallejo, Jefa del Departamento de Lenguas Modernas y Lingüísticas, de la Universidad de Concordia, en Montreal, los documentos requeridos para su investigación que auspiciaba el gobierno de la provincia de Québec con una beca.

Sin embargo, yo no hacía solo la labor de Asistente de Investigación que conllevaba compilar para el envío a Canadá de: reseñas periodísticas, sueltos, bibliografías, panoramas de literatura, antologías, tesis de grado, historias de literatura, entrevistas, etc., sino que además participaba con la responsabilidad de coordinar en Santo Domingo las visitas y las conferencias que Vanderplaats dictaba en la Biblioteca Nacional, en los meses de julio y agosto, para ofrecer al público un adelanto de sus investigaciones en los archivos y bibliotecas de República Dominicana.

Además, debo confesar que me había enamorado del proyecto de ir tras la huella, el rastro de mujeres escritoras que tuvieron que emigrar de la reciente proclamada República Dominicana en el siglo XIX, forzadas por la opresión política.

La otra orilla del lenguaje

La historia del complejo proceso migratorio de escritoras dominicanas en el siglo XIX es, una historia de resistencia, de búsquedas y de complejidades.

El siglo XIX fue una época muy convulsionada; las guerras intestinas configuraron nuestra idiosincrasia como nación, luego de la proclamación de la Independencia en 1844 de los habitantes de la parte Este de la Isla de Santo Domingo. En medio de las luchas sociales y políticas surge un discurso literario de influencia romántica de mujeres que se adhieren o internan a través de sus textos literarios en la confrontación patriótica.

Los textos de las autoras de Santo Domingo que migraron, entonces, tienen múltiples lecturas. Por un lado, plantean de manera enunciativa la otredad genérica de la identidad femenina, orquestada en una paradójica existencia, y por el otro, se expresan afligidas por el destierro, el exilio o la ausencia del compañero, algún familiar o ellas mismas. Cinco sucesos vinculados con la lucha patriótica, a la encarnizada persecución política, a la efusión de sangre dominicana, a los intentos de sedición, a las contiendas fratricidas y a las convulsiones sociales provocan la emigración constante de 1844 a 1900 de mujeres dominicanas y sus familias a las islas vecinas:

la Batalla de Las Carreras de 1849

la Conspiración del 25 de marzo de 1855

la Revolución del 7 de julio de 1857

la Anexión del 18 de marzo de 1861

la Restauración del 16 de agosto de 1863.[1]

Entre 1844 y 1899 muchas mujeres migraron: febreristas, independentistas, santanistas, baecistas, próceres y escritoras. Muchas de estas escritoras permanecen aún anónimas y olvidadas en el polvo del tiempo; las que padecieron el destierro y fueron víctimas de una emigración involuntaria murieron en playas extranjeras como Saint Thomas, Curazao, Venezuela, Puerto Rico o Cuba.

El saber de la mujer

En 1860 en Santo Domingo había veinticinco escuelas de niñas con 322 niñas registradas, y en las cuales 131 varones cursaban el inicio de sus estudios primarios. La documentación de que se dispone arroja los siguientes datos sobre la escritura y el saber de la mujer a fines del siglo XIX en la convulsionada y empobrecida República Dominicana. En 1883 estaban abiertas sólo cinco escuelas municipales de niñas,[2] entre otras, la de Regina, de las Mercedes, de la Misericordia, a lo cual hay que añadir que en ese siglo sólo tres mujeres dieron a la luz sus creaciones literarias en forma de libro: Salomé Ureña (*Poesías, 1880*), Josefa Antonia Perdomo (*Poesías de la Señorita Josefa A. Perdomo, 1885*), y Amelia Francasci (*Madre culpable: novela original, 1893*).

Salomé Ureña de Henríquez abre las puertas en Santo Domingo del *Instituto de Señoritas* el tres de noviembre de 1881, en la calle San José número 13. Bajo la dirección de Ureña se gradúan el 17 de abril de 1887 las primeras Maestras Normalistas Leonor M. Feltz, Luisa Ozema Pellerano, Mercedes Laura Aguiar, Ana Josefa Puello, Altagracia Henríquez Perdomo y Catalina Pou.

En el siglo XIX sólo tres mujeres dieron a la luz pública sus creaciones literarias en forma de libro: Salomé Ureña (*Poesía, 1880*), consagrada al porvenir y a la gloria de su misión patriótica y redentora, que vivió en medio de la angustiosa situación de la patria, en el tropel de las brumas políticas, el despotismo y el inicio de la conciencia crítica ante la tiranía de la ignorancia; Josefa Antonia Perdomo (*Poesías de la Señorita Josefa A. Perdomo, 1885*), la cantora de alma mística, iluminada por el éxtasis del creador, y la contemplación que inspira su alta poesía y devota admiración a la Virgen, y Amelia Francasci (*Madre Culpable: novela original, 1893*), de pensamiento extraño y curioso, amiga de "Pierre Loti, el incomparable prosista taumaturgo" como le llamara la escritora puertoplateña Mercedes Mota ("La Condesa Mathieu de Noailles" en *La Cuna de América* [27-VII-1913], número 14, año III, pág. 60), cuya casa era una cámara de enaltecidos encantos y seductores aromas, al lado del viejo templo colonial de la Catedral Santa María la Menor.

Las intelectuales más activas de la época que compartían aficiones como la lectura, la escritura, el magisterio, la membresía en asociaciones literarias, fueron Josefa Antonia Perdomo (1834–1896), Salomé Ureña (1850–1897), Amelia Francasci (1850–1941), Virginia Elena Ortea (1866–1903), una criatura excepcional de singular nostalgia, y Encarnación Echavarría Vilaseca de Del Monte (1821–1891).

La República Dominicana mostraba en la década del 80 como avances la instalación del *Teléfono* entre Puerto Plata y Santiago (1885), del *Ferrocarril* de Sánchez a La Vega (1887) y la primera línea telegráfica (1896). En 1870 María del Socorro Sánchez funda en Santiago el colegio *El Corazón de María,* y posteriormente, en 1882, en Santo Domingo el colegio de niñas *La Altagracia,* teniendo lugar la primera graduación de maestras el cuatro de junio 1887.

En el siglo XIX en la República Dominicana publicaron poemas, cuentos, cartas y artículos de opinión sólo 38 mujeres, en *El Oasis* (1854–1855, 1856), *El Porvenir* (Puerto Plata, 1872), *El Correo del Ozama* (1875), *El Sufragio* (1878–1879), *Listín Diario* (1889), *Revista Ilustrada* (1898–1900), *Letras y Ciencias* (1892–1898), *El Orden* (Santiago de Los Caballeros, 1875), *La Crónica* y *El Eco de la Opinión.*

De 1870 a 1890 dieron a conocer sus creaciones poéticas Josefa Perdomo (1854), la primera mujer en publicar un poema, Josefa del Monte (1875), Concepción Agüero de B. (1879), María del Pilar Sinués de Marco (1878) y Encarnación Echavarría de Del Monte (1882), Salomé Ureña (1870).

Josefa Antonia Perdomo y Heredia (1843–1896)

Muy poco ha dicho la crítica especializada sobre su obra poética, no obstante haber ocupado en la vida intelectual del siglo XIX, a partir de la década del 50, un lugar de preeminencia en la literatura femenina, que compartiría, posteriormente, en los años 80 con Salomé Ureña de Henríquez.

Perdomo pertenecía a una elite intelectual y al movimiento cultural que se desarrollaba a *Orillas del río Ozama,* en la ciudad intramuros de Santo Domingo. La crítica académica ha clasificado su poesía en dos renglones: *su poesía mística* y *su poesía patriótica,* a la cual nosotras añadiríamos en su prosa de estilo clásico y de tono intimista, *su poesía familiar* (muy reducida por cierto), y aquellas prosas líricas donde re-afirma su ausentismo del placer, su sola voz al lado de los amigos, y su introspección contemplativa hacia la naturaleza.

Perdomo publicó su primer poema "Delicias del campo" en 1854 en *El Oasis* bajo pseudónimo de Laura. Su tío, Manuel de Jesús Heredia fue su mentor. Posteriormente aparecen algunas composiciones suyas en *Las Flores del Ozama,* así como en otros periódicos y revistas de la época. Su obra poética fue recopilada en un volumen que se editó en 1888 en la Imprenta García Hermanos con prólogo del laureado poeta y escritor José Joaquín Pérez bajo el título de *Poesías de la señorita Josefa Perdomo.*

Cuatro textos patrióticos nos parecen significativos porque, ineludiblemente, en ellos se puede reconocer su pensamiento o tendencia ideológica-política: *A mi Patria* (16 de agosto de 1883), *Triunfo de la Patria* (1878), *Al*

Sr. D. Ignacio M. González, con motivo de la Revolución gloriosa de noviembre (refiere el movimiento del 25 de noviembre de 1873 que puso fin a los seis años del gobierno de Buenaventura Báez, dictador al cual Perdomo fue opuesta), y el texto *A la revolución del 7 de julio de 1857.* A estos añadimos la "sentida poesía" que escribiera en 1864 para despedir a Carlos de Vargas y Cerveto, Capitán General de Santo Domingo (1863–1864), durante la época de la Anexión, que pone en evidencia su simpatía por la Anexión y por la madre patria, y su adhesión a las ideas proteccionistas de los sectores más conservadores de la jerarquía política.

Virginia Elena Ortea

Virginia Elena Ortea nació en la ciudad primada de Santo Domingo de Guzmán el 17 de junio de 1866. Por su línea materna descendía de emigrantes irlandés—los Kennedy—que llegaron a la isla a fines del siglo XVIII. Su vida se desarrolla entre Santo Domingo, Puerto Rico, Puerto Plata y Nueva York, ciudad a la cual viaja en vapor en dos ocasiones para encontrarse con su padre. Era hija del periodista Francisco Ortea, quien huyendo a las persecuciones políticas emigró junto a su familia a Mayagüez, Puerto Rico, en 1879.

Virgina Elena inicia allí su vida literaria, época en que publica con el pseudónimo de Elena Kennedy, y conoce en el Ateneo de San Juan, al escritor Manuel María Sama, amigo entrañable de su tío el poeta Juan Isidro Ortea (fusilado en 1881), con quien se aduce tuvo una atormentada relación amorosa. Ortea escribió poemas, cuentos, dramas, artículos periodísticos y de costumbres, crónicas, una zarzuela y el texto inconcluso de una novela: *Mi hermana Catalina.*

En 1890 regresa temporalmente a Puerto Plata, ciudad de la cual parte posteriormente en 1894. Ella es la primera escritora, del siglo XIX, de quien se tiene noticias de haber sido laureada en un concurso literario, con su composición en prosa *En tu glorieta* en 1899, de quien pensaba el jurado era "un autor que se oculta bajo el pseudónimo de mujer". Su zarzuela en dos actos Las Feministas—hallada inédita en el fondo de un viejo baúl familiar, de su sobrino nieto el pintor Carlos Mena Ortea—con música del maestro Rodríguez Arresón fue presentada en Puerto Plata en octubre de ese mismo año, al igual que su diálogo alegórico con motivo de la inauguración del Ferrocarril construido para unir las ciudades de Santiago y Puerto Plata en 1897.

En 1901 publica con prólogo del reconocido historiador Américo Lugo, su única colección de textos narrativos breves titulada *Risas y Lágrimas,* falleciendo dos años después, se presume que de una afección pulmonar aguda, el 30 de enero de 1903, "A orillas del mar Atlante, en la ciudad querida, nido de (su) alegre infancia", Puerto Plata. Su muerte provocó muchos sentimientos de dolor, publicando la *Revista Ilustrada* un número especial, con manifestaciones de admiración de sus amigos, entre ellos, el escritor Tulio Manuel Cestero.

De este intercambio de fondos documentales para las Bibliotecas de Vanier y Webster de Concordia University, han salido a la luz pública tres libros—*Yo con mi viveza: Textos de conquistadoras, monjas, brujas, poetas y otras mujeres de la colonia* (Fondo Editorial Casa de las Américas, La Habana, Cuba, 2003); *Las madres de la patria y las bellas mentiras* (Ediciones Universal, Miami, 1999), y *Virginia Elena Ortea, Obras* (Centro de Solidaridad para el Desarrollo de la Mujer, Santo Domingo, 1997).

NOTAS

1. Batalla de Las Carreras. Durante el gobierno de Manuel Jimenes, instalado el 4 de septiembre de 1848, a principios de 1849 se produce la invasión del Emperador Soulouque al territorio dominicano. El 3 de abril el Congreso, ante las imperiosas circunstancias políticas, decreta que el general Pedro Santana "se ponga inmediatamente a las órdenes del gobierno", quien luchará al frente de sus hateros triunfando en *Las Carreras,* el Waterloo haitiano, el 21 de abril de 1849. Santana asume el poder político, cayendo Jimenes ante el despotismo santanista.

La Conspiración de 1855. En este año se produce un atentado de rebelión contra el gobierno de Santana. Esta conspiración arrastra al exilio a más de cien ciudadanos dominicanos, entre ellos a los poetas Félix María del Monte, Nicolás Ureña de Mendoza (padre de la poeta Salomé Ureña de Henríquez), Antonio Delfín Madrigal, José María González, entre otros, refugiándose en la nostálgica Saint-Thomas, para "enton (ar) ansioso (s) el canto sobrehumano que del letargo mísero a la vida vuelva la Patria excelsa" (Emilio Rodríguez Demorizi, *Santana y los poetas de su tiempo* [Santo Domingo: Editora del Caribe, 1969], p. 125).

La Revolución de 1857. *El Ozama piensa, el Cibao trabaja.* El 7 de julio de 1857 se produjo en el Cibao contra el gobierno de Buenaventura Báez (acusado, entre otras cosas, de usar el dinero de la Hacienda en provecho propio y en perjuicio del Estado). El levantamiento ocurrió en el fuerte de San Luis, en Santiago, dando lugar a la primera guerra civil de la República, a la cual se une Santana (el Hatero de *El Prado*), el 24 de agosto, al retornar de su destierro en la isla Saint-Thomas por Puerto Plata en la goleta española *Otilia,* por mandato del gobierno de Santiago que lo nombra el 27 de agosto General en Jefe del Ejército del Sudoeste.

Siendo instalado como Presidente del Gobierno Provisional el General José Desiderio Valverde, el día 8 de julio de 1857, que trajo posteriormente como consecuencia la instalación de un gobierno liberal en la ciudad de Santiago en 1858, designada como capital de la República, y que votara la *Constitución Liberal* de Moca del 19 de febrero de 1858. A la "revolución del 7 de julio", la poeta Josefa Perdomo escribe el primer elogio (ibid., p. 212).

Buenaventura Báez firma la capitulación ante el gobierno de Valverde el 12 de junio de 1858, y se embarca a Curazao en la goleta *27 de Febrero* en compañía de su ministro Félix María Del Monte. También se ausenta la poeta Francisca Cleofás Valdez de Mota, quien "encerróse en sus habitaciones hasta perder la vista" (ibid., p. 359), como gesto de dolor por la muerte de su esposo Félix Mota y Veloz (1822–1861), en el patíbulo.

La Anexión a España de 1861. Santana "el hombre de las circunstancias" le había dado la espalda al poder en 1848 y 1856. Desde julio de 1858 ocupa la presidencia de facto. El 31 de enero de 1859 toma el *Libertador* posesión del Poder Ejecutivo. "Yo no soy el hombre de las palabras, sino de los hechos", diría. Debido a las contiendas políticas, la nación estaba en el abismo económico. Había una "anárquica vocación del puedo al desorden y al ocio" (ibid., p. 237). La honda división política de una desmedida fracción de la sociedad había desequilibrado la idiosincrasia dominicana. La alternativa entonces fraguada por los partidarios de los caudillos era estar "arriba o abajo".

Este es el último período administrativo de Santana, que para asegurar la integridad del territorio, su tradicional hispanidad y la fuerza espiritual de la nación trastornada por el bárbaro vecino como diría Emilio Rodríguez Demorizi: "desvía el rumbo de su política estimulado por propios amigos, empujado por las imperiosas circunstancias y por el cansancio de la lucha en la defensa de la nación y de la paz, dirigiendo la nave de su destino político, de su propia vida y de su gloria, hacia el único puerto de salvación que vislumbran sus fatigados ojos: España" (ibid., pp. 237–238).

2. Las directoras de las escuelas fueron Francisca de la Concha, Teresa Valencia, Altagracia Quero, Dolores Guerrero Vda. Sánchez y Lucía Fernández de Castro. En 1893 en la ciudad de Santo Domingo, de acuerdo a Alemar en *Entre papeles viejos,* contábamos con 21 escuelas establecidas, para un total de 669 alumnos: 355 varones y 314 hembras. El colegio San Luis Gonzaga (1866) fue el primero autorizado en 1878 a conceder título de Bachiller. En la ciudad intramuros se destacan como Maestras de Escuelas, en 1858, María Josefa Loynaz del Castillo en San Carlos, Jerónima de Soto y Teresa Hernández.

Ana Moscoso de Sánchez establece en San Pedro de Macorís el *Instituto Preparatorio de Señoritas* en 1898, siendo la primera Escuela Normal de Señoritas de allí, donde estudiara la médica dominicana Evangelina Rodríguez Perozo. La ciudad disponía de cuatro librerías. *Librería Sardá* (1853), propiedad de Francisco Sardá y Carbonell; *Librería La Ilustración* (1861) abierta en la calle de Regina número 43, frente a la Iglesia; *Librería La Retreta* (1869) de García Hermanos, ubicada en la Plaza de Armas número 20, frente al Parque Colón; *Librería de Cos* (1881) de José María Cos, en la calle del Estudio.

BIBLIOGRAFÍA

Henríquez Ureña, Max. *Panorama histórico de la literatura dominicana.* Santo Domingo: Editora Librería Dominicana, 1965.

Llorens, Torres. *Antología de la poesía dominicana, 1884–1944.* 2d ed. Santo Domingo: Sociedad Dominicana de Bibliófilos, 1984.

Penson, César Nicolás, et al. *Reseña histórico-crítica de la poesía en Santo Domingo.* Santo Domingo: Imprenta Quisqueya, 1892.

Pérez, Carlos Federico. *Evolución Poética dominicana.* Buenos Aires: Editorial Poblet, 1956.

Rodríguez Demorizi, Emilio. *Santana y los poetas de su tiempo.* Santo Domingo: Editora del Caribe, 1969.

Vicioso, Abelardo. *Santo Domingo en las letras coloniales (1492–1800).* Santo Domingo: Editora de la Universidad Autónoma de Santo Domingo, 1979.

Contributors

Holly Ackerman, University of Miami

Jesús Alonso-Regalado, University at Albany, SUNY

Elsa Barberena, Universidad Nacional Autónoma de México

Carmen Block, Universidad Nacional Autónoma de México

David Block, Cornell University

Donna Canevari de Paredes, University of Saskatchewan

Micaela Chávez Villa, El Colegio de México

Víctor J. Cid Carmona, El Colegio de México

Allison Dolland, University of the West Indies, St. Augustine Campus

Georgette Magassy Dorn, Library of Congress

Nelly S. González, University of Illinois, Urbana-Champaign

Pamela M. Graham, Columbia University

Elda Mónica Guerrero, Asociación Mexicana de Bibliotecarios, A.C.

Kathleen Helenese-Paul, University of the West Indies, St. Augustine Campus

Yacoob Hosein, University of the West Indies, St. Augustine Campus

Juanita Jara de Súmar, McGill University

Sean Patrick Knowlton, University of Colorado at Boulder

Jaime Manrique, Columbia University

Nashieli Marcano, University of Akron

Nicole Michaud-Oystryk, University of Manitoba

Ulrike Mühlschlegel, Ibero-Amerikanisches Institut PK, Berlin

Ylonka Nacidit-Perdomo, Biblioteca Nacional, República Dominicana

DOROTHY M. PALMER, University of the West Indies, Mona Campus

RAFAEL E. TARRAGÓ, University of Minnesota

GABRIELLE M. TOTH, Chicago State University

Conference Program

Sunday/Domingo 3/19/06

8:00 A.M.–5:00 P.M.	Registration/Inscripción
8:30–10:30 A.M.	LAMP (Latin American Microform Project)
10:30 A.M.–12:30 P.M.	Regional Meetings/Grupos Regionales LANE (Latin America North East Libraries Consortium) CALAFIA (California Cooperative Latin American Collection Development Group) MOLLAS (Midwest Organization of Libraries for Latin American Studies) LASER (Latin American Studies Southeast Regional Libraries Consortium)
12:30–2:00 P.M.	Lunch/Almuerzo
2:00–4:30 P.M.	Latin Americanist Research Resources Project (LARRP)
4:30–5:00 P.M.	Coffee Break/Descanso
5:00–6:00 P.M.	Policy, Research and Investigation Audiovisual Serials Reference
6:00–7:00 P.M.	Membership Bibliographic Instruction Hispanic American Periodicals Index (HAPI) Gifts and Exchanges
7:45–8:00 P.M.	Bus/Taxi to Catholic University Campus for Welcoming Reception
8:30–10:00 P.M.	Reception at Catholic University Campus

Monday/Lunes 3/20/06

8:00 A.M.–5:00 P.M.	Registration/Inscripción
7:45–9:00 A.M.	Investment Working Group
8:00–9:00 A.M.	Task Force on Vendor Relations

9:00–10:00 A.M.	Marginalized Peoples and Ideas Enlace Nominating Finance (I)
10:00–11:00 A.M.	Acquisitions Cuban Bibliography Iberian Studies Interest Group (ISiS) Cataloging
11:00 A.M.–noon	Electronic Resources
Noon–1:30 P.M.	Lunch/Almuerzo
1:30–2:30 P.M.	Libreros-Librarians-Publishers
2:30–4:30 P.M.	Executive Board (I)
5:00–7:00 P.M.	Book Exhibit Opening/Inauguración del Salón de Expositores
8:00 P.M.	Transportation to Centro Historico Museo de las Casas Reales
8:30–11:00 P.M.	Reception hosted by Ministry of Culture

Tuesday/Martes   3/21/06

8:00 A.M.–5:00 P.M.	Registration/Inscripción
8:00–9:00 A.M.	Access and Bibliography Latin American Resources Forums Interlibrary Cooperation
9:00 A.M.–6:00 P.M.	Book Exhibit/Salón de Expositores
9:00–9:45 A.M.	**Opening Ceremony/Ceremonia de Apertura**

Rapporteur: *Darlene Hull,* Libros de Barlovento

Frederick Emam-Zade
Director, Fundación Global Democracia y Desarrollo

Adán Griego
SALALM President, Stanford University

Aída Montero
Comité Local, Fundación Global Democracia y Desarrollo

Dulce María Núñez de Tavera
Secretaria Asociación de Bibliotecas Universitarias
Dominicanas (ABUD), Directora del Sistema de Bibliotecas de
la Pontificia Universidad Católica Madre y Maestra

José Rafael Lantigua
Ministro de Cultura de la República Dominicana

Radamés Mejía
Vicerrector, Pontificia Universidad Católica Madre y Maestra

Tony Harvell
University of California, San Diego
José Toribio Medina Award Announcement

9:45–10:30 A.M.   **Keynote Speech/Conferencia Magistral**
Jaime Manrique, Columbia University
"El escritor transnacional"

10:30–11:00 A.M.   Coffee Break/Descanso (Sponsored by/Patrocinado por
ProQuest)

11:00 A.M.–12:15 P.M.   **Panel 1: Latin America and Europe/América Latina y
Europa**
Moderator: *Geoff West,* British Library
Rapporteur: *Patricia Figueroa,* Brown University

Peter Altekrüger, Ibero-Amerikanisches Institut de Berlín
"Revistas teatrales y de novelas cortas del Género Chico:
Argentina 1900–1940. Una 'nueva' colección del Instituto
Ibero-Americano"

Pilar Cagiao Vila, Universidad de Santiago de Compostela
"Emigración y cultura: la Biblioteca América de Galicia"

Gabriela Dalla Corte, Universitat de Barcelona y Casa
América Catalunya
"La Casa de América de Barcelona frente a la Guerra Civil
Española: emigración y exilio (1929–1939)"

Lluis Agustí Ruiz, Instituto Cervantes, New York
"El Instituto Cervantes y su red de bibliotecas"

11:00 A.M.–12:15 P.M.   **Panel 2: The Future of Library Collections: Librarian
Views of Bookdealers' Roles and a Vendor's Perspective/El
Futuro de las colecciones de bibliotecas: perspectivas de los
bibliotecarios acerca del papel los libreros y reflexiones de
un librero**
Moderator: *Daisy Dominguez,* Lehman College, CUNY
Rapporteur: *Nerea Llamas,* University of Michigan

S. Lief Adleson, Books from Mexico
"¿De la artesanía a la industria? Cambios en las actividades
profesionales de los bibliotecarios y bibreros"

César Rodríguez, Yale University
Lynn Shirey, Harvard University
"Cooperative Acquisitions at Harvard and Yale: Can We Really Do It?"

Teresa Chapa, University of North Carolina, Chapel Hill
"Bibliodiversidad: A Solution for Independent Publishers?"

11:00 A.M.–12:15 P.M. **Panel 3: Digital Library of the Caribbean (DLOC)/ Biblioteca Digital del Caribe**
Moderator: *Catherine Marsicek*, Florida International University
Rapporteur: *Sarah Leroy*, University of Pittsburgh

Jean-Wilfrid Bertrand, Les Archives Nationales d'Haiti
"Les Archives Nationales d'Haiti and the Digital Library of the Caribbean: A New Step to Regional Cooperation and Integration." Becario de Enlace

Maureen C. Newton, (Guyana)
"Preserving Caribbean Culture: CARIFESTA." Becaria de Enlace

Abul Bashirullah, Universidad de Oriente
"Digital Library of the Universidad de Oriente, Venezuela"

12:15–2:00 P.M.   Lunch/Almuerzo

2:00–3:30 P.M.   **Panel 4: The Exports of Migration/Las exportaciones de la migración**
Moderator: *Luis Gonzalez*, Indiana University
Rapporteur: *Nashieli Marcano*, University of Akron

Molly Vitorte, Stanford University
"Remittances to Mexico and Latin America"

David Block, Cornell University
"*Maladie sans frontières:* The Latin American Cholera Pandemic of 1991–1995"

Gustavo von Bischoffshausen, Universidad Nacional Mayor de San Marcos
"Imigración y cocina en el Perú." Becario de Enlace

Gabrielle M. Toth, Chicago State University
"Dubious Exports: U.S. Gangs in Latin America, a Bibliography"

2:00–3:30 P.M.   **Panel 5: Migration: The Mexican Experience/Migración: la experiencia mexicana**
Moderator: *Olga Espejo*, University of Miami
Rapporteur: *Cecilia Sercan*, Cornell University

Heshmatallah Khorramzadeh, El Colegio de México
"La Migración en el Norte y Sur de México"

Anne Barnhart, University of California, Santa Barbara
"Multicultural Archives at the University of California, Santa Barbara: Chicano Collections"

Elsa Barberena, Universidad Nacional Autónoma de México
Carmen Block, Universidad Nacional Autónoma de México
Elda Mónica Guerrero, Asociación Mexicana de Bibliotecarios, A.C.
"La imagen como documento de la migración: colecciones en las bibliotecas mexicanas"

Micaela Chávez Villa, El Colegio de México
Victor Julian Cid Carmona, El Colegio de México
"El Colegio de México: legado de la migración"

2:00–3:30 P.M.   **Panel 6: Digital Projects/Proyectos digitales**
Moderator: *Katherine McCann,* Library of Congress
Rapporteur: *Geoff West,* British Library

Georgette Dorn, Library of Congress
"La Biblioteca del Siglo 21: digitalización de materiales originales lusohispanos en la Biblioteca del Congreso"

Craig Schroer, University of Texas, Austin
"Archiving Digital Latin American Government Documents"

Stephanie Wood, University of Oregon
"Virtual Mesoamerican Archive"

Dr. Frank Moya Pons, University of Florida
"OGM Central de Datos: digitalización y marketing de archivos de periódicos en el Caribe"

3:30–4:00 P.M.   Coffee Break/Descanso (Sponsored by/Patrocinado por Thomson Gale)
Poster Sessions with Local Institutions/Poster Sessions de Instituciones Locales

4:00–5:30 P.M.   **Panel 7: Bibliographic Instruction/Formación de usuarios**
Moderator: *Peter Stern,* University of Massachusetts, Amherst
Rapporteur: *John Wright,* Brigham Young University

Alma C. Ortega, University of San Diego
"Building Alliances with Latin American Studies Faculty"

Sean Knowlton, University of Colorado, Boulder
Irene Münster, Inter-American Development Bank
"Digital Resources for Undergraduates: An Update on the *Choice Project*"

Martha E. Mantilla, University of Pittsburgh
"Challenges of Design/Currency of Web Pages"

Sarah Aponte, Dominican Studies Institute Library, CUNY
"Dominican Studies: Resources in the Diaspora"

4:00–5:30 P.M.   **Panel 8: Latin American Collections: An Update/Informe: Colecciones Latinoamericanas**
Moderator: *Gayle Williams,* Emory University
Rapporteur: *Victor Julian Cid Carmona,* El Colegio de México

Hortensia Calvo, Tulane University
"*Nombrando la Espuma:* Katrina, New Orleans and the Latin American Library at Tulane"

Françoise Beaulieu Thybulle, Bibliothèque Nationale d'Haiti
"Haiti's Bibliographic Treasures and Its Literary Patrimony"

Diomedes Núñez, Biblioteca Nacional de la República Dominicana
"La Biblioteca Nacional de la República Dominicana: evolución y nuevos desafíos"

Fernando Acosta Rodríguez, Princeton University
"Archivos ocultos del Caribe en Princeton"

Dulce María Núñez de Tavera, Pontificia Universidad Católica Madre y Maestra
"Colecciones especiales de la Pontificia Universidad Católica Madre y Maestra"

4:00–5:30 P.M.   **Panel 9: Caribbean Diasporas/Diasporas caribeñas**
Moderator: *Víctor Federico Torres,* Universidad de Puerto Rico, Río Piedras
Rapporteur: *Daisy Dominguez,* Lehman College, CUNY

María Elizabeth Rodríguez, Fundación Global Democracia y Desarrollo
"Creando sinergias entre migración y desarrollo: el caso de la República Dominicana"

Pamela Graham, Columbia University
"La Casa de la Cultura Dominicana in New York City"

Rafael Emilio Yunén, El Centro Cultural Eduardo León Jimenes, Santiago de los Caballeros, República Dominicana
"Banco de datos y materiales de arte y cultura: reafirmando la identidad dentro y fuera del Caribe"

Carlos Dore, Fundación Global Democracia y Desarrollo
"República Dominicana y Haití: el problema como oportunidad"

5:30–6:45 P.M.	**Panel 10: Film as a Mode of Representation/El cine como medio de representación** Moderator: *Laura D. Shedenhelm,* University of Georgia Rapporteur: *Claude Potts,* Arizona State University *Jesús Alonso-Regalado,* SUNY, Albany "Cine digital de acceso libre en el Internet: producciones españolas y latinoamericanas"
Documentary/ Documental	*Dominican Baseball Players/Peloteros Dominicanos* (Univision, 17 minutes). Presented by *Laura D. Shedenhelm,* University of Georgia
Brazilian Short/ Corto Brasileiro	*O Rio Severino* (11 minutes). Presented by *Patricia Figueroa,* Brown University
5:30–6:45 P.M.	**Panel 11: Crossing Borders: Latin America and Canadian University Libraries/América Latina en las bibliotecas canadienses** Moderator: *Denis Lacroix,* University of Alberta Rapporteur: *Eudoxio Paredes-Ruiz,* University of Saskatchewan *Donna Canevari de Paredes,* University of Saskatchewan "Spanish in Saskatchewan: Newcomers Influencing the Development of Curricula and Library Collections in Latin American and Iberian Studies at the University of Saskatchewan" *Juanita Jara de Súmar,* McGill University "Latin American Collections in Two Montreal Universities: A Preliminary Survey" *Nicole Michaud-Oystryk,* University of Manitoba "Immigration and Globalization: Meeting the Needs of an Emergent Clientele" *Ylonka Nacidit-Perdomo,* Biblioteca Nacional de la República Dominicana "Diálogo a través de las fronteras: reformulaciones femeninas del pasado"
5:30–6:45 P.M.	**Panel 12: Inside and Outside Academe: From Proposals to Concrete Projects/Dentro y fuera de la academia: de propuestas a proyectos concretos** Moderator: *Paloma Celis Carbajal,* University of Wisconsin–Madison Rapporteur: *Carlos Delgado,* University of California, Berkeley

Sean Knowlton, University of Colorado, Boulder
"Preparing Latin Americanists for Careers in Academic Librarianship: A Paradigm Shift for Collaboration in Higher Education"

Cecilia Pilar Jaña Monsalve, Escuela de Bibliotecología, Universidad Tecnológica Metropolitana
"Proyecto de diplomado en gestión y formación de proyectos culturales: Chile." Becaria de Enlace

Célida Álvarez Armenteros, Casa de las Américas (Cuba)
"Proyecto de remodelación y ampliación de la Biblioteca de Casa de las Américas." Becaria de Enlace

Jorge Matos, Centro de Estudios Puertorriqueños, Hunter College, CUNY
"The Centro Library and the Archives of the Puerto Rican Diaspora"

7:30 P.M.	Taxi/Bus to Centro Histórico for Libreros' Recepción
8:00–10:30 P.M.	Libreros' Reception/Recepción de libreros de SALALM (Location To Be Announced)

Wednesday/ Miércoles   **3/22/06**

8:00 A.M.–noon	Registration/Inscripción
7:45–9:00 A.M.	Finance (II)
8:00–9:00 A.M.	Library Operations
9:00 A.M.–2:00 P.M.	**Book Exhibit/Salón de Expositores**
9:00–10:30 A.M.	**Panel 13: Caribbean Migrations: The West Indies/ Migración caribeña: Las Indias Occidentales**

Moderator: *Enid Brown,* University of the West Indies, Mona
Rapporteur: *Holly Ackerman,* University of Miami

Margaret D. Rouse-Jones, University of the West Indies, St. Augustine
"Reverse Caribbean-African Migration: The Case of George James Christian of Dominica and the Gold Coast"

Elmelinda Lara, University of the West Indies, St. Augustine
"Venezuela-Trinidad Connection: An Exploration of Cross Cultural Currents"

Kathleen Helenese-Paul, University of the West Indies, St. Augustine
Yacoob Hosein, University of the West Indies, St. Augustine
Allison Dolland, University of the West Indies, St. Augustine
"The Presence of the Migratory Experience in the Special Collections at the University of the West Indies, St. Augustine"

Dorothy Palmer, University of the West Indies, Mona
"Trends in Jamaican Migration: A Look at the Political, Socioeconomic, and Gender Issues"

9:00–10:30 A.M. **Panel 14: Access and Control: Charting the Bibliographic Landscape/Acceso y control: trazando el panorama bibliográfico**
Moderator: *Ruby Meraz Gutierrez,* Hispanic American Periodicals Index
Rapporteur: *Norma Palomino,* Universidad Torcuato Di Tella

Floris Fraser, University of the West Indies, St. Augustine
"The Role of CARINDEX in Research on the Caribbean Diaspora"

Paul Losch, University of Florida
"LAPTOC: un modelo cooperativo de acceso a la literature periódica"

Snejanka Penkova, Universidad APEC (República Dominicana)
"LATINDEX: Indice Latinoamericano de Publicaciones Científicas"

Tina Gross, University of Pittsburgh
"Spanish-Language Subject Headings and the Sears List: An Inter-American History"

9:00–10:30 A.M. **Panel 15: Crossing Artistic and Social Boundaries/ Cruzando los limites artísticos y sociales**
Moderator: *Cecilia Puerto,* San Diego State University
Rapporteur: *Micaela Chávez Villa,* El Colegio de México

Elizabeth A. Marchant, University of California, Los Angeles
"Constructing Carmen Miranda: Memory and Documentary"

Tatiana de la Tierra, University at Buffalo
"*Para las duras*: cruzando las fronteras sexuales"

Nashieli Marcano, University of Akron
"Adaptación y traslación de la historia puertorriqueña en *La casa de la laguna* de Rosario Ferré"

10:30–11:00 A.M.   Coffee Break/Descanso
Poster Sessions with Local Institutions/Poster Sessions de
Instituciones Locales

11:00 A.M.–12:15 P.M.   **Panel 16: Women across Latin American Borders/La
mujer y las fronteras latinoamericanas**
Moderator: *Lesbia Varona,* University of Miami
Rapporteur: *Barbara Robinson,* University of Southern
California

Graciella Cruz-Taura, Florida Atlantic University
"Finding a Place in a Foreign Church: Cuban American
Catholic Women"

Nelly S. Gonzalez, University of Illinois
"How the Three Julias Got Their Fames"

Marian Goslinga, Florida International University
"Eliza Lynch: Female Migrant to the New World"

11:00 A.M.–12:15 P.M.   **Panel 17: Technology Panel/Mesa redonda sobre tecnología**
Moderator: *Tracy North,* Library of Congress
Rapporteur: *Myra Appel,* University of California, Davis

Orchid Mazurkiewicz, Hispanic American Periodicals Index
"Future of HAPI"

Martha Kelehan, University of California, Los Angeles
"Usability Challenges: Recommendations for the Redesign of
HAPI Online"

David Block, Cornell University
Claude Potts, University of Arizona
Miguel Valladares, Dartmouth College
"SALALM's New Home Page"

Patricia Figueroa, Brown University
"Latin American Travelogues"

11:00 A.M.–12:15 P.M.   **Panel 18: Cuban Diaspora/Diaspora cubana**
Moderator: *Martha E. Mantilla,* University of Pittsburgh
Rapporteur: *Nancy Hallock,* Harvard University

Rafael E. Tarragó, University of Minnesota
"Escritores cubanos en Europa: Cabrera Infante en Londres y
Zoé Valdés en París"

Ulrike Mühlschlegel, Ibero-Amerikanisches Institut de Berlín
"Cuba en Alemania: situación socio-demográfica y
bibliográfica"

Holly Ackerman, University of Miami
"Cuban Rafters: Ten Years After"

12:15–1:30 P.M.	Lunch/Almuerzo
1:30–2:00 P.M.	Town Hall Meeting
2:00 P.M.	Exhibits Close/Clausura del Salón de Expositores
2:00–3:00 P.M.	Business Meeting
3:00–3:30 P.M.	Closing Session
3:30–4:30 P.M.	Executive Board Meeting (II)
5:00–6:00 P.M.	Optional Visit to Local Libraries
8:00–10:00 P.M.	Closing Reception/Cena de Clausura